Additional praise for
THE KING AND QUEEN OF MALIBU

"Well written and thoroughly researched, Randall's exploration of land ownership in America and the American dream addresses issues of sexism, classism, love, and the preservation of natural beauty."

—*Publishers Weekly*

"*The King and Queen of Malibu* is an irresistible and compelling tale of a strong-willed and fabulously wealthy woman who sought to keep the beaches and mountains of Malibu as her private enclave."

—Meryl Gordon, author of *Mrs. Astor Regrets*

"David Randall's *The King and Queen of Malibu* is a compelling love story about an unlikely couple and at the same time a rich and instructive tale about the American Dream crashing head-on into the march of American progress. Always fascinating and elegantly written, it totally absorbed me in the unfolding drama."

—Howard Blum, *New York Times* best-selling
author of *Dark Invasion* and *American Lightning*

"Anchoring himself in exhaustive research, David K. Randall enshrines this paradigmatic American story in a compelling narrative that at once explores the power and the limits of the Southern California dream."

—Kevin Starr, University of Southern California

"David K. Randall's *The King and Queen of Malibu* is a vivid narrative of a strong-willed woman in a man's world. May Rindge, the landlady of her private Malibu paradise, was feared, even hated, but also respected. Randall tells the true story of a bloody feud that needs no invention."

—Bill Dedman, coauthor of *Empty Mansions*

"David Randall has unearthed a rowdy origin story for Malibu, vividly proving that movie stars weren't the first people to bring drama to that fabled stretch of coastline. This thrilling book shows that before Barbie and surfers showed up, the beach was a battleground."

—Monte Reel, author of *Between Man and Beast*

THE KING AND QUEEN OF MALIBU

ALSO BY DAVID K. RANDALL

Dreamland: Adventures in the Strange Science of Sleep

THE KING AND QUEEN OF MALIBU

The True Story of the Battle for Paradise

David K. Randall

W. W. NORTON & COMPANY

Independent Publishers Since 1923

NEW YORK LONDON

To Megan, Henry, and Isla

For information about permission to reproduce selections from this book,
write to Permissions, W. W. Norton & Company, Inc.,
500 Fifth Avenue, New York, NY 10110

For information about special discounts for bulk purchases, please contact
W. W. Norton Special Sales at specialsales@wwnorton.com or 800-233-4830

Manufacturing by Berryville Graphics
Book design by Lovedog Studio
Production manager: Julia Druskin

Library of Congress Cataloging-in-Publication Data

Names: Randall, David K.
Title: The king and queen of Malibu : the true story of the battle for paradise /
David K. Randall.
Description: First edition. | New York, N.Y. : W.W. Norton & Company, 2016. |
Includes bibliographical references.
Identifiers: LCCN 2015038696 | ISBN 9780393240993 (hardcover)
Subjects: LCSH: Rindge, Frederick Hastings, 1857–1905. | Rindge, May, 1864–
1941. | Malibu (Calif.)—Biography. | Malibu (Calif.)—History. |
Pioneers—California—Malibu—Biography. | Frontier and pioneer life—
California—Malibu. | Social change—California—Malibu—History. |
Economic development—California—Malibu—History.
Classification: LCC F869.M27 R36 2016 | DDC 979.4/93040922—dc23
LC record available at http://lccn.loc.gov/2015038696

ISBN 978-0-393-35394-5 pbk.

W. W. Norton & Company, Inc.
500 Fifth Avenue, New York, N.Y. 10110
www.wwnorton.com

W. W. Norton & Company Ltd.
15 Carlisle Street, London W1D 3BS

1 2 3 4 5 6 7 8 9 0

CONTENTS

Introduction

THE BEACH

ON A ROCK-STREWN BEACH TWENTY MILES OUTSIDE of Los Angeles, three men drenched in sweat and grease worked quickly by the light of the sun fading over the Pacific. They prodded three hulking Model T's into a line across a barren road and began threading chains between their axles, forging a barricade out of glass and steel. The waves crashing a few feet away covered everything with a cold mist and silenced any small talk.

It was July 29, 1917, and time was running short. As the chains jangled into place, each man stole glances at the shadows stretching across the beach and into the mountains. Somewhere out there amid the dark canyons were guards patrolling on horseback, each armed with a shotgun and instructions to use it. That the spot the trio had staked out was technically public land might matter in the eyes of God and the law, but it wouldn't bring much consolation to a dead man. Everyone knew that Rindge's men didn't fire warning shots.

A pair of headlights glimmered in the distance. Seconds later, the men could see a car speeding toward them, throwing up a black cloud of dust that hung in the air like an omen. It wouldn't be long now. Rindge was on her way.

DURING THE FIRST PART of the twentieth century, the perfect beaches of Malibu were the last place you could expect to find a celebrity. All of it—the sheer bluffs, the deep canyons, the south-facing shoreline that let you lie on the beach all day long without ever having to squint directly into the sun—was one private ranch, a wild kingdom hugging the edge of the continent. Running nearly twenty-five miles along the coast and stretching only two miles across at its widest point, it owed its borders to a time when Southern California was a half-forgotten outpost on the far side of the Spanish Empire. The crown, faced with colonizing a place where land was so plentiful as to render it nearly worthless, offered vast tracts, known as ranchos, to military officers and noblemen in an effort to put a Spanish stamp on the dry valleys surrounding the tiny settlement known as Los Angeles.

The Rancho Topanga Malibu Sequit, which in time would become the city of Malibu, was one of the first created, and even in a region widely thought of as inhospitable, it seemed the least fit for human enjoyment. The sharp peaks of the Santa Monica Mountains nearly sealed it off from the rest of Southern California, while bears and mountain lions roamed its seventeen steep canyons. Great boulders lay scattered across its beaches like marbles discarded by a wanton giant. Anyone who wanted to reach the Malibu, as the rancho was often called, had to first consult a tide chart and set off on horseback at the right time along the beach. A late start would result in finding yourself marooned on the coastline, the path forward and back flooded by the drift of the ocean. Attempting to cross the mountains, meanwhile, meant fending off rattlesnakes and bandits, both of which were in ample supply.

That this unwelcoming place would in time become known as a paradise filled with movie stars and billionaires was the result of one of the longest and most bitter battles over land in American history. It was a clash that pitted one of the wealthiest families in the country against the encroaching modern world, all set against a backdrop in which Los Angeles seemed to morph overnight from a dusty cow town into a global metropolis. Their fight would go all the way to the Supreme Court, and would culminate in a landmark decision that continues to shape the public's right to access beautiful places. In the process, the battle for Malibu would create the Pacific Coast Highway, a road that has since become a symbol of the good life in California.

At the center of it all were Frederick and May Rindge, a pair who would have needed no introduction in Los Angeles at the turn of the century. Newspapers tracked nearly every aspect of their lives, going so far as to once report that Frederick had stayed home from work with a cold. The couple arrived in the city as newlyweds in 1887, just a few months after a bidding war between the railroads in Los Angeles sparked one of the most frenzied housing bubbles the country had ever seen. It was a marriage of opposites: he was a Harvard-trained confidant of presidents and senators, the rare dreamer who knew what he was doing; she was a midwestern farmer's daughter, raised to be suspicious of the seasons. Resolute where he was romantic, guarded where he was generous, May seemed molded from a different clay than her husband. Yet the bond between them would prove to shape history in ways that no one would have expected.

In their first days in the city, Frederick, the only surviving heir of an immense Boston fortune, could barely contain his desire to make a mark in a place that seemed only one step removed from the frontier. Within a decade, he owned more businesses than perhaps any other single person in California, putting the Rindges atop the booming city's hierarchy. He soon purchased the thirteen-thousand-acre Malibu rancho as a country home for his growing family. It was a day's ride on horseback from Santa Monica and contained not much more than cattle and fallow fields of lima beans, but he had no need for the ranch to produce income. Frederick, a deeply religious man, saw in its pristine beauty the work of God, and resolved to keep it untouched while Southern California boomed all around.

He would have little time to fulfill his wish, however. With Frederick's sudden death in 1905, May Rindge took control of a fortune that would be worth nearly $700 million in today's money. She vowed to keep Malibu, the place where she had spent the best days of her life with Frederick and their three children, as an unbroken reminder of her husband's love. Her resolve would be challenged within days of his funeral, beginning the struggle that would mark the rest of her life. Over the next decades, May fended off attacks from aggressors ranging from the most powerful railroad bosses in the state, to a mob of armed homesteaders, to fractures within her own family, all in effort to preserve Malibu as she had first glimpsed it while riding in a horse-drawn carriage with Frederick at her side.

This is the story of how the Rindge family came to own and ultimately lose their grasp on Malibu, eventually turning a rugged ranch in the middle of nowhere into a global symbol of fame and fortune. It is a tale of creation and destruction, of triumph and heartbreak, all of which takes place along a stretch of coastline of unparalleled majesty. And, strangely, it is a tale that has largely been forgotten, despite its impact. After the news of May Rindge's death was splashed across the front pages of Los Angeles' newspapers in 1941, her story was largely pushed aside and replaced with a new mythology of surfers and sunshine that better suited the times. Gidget's arrival on a surfboard in the 1950s beamed a different, happier version of Malibu across the world, enriching the name with a romance that has helped sell everything from Barbie dolls to family sedans. Few driving up and down the Pacific Coast Highway today know anything about the epic fight that created the road, even as the highway itself continues to draw millions of tourists from across the globe.

Until not long ago, I was one of them. I grew up in a suburb about fifty miles outside Los Angeles, and as soon as I could drive, I spent most of my time rolling up and down PCH, looking for waves. It was only after I moved across the country and found myself stuck in a small apartment during one of the worst blizzards to hit New York City that homesickness compelled me to seek out the origins of the road that played a starring role in my childhood. As I read through old issues of the *Los Angeles Times* and other newspapers from the turn of the century, I kept finding mentions of a long-simmering standoff at the gates of Malibu. I soon found myself immersed in a Los Angeles before freeways, before surfers, and before celebrities. In a place famous for reinventing itself with every passing fad, I had stumbled on the story that underpinned it all.

The book that follows is a result of several years of research, in archives both public and private. It traces the path of one family over a roughly seventy-year span as the country swept off the last vestiges of the Civil War and transitioned into what we recognize as the modern age. The story of Malibu stretches from the halls of Harvard to the Old West in New Mexico, from a cult tucked amid the hills north of San Francisco to a gold mine near the Oregon border, and culminates in the glamour of early Hollywood. It is a tale that could have happened only during the brief sliver of history in which the advent of railroads and the automobile meshed with the limitless American frontier and anything seemed possible. At its heart is the story of a marriage between two people whose temperaments and backgrounds could not have been more different, and yet each filled in what the other was missing. Without him, May would have never left a dreary Michigan farm, where she was lost among a jumble of siblings, and entered a world of wealth beyond her imagination. And without her grit, Frederick's dream of preserving the beauty of Malibu would have never been realized, because only she was willing to shoulder the cost.

But all of that would come years in the future. The story of Malibu starts with a young man just outside Boston, walking out his family's front door and into the great world beyond his window.

THE KING AND QUEEN OF MALIBU

Chapter One

A GREAT BEAST AWAKENING

NO ONE THOUGHT THE BOY WOULD LIVE THIS LONG.
Death seemed to hang in the air at the Rindge estate, a towering brick mansion perched at the corner of Dana and Harvard Streets in Cambridge. Already, Samuel Rindge had buried two of his children before they reached the age of six. Now he had to write another one of the letters that were becoming a painful constant in his life.

"Dear Aunt Margret," he scrawled in his pristine, looped script, a skill born from tending the books of his growing business empire. "Little Henry died this afternoon and we now calculate to have the funeral Sunday afternoon early. Mary still continues very sick. Frederick is doing well. Yours affectionately, Samuel B. Rindge."

As he wrote the letter, Samuel began the grim calculation of which child he would have to bury next. Even with Mary's current condition, he assumed that Frederick would be the one to not survive the winter. Though the boy was in stable health at the moment, the doctors had discovered that, like his brothers and sisters already gone, he had contracted rheumatic fever, a deadly disease that in 1863 seemed to have no cure. As an infant, Frederick spent the first months of life gasping for air while his chest fluttered, his heartbeat so weak that you could barely feel it one minute and pounding so hard it seemed ready to burst out of his chest the next. His joints were often swollen and hot to the touch, and he could barely move his arms or legs without howling in pain. On the worst nights, his body quaked in spasms, followed by hours of uncontrollable crying. Growing into a toddler did little to quell his suffering. While other boys spent the humid New England summer exploring the nearby Boston Common or wading in the banks of the Charles River, Frederick was often stuck looking out his window at life in full bloom, betrayed by his body. Every time he seemed like he was finally close to a full recovery, the disease returned with a renewed vengeance, as if determined to finish the job.

Mary died unexpectedly three days after Henry's funeral, again forcing Samuel to carry a coffin that was much too light. Frederick was soon the only child left out of the six siblings who had once roamed the halls of the Rindge mansion. Samuel and his wife prayed that God would spare their only remaining son, all the while chasing away thoughts of the inevitable. A year passed, and then two, and then three. In the constant fight between Frederick's body and his spirit, the will to live continued to win, though just barely. The simple act of breathing turned into a demonstration of defiance, evidence that he would not succumb to a disease he did not understand. With his chance of survival uncertain, Frederick found comfort in the Bible, devouring the tales of men defeating long odds because they had God on their side. With each example of the power of faith, the boy felt less alone. He reasoned that he was no longer just a child fighting off a disease he couldn't comprehend; he was a young man God had decided to test, and he was determined to pass. In a house that seemed marked by death, the Bible pointed a way to eternal life.

The daily study sessions started to frame his life in ways that his parents had never anticipated. The family could trace its lineage to the arrival of the English on the Massachusetts shore. Daniel Rindge had wielded a sword in the first skirmishes between Puritans and the native Wampanoag and Narragansett tribes in the seventeenth century, while his nephew, John Rindge, marked out the boundary between the colonies of New Hampshire and Massachusetts on foot at request of the king. A hundred years later, their grandsons aimed bullets at the British in the Battles of Lexington and Concord, the first action in what became the Revolutionary War. Religion was a part of the family identity, but only a fraction of the whole. New England pragmatism ruled their daily life.

Frederick, however, set about on a different course. He began wearing his faith openly, eager to share the tales of triumph that buoyed his spirits when he was close to sinking. He sought out maxims and proverbs, reveling in the structure and certainty they offered when doctors could not tell his parents whether he would survive long enough to see another summer. Even as his body continued to disappoint him, Frederick kept an eye on the horizon, hewing as closely as he could to Christ's teachings out of hope that his faith would be rewarded. Each new day seemed like a promise that it would be. His very presence continued to confound doctors, who saw no reason why this particular boy was still living when so many others with rheumatic fever quickly fell to the disease. Yet there he was, slowly growing into a man before their eyes.

ON A BRISK FALL DAY in 1875, Frederick Hastings Rindge began his adulthood by walking out the family's front door and heading off in the direction of Harvard. He was eighteen, handsome, and, to the eternal joy of his mother, Clarissa, who continued to worry about his health, had recently developed a full belly, which only made him look more like the wealthy heir he was. Following the fashion of the day, he wore a long black overcoat over his triple-pleated shirt, which he topped with a patterned silk ascot and crowned with a black top hat. He sported a bushy black beard that covered his face almost to the nose, the effect of which was lessened by the fact that his round cheeks and large brown eyes made it seem as if he were always on the verge of smiling. If his clothes weren't enough to identify him as a young gentleman, then the walking stick would have tipped the balance. Long, slender, and culminating in a gold ball, its every strike on the pavement ticked off another one of the dwindling number of steps remaining between his childhood and the rest of his life.

The countless hours spent cooped up in his room as a child now gave him a certain air of restlessness, a sense of motion that could be felt in his presence even when he was still. Some of it was simple ambition. As he took his first steps toward the Harvard campus, Frederick was eager to prove that he could not only beat the disease that still lingered in his body but defeat whatever lay next. Yet there was something else, something left unsaid after every grin and laugh and greeting that drew people into his orbit and made them want to stay there. For all of his physical weakness and the number of funerals he had already been to in his short life, his spirit remained unblemished, emanating a sense of optimism that made it seem inevitable that better days lay ahead.

He had plenty of reasons to be confident. Over the last decade, his father had built a prosperous business loading glassware, popcorn, and other small items onto the packed clipper ships venturing around the horn of South America en route to California, where the discovery of gold twenty-six years earlier still continued to draw dreamers ready for a fresh start on the West Coast. While never a warm man, Samuel showed his affection for Frederick by schooling him in the dismal science of bookkeeping, illustrating how a rigid appreciation of even the smallest transaction could snowball into a larger fortune. He demonstrated how to use an account ledger, how to record each and every purchase a person made, and how and when it was appropriate to dip into your reserves to keep the books balanced. It wasn't exciting by itself, he counseled his son, but these skills often meant the difference between success and ruin.

That comfort with numbers had one day changed Samuel's life. At fifteen, with a loop of curly dark hair ringing his ears, he had started working as a gofer, a job that at the time went by the decidedly unglamorous term of "boy," in the counting room of the firm Parker & Blanchard, one of several importer-exporters nestled near the city harbor. He did a lot of everything—opening the office doors in the morning, sweeping floors, carrying bundles of merchandise taller than his own head—all for salary of fifty dollars a year and a hot lunch, an attractive combination to a young man who had no family money to speak of. From the beginning, Samuel seemed to have an innate understanding of the art of trading. Within a few years he had his own desk, and by his twenty-fifth birthday he had become a partner, making deals to buy and sell merchandise all over the world.

His material success readily transferred into a jump in the family's social standing. Invitations to charity balls and fund-raising teas began flooding into the Rindge home, each organization hoping that some of the family's billowing wealth would make it their way. Soon Rindge's comings and goings became a regular feature in Boston's newspapers. For a man with deep roots in Massachusetts, though, nothing compared to the opportunity to represent the city of Cambridge at the centennial celebration of the Battles of Lexington and Concord. Samuel stood beaming on stage throughout the parade, listening to the marching bands and long-winded politicians, all the while secure in the knowledge that he had at long last joined the city's elite. As the power of the Rindge name grew, Samuel understood that his son would have a job waiting for him at any firm in Boston after graduation.

Even if given a choice in the matter, Frederick couldn't have picked a better time to be young. Already there were whispers that, after years of depression, the country was on the brink of an explosion of wealth like nothing the world had ever seen. For this, it could thank the locomotive. Railroads opened up the landscape, uncorking a restless population that was still recovering from the damages wrought by the Civil War and linking the riches of the two coasts. Train cars full of men and women ready for a new life headed west, replaced by those carrying gold, silver, and other riches from the frontier chugging their way back east. America soon had more than half of the total length of train tracks laid around the world, and the country couldn't wait for more. The railroads became so important to the national economy that they would soon change time itself. On November 18, 1883, the U.S. Naval Observatory in Washington, the nation's official timekeeper, introduced the concept of time zones across the country, ending the patchwork system of local times, which was driving schedule makers mad. From now on, clocks in places as far apart as Chicago and West Texas would strike noon at the same instant, regardless of where the sun happened to be in the sky.

Money became the sum total of American ambition, even if it meant stealing or swindling a little bit in the process. As Mark Twain, who gave this new Gilded Age its name, put it, "What is the chief end of man? To get rich. In what way? Dishonestly if we can; honestly if we must."

Boston in particular was a place where a man blessed with desire and the right connections could go far and enjoy every minute of it. Opportunity seemed to waft through the city like an early morning fog. The drum of hammers announced the arrival of buildings sprouting up in the heart of downtown, which just three years earlier had been the site of the city's worst man-made disaster. A fire that began in the basement of a five-story warehouse shortly after seven in the evening sent embers flying across the city's narrow streets and onto the nearby roofs of wooden buildings that dated to before the revolution. The fire department wasn't of much help. A particularly nasty equine flu had lodged itself in the city's stables, incapacitating the horses required to pull the department's fire trucks and ladders. Ad hoc teams of men banded together to lug each piece of equipment to the fire, in a slow and disorganized process that allowed the blaze to widen further. A group of property owners, fearful that the flames would spread beyond the financial district, took it upon themselves to load kegs of gunpowder into a block of buildings and blow them sky-high, hoping that the rubble would form a firebreak. Instead, the uncontrolled explosion simply egged the fire on. When it was finally contained, the next morning, more than seven hundred buildings downtown had been demolished and thirty lives lost.

A new city was now emerging from the ashes of its colonial past, stretching and growing like a great beast awakening. It was a place where the old ways of doing things—and the people who did them—seemed to change overnight. Immigrants steamed into Boston Harbor and made their way into the city to find their fortunes, elbowing past men from the countryside drawn by the lure of a job in an office or a factory instead of the field. By the end of the decade, more than one in five men and women walking on the streets of Boston would hail from Ireland, and the number of Germans and Italians they passed each day steadily increased as well. With a job readily available for anyone who asked, the number of people moving to cities topped the number of those staying on farms for the first time in the nation's history, and the ratio would never again favor rural life. With its swelling population, Boston had to expand out of its tightly packed seaport or else start building on top of itself. The first horse-drawn streetcars soon began running from Central Square in Cambridge to Bowdoin Square in Boston, drawing residents out of the city proper with the promise that they could easily get back into town. By the end of the century, Greater Boston would encompass a new ring of thirty-one suburbs sprawling over a ten-mile radius.

It was an age of expansion, when for the first time in history it was possible to cross a continent in about a week's time and refashion your life in any way you chose. Genius, too, seemed to be found behind every door. Two miles away, a Scottish professor at Boston University named Alexander Graham Bell had just a few months before lined a mass of wires between two rooms of his fifth-floor workshop and gone to work coaxing sound out of them. When his assistant heard the command "Mr. Watson, come here, I want to see you" bleating from the receiver, the telephone was born. As Frederick walked the Harvard campus, he could find himself in the wake of Richard Henry Dana Jr., whose memoir of his journey to the then-barren shores of California, *Two Years Before the Mast,* was already considered an American classic, and who had now settled into private practice and regularly attended meetings at Harvard Law School.

Frederick could see that his restlessness was neatly suited for the times. Like many young men living on the East Coast, he thrilled to the chance of adventure and the unimaginable wealth that seemed to beckon from the frontier. Yet unlike most of them, he was already firmly nestled in luxury. A life of privilege in Boston was all but assured, Harvard degree or no. Still, Frederick couldn't quite keep his eyes off of the horizon, still pulled by an urge to discover what was far beyond his window.

He had been west once before. When he was twelve, he had sat next to his parents in a swaying cabin on the first train to travel the length of the transcontinental railroad, a colossal feat of engineering that carved a path across the country and suddenly made the empty spots on the map seem within easy reach of the cities of the East Coast. His parents had booked the journey in hopes that the fresh air of California, already believed to be magical, could finally cure their son. Frederick spent the entire trip with his face pressed against the window, watching the growing nation unfurl in front of his eyes. The wonders began as soon as the train passed Chicago and entered a west that was still wild. Great herds of buffalo spanned the prairie and seemed to move with one brain, their numbers so endless that Frederick gave up trying to count them. Oceans of grass, each stalk nearly as tall as his head, suddenly gave way to snow-capped mountains, their peaks cutting into the sky. Smoke from native villages hung in the air, the only sign of human habitation on the limitless landscape. Chugging westward underneath brilliant blue skies, the train in which the young boy sat was the first link between the coasts, and with each mile, it propelled the nation further into a new era.

THE WEST WAS SURELY on Frederick's mind as he walked the final steps across Harvard Square and into his new life as a university student. Yet once there, he directed all of his efforts to what was then considered the chief reason for a college education. He began forging connections with other young men who hailed from prestigious families, effectively cementing his father's efforts to move the Rindge name into a higher social register. Harvard's student life at the time was rigid and competitive; making the right friends or joining a certain club could—and did—have an outsized effect on a young man's future.

The sorting process began early in freshman year. Frederick quickly joined the Art Club, the Glee Club, and the Hasty Pudding Club, each one a building block in his plan to be recognized as one of the chosen of the chosen. He squeezed into a train car packed with men wearing bowler hats and silk ties to travel down to Hamilton Park in New Haven, where, along with two thousand other spectators, he paid fifty cents to watch Harvard line up against Yale in the first ever football game between the two schools. In another first for the fledgling sport, each team took the field in matching uniforms rather than a mishmash of gear. The men from Harvard sported crimson knee breeches, shirts, and stockings, while the team from Yale wore dark pants, blue jerseys, and yellow hats. Despite constant bickering between players, spectators, and even referees over the rules, Harvard won 4–0 in a game that was closer to rugby than anything that could be called football today.

In his sophomore year, Frederick was tapped to join the Institute of 1770, then one of the most important social honors on campus. The purpose of the grandly titled club was to identify the one hundred members of each class most fit to join society, all by a process of cascading elections. Members of the previous year's class would choose the first ten members of the next. These ten men would then tap the next ten of their class, and so on until there were a new one hundred ready to take their place atop the school's hierarchy. With membership a prerequisite to join the Porcellian, the Fly, or another one of the prestigious and secretive final clubs that counted multiple congressmen and senators in their alumni rolls, the names of those admitted to the Institute of 1770 were printed in Harvard's own *Crimson* newspaper and in Boston's broadsheets every year, listed in the precise order in which the young men were chosen.

His status secured, Frederick opted to become a member of the A.D. Club, one of the oldest and most exclusive final clubs on campus. He spent long hours in the club's two-room headquarters on Brattle Street, just off Harvard Square, drinking beer and wine and playing hands of whist with his classmates. Frederick soon began spending more and more of his time with a wild New Yorker who could also understand the dark irony of passing one's childhood trapped in a mansion. Like Frederick, Theodore Roosevelt knew what it was like to feel cheated by his body. Yet where Frederick had turned to religion as a salve for his wounds, Teddy had resolved to overcome his asthma and weak frame through sheer brawn. As a teenager, he had decided to "make his body," as he would later call it, convincing his father to install a gymnasium in the family home on East Twentieth Street in Manhattan. There, he spent nearly every available hour of his late adolescence lifting weights and practicing gymnastics. He was soon well enough to travel with his family on a tour through Europe and the Middle East. That success did little to deter him from continuing the punishment of his body in order to refashion it more to his liking. He hurled stones, hiked mountains, pursued game through forests. Once enrolled at Harvard, he began boxing and wrestling, as if determined to beat any lingering specks of physical weakness into submission.

As it would for countless others, Teddy's lust for life stirred something inside Frederick. He could not match Roosevelt's seemingly inexhaustible physical energy; nor could he even try to: defeating his rheumatic fever was on another scale entirely from Teddy's single-minded conquest of asthma. Yet while he would never be an athlete, Frederick realized that he, too, was strong enough to travel the world and seek out the experiences that would give him the sense of making up for lost time. His tales of traveling the West by railroad car and the sights and sounds of San Francisco already enthralled Teddy; now he was determined to add to his stable of stories so as to keep pace with his friend.

THE QUESTION OF WHERE to go was easy. As millions of immigrants steamed toward the United States from Europe, Americans of means headed in the opposite direction. Despite its wealth, the young United States was widely considered to be sorely lacking in culture. Its few museums could not compete with the glories of the Louvre; its wooden churches were nothing in contrast to the immensity of St. Peter's Basilica; it had no Shakespeare or Milton to call its own. In his infamous list of the things the United States was lacking compared with what he called "the denser, richer, warmer European spectacle," Henry James included "no sovereign, no court, no personal loyalty, no aristocracy . . . no castles, nor manors, no old country-houses . . . no cathedrals, nor abbeys . . . no great universities nor public schools."

Traveling abroad offered a clear way to demonstrate one's refinement and taste at a time when it seemed like just about anyone could strike it rich. The docks of New York became stuffed with steamships, heading off to all parts of the globe. "The American is a migratory animal," wrote Robert Tomes in *Harper's New Monthly Magazine* in 1865. "He walks the streets of London, Paris, St. Petersburg, Berlin, Vienna, Naples, Rome, Constantinople, Canton and even the causeways of Japan with as confident a step as he treads the pavements of Broadway." Firsthand tales of tasting exotic foods and touring ancient sites became a standard feature in newspapers, written largely by tourists sending flowery dispatches back home. Professionals, too, realized that travel would sell. Nearly every notable American writer published an account of their voyage abroad, from Nathaniel Hawthorne, who wrote *Our Old Home*, to Frederick Douglass in *My Bondage and My Freedom*.

With the world open to them, Americans opted for the Continent most of all. "Europe is the biggest show I ever went to," one writer at the time noted. The newly rich, unsure of where to go and how to act, turned the guidebook industry into a can't-fail proposition. Nearly two thousand travel books were published in the United States between the Civil War and 1900, and nearly all of them did well. Even unedited collections of letters and outdated newspaper articles sold by the tens of thousands. The sights Americans were expected to see, and the feelings they were supposed to have when they saw them, were all prescribed by George P. Putnam's *The Tourist in Europe*, the most popular guidebook at the time. Itineraries listed what was mandatory and what could be skipped, which hotels to stay at and which to avoid, and even the prejudices one should follow. "Verily, the lower classes of the French are a filthy people," Putnam advised. With his guidebook in their hand, the "American who conducts himself as a patriotic and gentlemanly American should do, has no reason to be ashamed of his name or nation," Putnam counseled. Rather, he "belongs to nature's nobility."

On June 20, 1878, at the age of twenty, Frederick hustled across the docks in New York Harbor alongside a classmate from Harvard by the name of Washington Butcher Thomas, carrying Putnam's guidebook in his satchel. Once they found the right pier, Frederick pushed forward down the gangplank toward the long black hull of the SS *Baltic*, then one of the largest, fastest, and most luxurious ships in the world. A brilliant red flag sporting two tails flew high above its deck, with a star in its center that identified the ship as part of the White Star Line. Built in 1871, the ship sported four towering masts and a stout steam funnel looming above its deck. The ship was one of the first to cut the travel time between New York and Liverpool to under ten days, and it still regularly made the voyage across the Atlantic at a rate seven hours faster than any of its competitors.

Yet speed alone was not the main draw. It was luxury. The ship had more than a hundred first-class cabins, each adorned with deep polished wood and Italian marble. Its public rooms, meanwhile, were "rich enough for a nobleman's villa," wrote Benjamin Silliman, a professor at Yale who made a trip across the Atlantic on the *Baltic*. More than fifty mirrors lined the halls of the various saloons, making it possible for Silliman to look up from reading and count six replicas of himself reflecting back. The food, too, was opulent. A gong announced the arrival of each serving, and seemed to ring continuously from eight in the morning until nearly midnight over the nine days that Frederick was at sea. A typical first-class menu offered, in the words of a historian of the competing Cunard line of ships, which tried to match the White Star's level of luxury, "two soups, six varieties of boiled meat, three fish dishes, nine kinds of roasted meat, nine entrees with elaborate French names, two vegetables, two salads, eight choices for dessert, fruits and nuts, and coffee and frozen lemonade." Wine and spirits cost extra but flowed abundantly, leaving many passengers stumbling bleary-eyed to breakfast the next morning with a request for the strongest coffee the cook could muster.

The ship docked at Liverpool on June 29, and the two young men immediately got to work enjoying themselves. On their first day, they bought silk cravats and white gloves, gold-plated opera glasses and strong beer, and roamed the city of London. They spent their first night on the town in pit seats at a production of *Our Boys* at the Vaudeville Theatre, a comedy that was the longest-running play in the world at the time and dealt chiefly with the theme of wayward sons and their responsibilities to their fathers. With his own father's voice no doubt in his head, Frederick dutifully entered every transaction of his journey in his diary that night. He spent three pounds, six shillings on a haircut in the morning, six pounds for dinner at the London immediately before the production, and one pound on the account book in which he kept track of everything.

It was a habit he would keep for the next eight weeks, maintaining a running tally of his adventures as the pair traced a path through the Continent laid out by their guidebooks. He noted the ten pounds he spent for a suit on Savile Row, the two francs he spent on beer and champagne at lunch after touring the World's Fair in Paris, the two *décimes* he paid for a beach chair in the seaside resort town of Cabourg, on the Normandy coast. In Cologne he spent three German marks on a carved head of Christ; the next day, he paid fifteen for an enamel snuffbox engraved with the face of Frederick the Great. Alongside Thomas, Frederick gawked at the giraffes at the London Zoo (six pence), bowled with coconuts on the lawn of Hyde Park (three pounds), and watched a dog show on the Isle of Jersey (six pounds). In his final weeks alone, he spent one franc to secure a ride on a donkey to the remote town of seaside village of Dives-sur-Mer, ten pounds on a tour of Shakespeare's house and tomb, and one German mark to tour three ruined castles perched above the Rhine.

Returning to Harvard and the confines of a class schedule was the last thing Frederick wanted to do. He had kept his illness at bay and survived longer than anyone had ever thought possible—including, if he had to admit it, himself. Until now, that had been enough. He had trained himself into greeting each new day as an unexpected gift, and his ability to enjoy each one had fueled his optimism that there would be more to come. But while he continued to give thanks to God for the air in his lungs and readily shared his faith with anyone who asked, Frederick had tasted an unstructured life for the first time and didn't want to return to his pen, no matter how gilded.

There would be hardly any time for him to grow bored, however. With little warning, his illness reasserted itself with an unrestrained rage. He was soon too weak to attend classes, and then found that he could barely walk without assistance. The act of drawing a new breath into his lungs took every last bit of energy he could summon. Exploring the world was no longer on his mind; all of his thoughts once again narrowed to survival. His father moved him back into the family mansion on Dana Street, where Frederick again passed his days and nights in his cramped childhood bed. After the worst of an attack would pass, Frederick would spend the dark hours of the night staring out his window into the skies, wondering where to go next. He busied his mind imagining the ways he could make a mark with his life, never knowing how short that life might be.

As winter approached, Frederick's doctor warned that the chill might be too much for his body to handle and suggested that he head south. With the discovery of the antibiotics and other drugs that would cure rheumatic fever still a generation away, science at the time believed that fresh, balmy air far from the stench of overcrowded cities had an unseen ability to heal the body that drugs or exercise alone could not match. It was a theory barely removed from the medieval belief that so-called bad air, or miasma, was the root of all disease. Frederick lived on the doorstop of the modern age, yet the distance remaining could often be deadly.

With no other options, Frederick soon found himself on a train heading south from Boston, with a nurse at his side. His life's true adventure had finally begun.

Chapter Two

OH, THE HAPPY VAQUERO!

A NYONE LOOKING FOR EXCITEMENT IN JANUARY 1879 would have steered far past St. Augustine's shores. Everything that seemingly could happen on this patch of Florida coast had already happened, and all of it a very long time ago. The small city owed its existence to Juan Ponce de León, a Spanish explorer who landed there in 1512 and claimed it, and all of the land he called Florida, for the Spanish crown. A settlement established at the spot in 1565 took the name of St. Augustine. For the next three hundred years, the town would shuffle between the great powers of Spain, Great Britain, and France before coming into the hands of the young United States. Massacres, shipwrecks, and pirates had each played starring roles in its history, but by the latter half of the nineteenth century all of that seemed to belong to a different world. The so-called Ancient City, the oldest surviving European outpost in the United States, had become little more than a balmy beach town that shuffled to the rhythm of the tides.

It was here that Frederick Rindge escaped to heal himself. The town was "dilapidated in its appearance, with the stillness of desolation hanging over it, the waters undisturbed except by the passing canoe of a fisherman, its streets unlivened by busy traffic, and at mid-day it might be supposed to have sunk under the enchanter's wand into an almost eternal sleep," noted a visitor who spent a winter there. Yet what it had going for it was that it was far removed, both physically and socially, from the bustling cities of the Northeast. Out went the relentless efforts to acquire wealth and shimmy up the social ladder, and in their place came an unruffled pace of life.

The air alone seemed enough to recharge a broken-down body. "Morning comes, and such a morning does not come anywhere but St. Augustine," noted the author of *Winter Cities in Summer Lands*, a guide to the tourism industry in Florida, which was still in its infancy. Within a decade of Frederick's arrival, Henry Flagler, a founder of the giant Standard Oil company, would make his own trek down the coast and pass through the city's stone gates while on his second honeymoon. Enchanted—and sensing a business opportunity—he bought up as much of it as he could. Flagler constructed luxurious hotels on each of the city's small squares and set to work building direct rail lines to St. Augustine from the North, all the while envisioning the town as a winter Newport where Gilded Age barons such as himself could escape the cold while maintaining in touch with high society.

At the time, however, Frederick was the lone outpost of East Coast finery. He rented a room at the St. Augustine Hotel, then the grandest place in town, and let himself sink into the dreamy stillness of the city. When he felt well enough, he wandered through its tiny downtown of narrow streets, each one darting beneath a canopy of thick Spanish moss draping the limbs of gnarled live oak trees. He strolled along the seawall, gazing at the ocean, and rested in the shadow of the gray watchtowers of the Castillo de San Marcos, an ancient stone fortress on the lip of the bay that was then known as Fort Marion. Sometimes he made his way to services at a black gospel church, where he sat in a pew, riveted by the music. Amused by the novelty of fresh fruit available in January, he bought crates of oranges and sent them, alongside stuffed alligators, to his classmates at Harvard, while keeping a sharkskin belt for himself. Slowly, he allowed his body to recover and felt his sense of purpose return.

With little else to do as his body continued to mend, he indulged in a curiosity about native life that he had carried with him since he had first spotted Indian villages far across the horizon while on the train to California. Frederick made the acquaintance of Peter Jones, locally famous at the time not only for being an ex-mayor of the nearby port city of Jacksonville but for being an ex-mayor several times over. He had twice served a term as the head of the city, and by the end of his life he would serve four more, a track record that left the impression that Jacksonville was continually looking for someone better but ended up going with what it knew in the end. Outside of work, however, he liked to explore the evidence scattered around St. Augustine and Jacksonville that mature civilizations had existed long before European sailors waded ashore.

Great earthen mounds, crafted out of a mixture of shells and sand and in some cases standing over sixty feet high, lay untouched along the river and on a few islands just off the coast. Though Jones and Frederick didn't know it at the time, these grass-covered monuments had once been the centerpieces of native Timucua villages, essentially acting as grand platforms from which temples and meetinghouses overlooked the community. The pair hired a group of African American laborers to go out to a mound on Jones's property six miles upriver from town, where they planned an amateur excavation of the site.

As the group rowed its way along the river, Jones hailed a passing boat steered by a man who seemed distinctly out of place. To Frederick's surprise, Jones unearthed a letter from his satchel bearing Russian post-marks and stamps, which he gave to the stranger without ceremony. He went on to tell Frederick that the mysterious man was a Russian of high family and good education who now lived on a small orange plantation. Frederick thought little more of the encounter until two months later, when he again set off on the river to investigate the mounds, only this time without Jones at his side. Once more the quiet Russian appeared on a passing boat, and called over to Frederick. Together, they went ashore and walked into a makeshift hut standing alone on the banks of the St. Johns River.

The man then began a haunting tale. He started off slowly, unraveling his story in a heavy accent born on the far side of the world. The man "did not in any way boast of his antecedents or speak as if he were anxious to arouse the sympathy of his listener, but in a quiet manly manner told me his history. The fact of my having been in and seen many places and things on the continent which he had, doubtless led to his desire to tell me that he had seen better days," Frederick remembered in his diary. The Russian, Frederick learned, had been born in St. Petersburg into a good family that was wealthy enough to send him on tours throughout Europe. He enrolled in a university in Berlin, intent on studying law. As if to answer a question dangling from Frederick's lips, the man proceeded to open a drawer in a dilapidated wooden cabinet, from which he drew his university degree and receipts for his paid tuition bills as evidence to back up his story. After his graduation, the man began working for the government, as was customary for recent law graduates at the time. He was sent to Poland, which was then part of the Russian Empire, to serve as a justice of the peace.

It wasn't until he arrived in the country that he realized what he had gotten himself into. The governor of the province took him aside and told him that in order to keep his job, he would need to decide in the favor of his home country in all cases concerning a Polish citizen and the Russian government. The young Russian took his role as an impartial judge seriously, however, and could not reconcile this order with his own higher moral code. In time, he heard several cases that pitted Polish citizens against the Russian government, and he decided for the Pole in each of them.

Soon a new directive came down from his superior: he was ordered to report to Siberia, where he would fill the same post as he was currently serving in Poland. Even then the cold northern reaches of Russia served as a convenient place to banish anyone who caused too much trouble. Rather than go where it was said that a man could see green grass for only two weeks of the year, the Russian returned home, where he expected to work in the family business. Yet after a falling out with his father over his decisions in Poland, he fled to New York, where he thought his facility with languages would help him find a job in a commercial trading house. His skills in English itself were lacking at the time, and he soon found himself in North Florida, where the only way he could find to support himself was to become a fisherman. He had lived the last three years in a shared wooden shanty, each day hoping for word from across the sea that he could safely return to his home. The last letter he had received, by way of Jones, had been from his stepfather, who'd told him that he had secured work for him in a private law office and that he was free to rejoin his family. His exile would soon be over.

At the time, most men who heard such a globe-spanning tale would leave with a renewed appreciation of their stable, even boring lives. Frederick, however, walked away from the Russian's crumbling shack with an ignited yearning for adventure. He couldn't help it. For as much as he'd envisioned that his time in Florida would be an escape from the restlessness that nagged him to the core, restlessness had once again found a way to intervene—this time in the form of a homesick Russian bearing stories of risk and danger and loss. The combination of thrills was simply undeniable to a man who still felt the pain of having been cooped up in his room as a boy. No matter where he went or whom he encountered, Frederick was often little more than a caged bird, impatient to roam. He marked the Russian's life story in his diary, eager to "fasten it in my memory" as a source of inspiration for the days ahead.

The happiness of a healthy body had always been just out of his reach. These last three months had finally turned that on its head. Frederick was now stronger than he had ever been in his life, yet he was living in the sleepiest place he could imagine. It didn't take long for him to start formulating an escape plan. Rather than return to Harvard and face the possibility of reliving the same cycle of sickness that had long plagued him, Frederick resolved to finally indulge the fantasy that had badgered him since he was a twelve-year-old riding along the great ribbon of train tracks spanning the continent. He would go west, where he would prove his strength—and try to make his fortune—on the frontier.

WITHIN THREE MONTHS, Frederick found himself on horseback on the outskirts of Denver, tending to a flock of sheep. It wasn't the kind of adventure he'd had in mind when he set out for the West, but already he could feel himself becoming unburdened by the expectations of life in the Northeast. He began writing nightly in his diaries, filling pages with descriptions of the untouched countryside and jotting poems to capture his moods as he felt himself morph into the cowboy he had always wanted to be. "Oh, the happy vaquero!" he would later write. "Who would be a banker when he could ride the smiling hills and hide himself and horse in the tall mustard! Who would be a slave to desk and electric light darkness in a back room when sunshine is free to all? Aye, a liberal competence is splendid, but slavery is often its price. But then, we cannot all be vaqueros!"

Except for its harsh winters, the fledgling city of Denver would have been a natural place for Frederick to settle. Ten years earlier, its population had numbered fewer than five thousand residents, yet it had quickly swollen to nearly forty thousand after the discovery of vast silver deposits across the state. Wealth, and the people who carried it, flowed into the city, where the tracks of the transcontinental railroad ran through its booming downtown and made it an outpost of civilization amid a still-lawless frontier. Just a hundred miles west lay the seemingly inexhaustible silver mines at Leadville; there Oscar Wilde, on an expedition to sample life in the rough-and-tumble mining camps, walked into a bar and saw a sign on the piano asking customers, "Please do not shoot the pianist. He is doing his best." Prospectors such as Horace Tabor, a once-struggling storekeeper whose luck in the mines earned him the sobriquet of "the Bonanza King of Leadville," decided to turn respectable with their millions and build palaces in the capital city of the state that made them rich. At the corner of Sixteenth and Curtis Streets, Tabor began construction of an opulent marble theater, topped by a silver dome, that spanned an entire block and could fit nearly two thousand into its red velvet seats. When the newly christened Tabor Grand Opera House opened in 1881, it was said to be the finest theater west of the Mississippi and instantly sent Denver's stock higher in the eyes of the country.

A man like Frederick, who carried a valuable East Coast pedigree and a letter of introduction that secured him an audience with one of Colorado's sitting U.S. senators, could have easily found work in a respectable position at any bank or insurance company in town. Instead, he chose to roam. He met up with Thomas Webb Preston, a friend from Harvard who was spending his summer away from Cambridge in Denver, and on July 7, they took a pair of mules by the names of Jimmy and Jack, two riding ponies, and a small wagon and set off on a trek across the wilderness of Colorado and New Mexico. It was a trip with no destination or plan other than to experience the wilds of the Rocky Mountains at a time when the country's open spaces were rapidly filling up with people. Their only companion was a cook named Isaac Brown, who prided himself on being a relative of John Brown, a white abolitionist who twenty years earlier had led a raid on a federal armory in Harpers Ferry, Virginia, in hopes of sparking a slave uprising throughout the South. As Frederick sauntered on horseback toward the green foothills with little more than a shotgun on his back and a few days' supply of water, he must have felt that his luxurious jaunt through Europe just one summer before was a false memory from a different life.

Atop a black horse he named Omega, he braved the Berthoud Pass, a doorway through the Rockies two miles above sea level that brought him onto the western side of the Continental Divide. For the first time since he'd been a child visiting San Francisco, the water flowing through the streams and rivers around him eventually wound its way into the Pacific Ocean, an undeniable signal that he had truly left behind the East Coast and all that came with it. The trio soon came upon Castle Rock, an outcropping of sheer rhyolite walls towering above a valley that reminded Frederick of the stone fortresses he'd seen lining the rivers in Germany the summer before. "Nothing more picturesque can be imagined, and they forcibly remind one of such castles as the Rheinstein, the Cat, and the Mouse Castles on the Rhine. We camped near them several times, and in the evening a full moon made a scene never to be forgotten," he wrote in his diary. Over the next few days, he waded in hot springs, caught and ate trout spawning in the Blue River, and killed porcupines for sport. The party soon wandered onto the ranch of an eccentric by the name of Jack Rand, a former sailor who lived alone on a sprawling estate in the wilderness. Rand, whose long gray hair was said to make him resemble a Greek oracle, gave Frederick an impromptu lesson in the coarse social customs of the West. "His welcome of coffee sans sugar or milk, and his brusque manner of acting the host, together with his disappointment of our not having whiskey, was rather startling," Frederick would write in his diary that night.

In Leadville, Frederick and Preston met up with Lewis Northey Tappan, a heavy-browed scion of the prominent Tappan family who had left his native Boston to become an abolitionist and politician in Colorado. Together, the three men of eastern privilege journeyed 250 feet down a cramped mine shaft, and later spent an afternoon in the makeshift casino of the mining camp, which Frederick found "not unlike similar ones at Monaco and Baden-Baden, substituting only the peasant for the prince."

Frederick and Preston then crossed the smaller peaks of the Gore Range, named after an infamous Irish nobleman who had trampled over the same path forty years earlier. With more than forty men and an untold number of barrels of gunpowder at his disposal, Sir George Gore spent three years killing most any animal that moved while on an epic hunting expedition through what is now Colorado, Wyoming, and Montana. Gore himself was said to have shot more than two thousand buffalo, fifteen hundred elk, and more than a hundred bears purely for sport, a massacre that appalled the local tribes, who relied on the animals for sustenance. When Gore finally reached the Upper Missouri

River with a massive haul of buffalo hides and antlers, the traders at the American Fur Company offered him a pittance for them as a retaliation for the troubles he had caused with the Indians. Gore did not take the insult well. The Irish nobleman turned "wrathful, effervescent, and reckless and heedless of the consequences" and "burned his wagons and all the Indian goods and supplies not needed, in front of the fort, guarding the flames from the plunder of whites and Indians," according to one of Gore's stewards who witnessed his rage.

Tensions with the local tribes had hardly improved when Frederick and Thomas Preston stumbled into a Ute village tucked beneath a willow grove, taking the natives—and themselves—by surprise. Perhaps sensing that the pair of young bluebloods were not part of any army expedition, a Ute chief, who gave his name as Little Joe, told them to stay awhile. Frederick found himself in the midst of a waking dream, surrounded by the Indians he had puzzled over in his mind since he was a child. He set about examining the village's canvas tepees inside and out, marveling at boxes made of elk hide and the children playing card games he could not understand. In return, he brought out a tennis racket and ball from among his supplies, a pairing the Utes had never before seen and found hilarious. "We were much surprised to find them such a well built, clean and intelligent looking race," Frederick wrote in his diary that night, echoing the casual racism of his age.

Within weeks, that jovial encounter would be shown to be a fluke. As Frederick and Preston left the village, a contingent of nearly two hundred cavalry were on the march from southern Wyoming, headed toward the very same spot in order to enforce a recent order that banned the Ute from owning horses. When the Ute warriors refused to give up their animals, the Battle of Milk Creek broke out, killing more than twenty men on both sides. The battlefield, enclosed by step ridges covered in sage brush, was less than ten miles from the village where Frederick had spent a lazy afternoon. "The very Utes we invited to breakfast with us would now take our scalps," a shaken Frederick wrote in his diary.

The pair made a hasty retreat down to the New Mexico Territory in order to escape any further bloodshed and, in that same spirit, declined an invitation from their stagecoach driver to watch the lynching of three men who had robbed a train. The offer wasn't out of the ordinary. On the map, the territory formed an almost perfect square tucked into the nook of Texas. Within that square, however, the U.S. government held a tenuous grasp of order, and gangs of well-armed men readily filled the gaps with their own notions of the law. The summer before Frederick rode a stagecoach down to New Mexico from Denver, a shootout between rival factions in remote Lincoln County had turned a young Irish gunslinger by the name of William Henry McCarty Jr. into the outlaw known as Billy the Kid.

Frederick, who considered New Mexico "the most foreign part of our country, with its Spanish-speaking people, its Santa Fe, and its Pueblos," stayed long enough to meet Lew Wallace, the governor of the territory, but didn't think much of the place. He had found himself in the wildest part of the West and wanted no part of it. The reliance on a bumpy stagecoach in place of trains for long-distance travel was "tiresome," he felt, and the mix of Mexicans and Indians in the territory combined to form "a most unintelligent looking race." After attending a Mexican wedding, he scoffed that the faces of the dancers were "so solemn that one would think that the dance was a punishment rather than a pleasure." Frederick returned to Denver two weeks later, where he holed up in a room in Charpiot's, Denver's most luxurious hotel, and put all of his energy towards forgetting what he'd seen.

"Why could we leave the comforts of Charpiot's for the bad beds and worse meals of New Mexico?" he wondered in his diary.

FROM THEN ON, Frederick Rindge hewed closer to the boundaries of what he knew as civilization. Again with Thomas Webb Preston at his side, Frederick rode to the ranch of Barney Day, a Civil War veteran who had left his native Ohio and settled in the high basin of Middle Park, underneath the southwest shadow of the Rockies. Day, now one of the county's first elected officials, thought of himself as a man whose mission in life was to bring order to chaos. His son, also named Barney, was said to be the first white child born in the Colorado Basin. The Day Ranch in time became known as a prime hunting ground where Denver's elite—and well-to-do tourists simply passing through—could sample the untamed fringes surrounding the city without fear of falling into anarchy. Frederick found himself in the company of Sir Charles Watson, an unhinged minor English aristocrat who, Frederick soon learned, had "been in Colorado for his health or rather to keep himself from the use of brandy, as he is more or less insane," as he succinctly put it in his diary. Watson's doctor, who had traveled with him from England, kept up a daily deception by giving him swigs from a bottle of colored water that Watson believed to be alcohol, and the rest of the hunting party joined together and kept up the ruse.

Months passed. Frederick spent his days hunting elk along the Gore Range and his nights in the company of Preston, Day, and whatever band of well-bred travelers happened to be visiting the ranch. In the nomadic world of the frontier, he had finally found a place where he felt comfortable enough to stay awhile. He drew up a financial plan, spent four hundred dollars to buy a flock of sheep, and got himself into the wool trade. It was the first time in his life that Frederick had started a business of any kind, and he found that a facility with numbers and a drive for profit flowed innately through his blood. He soon began making other long-range plans as the future, which for so long had seemed like an unkept promise, started to become real. "I have made arrangements with a Mr. Henry Harris to live in a cabin to be built by myself on his ranch and to take my meals with them the coming summer," Frederick wrote in his diary that fall, the pride of his newfound skills in self-reliance obvious on the page.

He continued to explore the small towns surrounding the Day Ranch, often heading out alone despite the coming chill of winter. Frederick spent Christmas Day of 1879 alone atop his black horse, Omega, cutting a path across drifting snow on his way back to Denver. He never fully explained to Preston why he opted for these trips of solitude, preferring to keep his reflections on the future to himself. Over six short months, he had transformed himself into the kind of man he had always wanted to be: physically strong, resourceful, and at ease with a gun on the open range. If not for the freezing weather, it would have been easy to grow comfortable and expect that his body would not fail him again.

As Frederick sat in his stately hotel room in Denver, he began sketching out his plans for the year ahead. "After much uncertainty and doubt, I have finally decided that it would be better for me to remain away from home some time longer; that I had much rather spend a few months in Southern California than to go home for that length of time only to return again in the spring. And with this determination and in fulfilling these plans, I am confident that, *deo volente,* I shall be surely strong enough to return to Boston by October and undertake with strength and pluck whatever business fate may place in my hands," he wrote in his diary.

The next morning, Frederick stood outside of Charpiot's, flanked by a stagecoach. Preston was on his way down. The two planned to share a train up to Cheyenne and celebrate the first day of 1880 together amid the prosperous company of men flittering through the city's mansions, each one built from the sales of supplies or beef to miners searching for gold in the Black Hills. From there, Preston would make his way back east; Frederick would continue going west to begin his new year in California. Frederick held a ticket to San Francisco and, as the railroads had yet to extend to Los Angeles, planned to reach Southern California by horseback.

Before that, however, he promised Preston that he would stop by a rural ranch outside San Francisco owned by one of Preston's relatives. It wasn't much, Preston allowed, but it would offer Frederick a chance to explore the Sonoma County foothills for a few days before continuing his journey.

It was an invitation that would change Frederick's life.

Chapter Three

THE PROPHET
OF PRESTON

WHATEVER FREDERICK RINDGE HAD THOUGHT HE would find when he stepped out of a stagecoach in the rolling green hills some eighty miles north of San Francisco, it surely wasn't this. In front of him stood what was clearly a two-story hospital, albeit one that had seemingly been dropped out of the sky and onto a hilltop overlooking the slender Russian River, miles away from anywhere. No doctors or nurses appeared to be tending to the motley collection of patients milling about the building. Men wearing silk hats and full suits sat next to those in dirt-encrusted denim wafting with the pungent smell of the nearby mining camps, where the only ones still trying to find gold were those too desperate to give up. Older women in bonnets laced with flowers paced next to young mothers shushing children covered by little more than rags. The only similarity that could be found among the men and women assembled in the wilderness was the sad fact that they amounted to "a lot of human wrecks," as one visitor to the place would later say.

It would have never occurred to anyone on earth that this place could be considered heaven. Anyone except for the hundred-odd men and women who had traveled from as far as the Washington Territory to seek treatment by a woman known to all as Madam Preston. She was the unquestioned leader of the colony where Frederick now found himself, and she would alter the course of his life in ways that he could have never foretold.

By the time Frederick met her, Emily Preston had already lived one of those lives that seems possible only in America in the second half of the nineteenth century. Born in 1819 on a farm in upstate New York, the then Emily Lathrop spent her childhood marinating among itinerant preachers and self-described prophets, all of whom claimed to speak directly with God. In time, the region would be seen as the center of what was called the Second Great Awakening, a burst of religious excitement spurred by men and women uneasy in a changing world of factories and technology. Not far away from her home in rural Schoharie County lived a commune of Shakers, a celibate sect named for their tendency to tremble during services. One hundred miles north, William Miller, a Baptist lay preacher, was gaining followers by prophesying that the world would end on October 22, 1844, leading a movement which eventually ended in what became known as the Great Disappointment. Four years after Emily's birth, a farmer living 150 miles to the west named Joseph Smith Jr. experienced a vision in which an angel named Moroni appeared to him and told him of a book of golden plates buried nearby, the basis of what became the Book of Mormon.

By the time she's reached adulthood, Emily had sailed around Cape Horn as a widow with two young children in tow and arrived in California just as the Gold Rush started to ebb. Within fifteen years she had been widowed once more and lived alone in a flat at 717 Bush Street, in San Francisco's posh Nob Hill neighborhood, alongside tycoons such as Leland Stanford and James Flood. It was there that she experienced her own spiritual revelation. Suddenly, she felt as if God had "removed a veil or something from the front of my eyes, which enabled me to read, in my real normal state, the open Book of Life—the words of God which fill the Universe," she would later write. "Besides the words of written language, I see infinite varieties of Photographs representing—I am told and believe—the real realities of things in the Universe, Heaven, Earth and Hell."

With her newfound gift that she called the Intelligence, she started running advertisements in San Francisco's *Daily Alta California* and other newspapers throughout the area, offering free lectures in which she promised to "read from Divine Photography a message to the people." The ads worked, and soon she was drawing audiences that numbered in the hundreds. Her followers crammed into the balconies of the Metropolitan Temple, a grand three-story auditorium at the corner of Fifth and Jessie in San Francisco, to hear the words of the woman who had become the city's most famous faith healer. "I promised the Great God that, if he would spare my life, I would read His messages to the people, here and in every part of the world, at His command," she explained to an awestruck audience made up of everyone from stevedores to politicians, each one in rapt wonder as to what secrets she would reveal next. While she had no formal training in medicine or religion, she relayed to the crowd that God himself had told her that it would be a heinous crime for her to remain silent now that he had revealed his plans. "He had told me for more than a year past, that I must go and tell the world, that there is a Hell, and there is a Heaven; and I have seen photographs of Heaven and Hell. I have been shown all the different conditions of people, for every grade of life has been laid open and plain before my sight, and having this sight, I am responsible if I hide myself away from the world," she said.

Among those in the crowd was a wealthy attorney by the name of Hartwell L. Preston who had spent the last ten years of his life wrestling with questions of faith that pushed him further and further from his Quaker upbringing. He was transfixed by what he heard, and after a brief courtship, the pair were married in Oakland the following year. They moved to a loping ranch outside the rural Sonoma County village of Cloverdale that Hartwell Preston had purchased years earlier. Sitting on the slope of a hill they called Oak Mountain, beyond a red covered bridge spanning the Russian River and down a winding path through hills so quiet that the strike of a horse's hoof sounded like gunfire, the ranch wasn't much more than a few simple buildings and an endless number of trees.

Preston's devotion to Emily, his wife and spiritual guide, became total. "If you believe the Messages are from God, when they tell you to do anything, however inconsistent with your ideas of propriety or dignity, ask no questions and make no objections. Obey instantly. If you are told to do a thing, go do it. The moment the order is given to do a thing, do it or you will never be in covenant relations with God nor have any atonement with Him," he wrote in a book the pair published about Emily's gifts, *The Hell and the Heaven.*

Madam Preston, as Emily took to calling herself, claimed that her divine gifts allowed her to " 'diagnosticate' cases at a distance," a skill that meant she could treat any illness, regardless of her physical distance from her patient. Letters, more than ten thousand in all, poured in from faraway places, each one filled with tales of unremitting pain. The list of remedies Madam Preston offered ranged from the rather innocuous—fresh air and guzzling from the mineral springs that ran across the ranch—to the decidedly more intoxicating, with wine cordials and marijuana among her prescribed solutions.

Her signature answer to nearly every question, however, was a medieval form of therapy known as blister treatment. A patient would be given instructions to wrap a bandage dipped in a secret batch of caustic chemicals around the part of the body that was causing pain, and to leave it there for more than a week. The site would inevitably fester, which, Preston counseled, was a sign that the sickness was being drawn out of the internal organs and to the surface of the body. When the blister popped, any offending toxin would then dissipate into the air, leaving the body healed.

In an era when medical science had yet to fully distinguish itself from outright quackery, Preston's methods seemed as promising as any other, particularly among those whose losing fights against chronic disease left them open to suggestion. After purchasing a tin full of her treatment, patients took to wearing several liniment-soaked bandages at a time, often causing deep blisters that left permanent scars. Their belief in Preston and her ability to commune with God led them to look past the disfigurement and ask for more. Men and women scarcely able to walk somehow conjured the ability to hike through a redwood grove to the Preston ranch and knock at the front door, begging for another tin of liniment. The constant presence of unannounced visitors soon prompted Hartwell Preston to build a twenty-room hospital on the edge of the ranch which doubled as a boardinghouse for those who made the pilgrimage to the home of the woman they considered their savior.

This was hardly the only place in Northern California where men and women went searching for an alternative to heal their pain. Colonies filled with those seeking an earthly utopia flourished in America in the waning years of the nineteenth century, but nowhere more so than California. Just three miles south of the Preston ranch, seventy French men and women settled what they called Icaria Speranza, in honor of Etienne Cabet, whose novel *Voyage en Icarie* had captured the imagination of French revolutionaries by arguing that all human vice was the result of a poorly organized society. By instituting a system of group ownership, the members of Icaria Speranza hoped to abolish inequality and all other social evils. Within a month of their arrival in Sonoma County, the would-be colonists planted zinfandel grapes they had brought with them from France and planned to establish their own winery to keep the colony going. Yet a dispute over whether tending a vineyard constituted private property would eventually split the colonists into two factions, leaving Icaria Speranza abandoned by 1886.

Whether it was the bucolic surroundings, the placebo effect of mixing feel-good medicine like wine and marijuana with painful blister therapy, or some combination of the two, patients who traveled to Madam Preston's ranch credited her with saving their lives and vowed to never leave. Preston, as the camp came to be known, slowly transformed from a working ranch into a homegrown religious sect centered on what its followers called the Religion of Inspiration. Each week, Madam Preston would stand in front of a congregation made up of her patients and read the divine messages she said she saw printed on walls of light in front of her. She asserted that any person could go to heaven "if their hearts are right," a message of welcoming salvation that resonated with a collection of men and women who had little reason left to hope. "This religion is to make you happy while you live, and to open every door for you; and when the time comes for you to die you will not be afraid," she told them. "This religion brings you everything; yet it is so little appreciated; but in time it is going to be taken up. This religion will be sought after by and by; it is going to open people's eyes, and they will see that they must come to God for inspiration and the love of heaven."

To her followers, Madam Preston was a prophet, and the community pulsated according to her whims. As the number of her followers grew, she took to wearing a white dress with a small train, a uniform that only accentuated her short height and wide frame. Bells hanging from the top of her home rang out to signal every meal, and anyone who stayed out past the final bell, at eight each evening, would be locked out until morning. All forms of dancing were outlawed, and anyone found having sex would be immediately banished. If a man traveled to the ranch but was unable to pay for treatment, she would offer her services in exchange for the promise of physical labor once he was healed. Within a few years of its founding, Preston grew to nearly 150 residents, who were able to support their own farm, school, and two orchestras while producing over ten thousand gallons of wine each year. Madam Preston and her husband overlooked it all from their two-story Italianate mansion at the crest of a hill, separated from her patients below by a tall iron gate. Every aspect of the house—from its stone walkway to the wood frame to the nine columns supporting its veranda—was painted a blinding white. A flock of white turkeys, tended to by her followers, strutted across its neatly trimmed lawn.

The swelling population soon attracted the attention of the local press, who puzzled over what to make of a woman who, in the words of one newsman, was "regarded by everyone acquainted with her as enveloped in an unfathomable mystery." In a full-page spread, the *San Francisco Chronicle* marveled at the power she held over her sect. "Is there anyone who will credit that somewhere in the world there is a woman who not only owns a townsite, but runs every enterprise of importance in it; who is Mayor and Council and School Board and preacher, who owns the water supply and provides work and wages for the inhabitants, who is their medical adviser and cemetery association and their spiritual guide; who develops their mental resources and directs their aesthetic tastes, who superintends the design and construction of houses and plans all their amusements and recreations? She has been found in California. As a matter of course, she could scarcely exist elsewhere." Outside of the commune, few living in Sonoma County believed in her powers, and yet many admired the care she provided to patients doctors had deemed incurable. "Those who would condemn her as an imposter on the strength of her pretense to divine inspiration and direct communication with the ruler of the universe, consider the good results of her teaching among those who believe, and are silent," noted the local *Healdsburg Enterprise.*

In contrast to her patients, many of whom were destitute, she often wore fine clothes and jewelry, making her seem all the more removed from their earthly concerns. Her eyes, too, glimmered with an otherworldly intensity. "The hold the doctress gained upon her patients would seem incredible were it not evident that her wonderful animal magnetism could be resisted only by an equally strong or a violently antagonistic nature concentrated in her eye," reported the San Francisco *Daily Examiner.* "They hold one's gaze with a weird but far from unpleasant fascination, and have that singular effect of following one that is often noticed in the eyes of a well-painted portrait. Their range of vision seems limitless and comprehensive. Her voice is unusually deep and mellow, while her speech is slow and almost hesitating, as if she desired before speaking to assure herself that each word has its proper place." When a new patient arrived in Cloverdale, he would be given a small glass of a concoction made mostly of port wine, while Madam Preston stared intently at him from across a desk. Minutes would pass wordlessly, an experience that more than one patient reported felt as if she were looking right through him. After this long pause, Madam Preston would say what the divine light told her his illness was and would prescribe one of her own liniments as a cure. "It is the Intelligence which guides me," she later said.

Only the State Board of Medical Examiners, as part of a push to rid the state of unlicensed practitioners, made any attempt to shut the commune down. Madam Preston would have none of it. "Her word was law," one patient would later remember. "She was very stubborn. She was a woman of few words but when she said a thing she meant it. She hated to give in." Drawing on the legal advice of her husband, she replied with a defiant letter in which she said she had never claimed to be a doctor or physician, and she vowed to continue working with her patients. "They all tell me the same story—and it almost breaks my heart," she wrote. "The Doctors! The Doctors! They use their little morphine syringes upon me and deadened my pain, until they got all my money and then turned me out to go to 'springs'!!! It is dreadful, Doctor, and we must try and cure them—some of them at least."

Less mysterious was the fact that dispensing cures was making her rich. "Mrs. Preston has become very wealthy in a few years from her practices, as it is claimed she was comparatively without means when she came to Cloverdale," the *Sonoma Democrat* wrote. "Most of [her patients] are very wealthy, and while she talks religion she is looking after the dollars and cents with a practical and business-like manner."

Frederick Rindge, the wealthiest person to ever step foot in Cloverdale, received outsized attention from the start and soon proved that he, too, was not immune to Preston's charms. Throughout his life, Frederick had relied on faith to compensate for the frailty of his body. In Madam Preston, he was confronted with the notion that faith could transform it. The mix of religion and medicine was intoxicating for a man who had searched his known world for a lasting cure to the illness he had carried with him since infancy. He spent weeks at the Preston ranch, exploring the hillsides on foot and paddling a canoe down the Russian River, all with one of Madam Preston's caustic liniments tied around his chest.

As a sign of gratitude for his care, he purchased sixty acres surrounding the ranch and told the Prestons to use it as they saw fit. He then footed the cost of the construction of a new church building in the middle of the encampment. When completed, it stood twenty-four by fifty feet and was topped by a three-story tower, where a bell engraved with the words "To God's glory, not ours" rang every half hour. If not for its sanctuary, built out of redwood from the nearby forest, the church could have been found in the center of any New England village, as if Frederick were attempting to relive his childhood in a place where he no longer had to fear his body. Inside, a dedication he'd penned was stenciled above a stone hearth. "Truth is our motto!" it began. "Purity is our pass-word into Eternal Life."

Over the next few years, wanderlust carried him as far away as Hawaii and back again. Yet Frederick always found a way to return to Preston. In time, it would prove to be his retreat from the pain inflicted by the wider world. His father, Samuel Rindge, passed away in 1883, and his mother died two years later. With her death, Frederick became the sole heir of an estate that would be worth approximately $140 million in today's dollars. When he returned to Cambridge for her funeral, he could look out the top-floor windows of his family home and still see the influence of his father all around him. The cramped office building where Samuel had worked as a curly-haired teenager now housed one of the most prosperous firms in the city, which counted itself lucky to have him as a partner until the end of his life. Lots to the immediate east of Harvard's campus that Samuel had long ago purchased and never developed stood vacant save for their hawthorn bushes, as if still waiting for a directive from his pen.

Frederick had more money than he could spend, had lived longer than he had ever dared to dream, and stood in a city where his last name would open any door. Yet he was still searching for the peace that had eluded him since birth. Frederick's pain was not lost on Madam Preston, who was nothing if not perceptive about the wants of those with money. She nurtured him when he returned from Cambridge, filling his spirit with a gospel of her own design. As for his more earthly needs, she delicately offered a suggestion: her niece May was a fine young woman—the type with whom Frederick could perhaps start a family of his own.

ALL OF HER LIFE, Rhoda May Knight had been known simply as May. Standing at nearly five-ten, she towered over her twelve siblings in the tiny farmhouse on the outskirts of the village of Trenton, Michigan. If not for her height, it would have been easy for her to get lost in the shuffle. Her father, James Knight, had sailed to the United States from Kent, England, as a child, and in adulthood carved out a small farm on which he tended to a flock of sheep, providing the sole means of support for his growing brood. May was the eighth child, and seventh daughter, in the family, and her appearance suggested nothing if not a young woman whom life had decided to test early and often. She was slow to smile and quick to anger, and when she did offer a halting laugh, little joy danced in her eyes. Her wide nose and deep-set eyes gave her face a flat quality, as if the prospect of expressing happiness had been extinguished and little could be done to rekindle it. The few pieces of nice clothing she owned hung awkwardly over her broad shoulders and narrow hips, making her seem all the more relegated to the margins during any gathering outside of the family home.

What she lacked in charm, however, she more than made up for in grit. From an early age, May was the stubbornest member of a family that prized self-reliance above all. In the Knight home, there were few books to go around, and the sheer number of mouths to feed required every child to pitch in not long after they took their first steps. May's mother, Rhoda Roxanna Lathrop Knight, kept the farm and family running from a rocking chair on the porch, issuing commands that prevented the entire system from venturing into chaos. Even so, the simple acts of eating, bathing, and finding a quiet place to sleep often devolved into a Darwinian struggle that rewarded the most unwilling to budge. May learned quickly that anything—from the food on her plate to the pillow on her bed—could vanish if she didn't zealously stand her ground.

It came as a surprise, then, to the teenage May when her parents offered her a choice between two birthday presents. Gifts of any sort were a rarity in a household where every last bit of material was repurposed into something else of value. As her parents laid out the options, she delighted in the novelty of selection: she could have either a new dress or a tattered set of books on arithmetic, which would allow her to become a teacher and take charge of her own life. In the end, it wasn't much of a decision for her at all. She opted for the books without ceremony, even then valuing a path toward independence over short-term luxury.

By the time May turned twenty-two, she was working as a math teacher at the local schoolhouse, while continuing to live on the farm. Her meager pay helped the family get by. One winter afternoon in early 1887, she returned home from work to word that she had received a letter from a stranger in California. At the time, May had never been more than a hundred miles from the farm, had never walked on the streets of a big city, had never seen much of the world outside of Michigan. The letter she held in her hand, with its offset San Francisco postmark, was as exotic as something imported from across the globe. She opened it carefully, pausing several times over the formal script that addressed her as "Dear Miss Knight."

It had come from a man named Frederick Hastings Rindge. He informed her that he had been a guest in the care of her aunt Emily in California and would shortly be setting off back east en route to his family home in New England. Rindge offered to meet her in Trenton in order to pay his respects to the niece of the woman he credited with saving his life. May wrote back her agreement at once. A second letter, this one from Denver, arrived in early April. Rindge apologized for his tardiness, pinning it on a rash of business he was conducting in the Rocky Mountains, and promised to meet her within weeks.

It would be the last time he wrote to her by her maiden name. Frederick arrived at the Knight farm to find a scene that had long been the subject of his dreams. The small house shook with the sounds of thirteen siblings crammed under one roof, each one wanting to catch a glimpse of the man from California. Children tumbled over each other on the steps of the porch, while, inside the house, the scene was nearly as chaotic, a whirlwind of food and conversation and laughter. Frederick had known only the stillness of an empty mansion echoing with the absence of his brothers and sisters who had never lived to adulthood. Here, for the first time, he glimpsed what it was like to be part of the tiny spiraling universe known as a family. Despite the dingy surroundings that spoke to a station in life far below what he was used to, he desperately wanted a part of it.

The next few days were dizzying even to those who lived it. Two days after meeting her in person, Frederick proposed to May in the Knight farmhouse. She accepted without hesitation, and they were married in a small ceremony on the property within a week. Even physically, the marriage was a union of opposites: May, tall and broad and calloused, stood several inches above the refined, lean gentleman who was soon pronounced her husband. Their demeanors, too, seemed arranged around opposite poles. More so than his wealth or privileged upbringing, kindness was the core of Frederick's life. The quality seemed to radiate from his body, making anyone seem comfortable in his presence, no matter their own wealth or lack thereof. May, meanwhile, a natural introvert, was not used to being described by anybody, much less in a flattering way. Anyone who burrowed past the surface of her hard demeanor would be surprised to find a woman who fiercely valued family, a quality Frederick intuitively grasped and felt drawn to. In May, Frederick had found his inverse: where he was idealistic, she was skeptical; when he saw the world as a place to be conquered, she knew that it should be feared. Despite those differences, the two formed each other's perfect complement. The link between them was fast, and would prove to be lasting.

One final matter remained unsolved after the whirl of the wedding: the question of where to live. Frederick knew that a man with a family could not very well continue his nomadic existence, shuffling among the booming towns of the West. Trenton, for all of the charms of the Knight household, was simply too small for his ambition. Cambridge, meanwhile, seemed a town already won, a place where Frederick could accomplish little that would not pale beneath the light of his father's memory. He ached to create his own family, and to prove himself worthy of the great fortune he had inherited.

There was one place where a man with that sort of eagerness for life could go and make his name: Los Angeles, already becoming known as the city of dreams.

Chapter Four

THE BOOMIEST BOOM

ON A CLOUDLESS SPRING DAY IN 1887, A BLACK train chugged across the plains of southern Wyoming, huffing pillows of white smoke into the sky. In the first-class Pullman Palace cars, men and women decked out in fine clothes sipped wine and discussed their prospects; farther in the back, a round of hollers and curses announced the winner of each hand of poker played by a scruffier sort unencumbered by family life. For the first few days out of Detroit, the bleat of the engine had overwhelmed most conversation, but by now each person was adept at making himself heard over the background roar. The speed, however, took some getting used to. A mountain peak would appear in the far distance, and the next thing you knew it was right outside, as if by magic. Every so often a white-knuckled gentleman holding a rosary could be heard muttering to anyone who would listen that man wasn't meant to go this fast. Even those who could barely stand the rush of moving along at the ungodly speed of seventy miles per hour weren't able to take their eyes off the windows for long. Outside the glass panes, a vivid panorama of the untouched plains rolled by, full of sights and sounds that few who lived in the cities east of the

Mississippi could ever conceive of. The train passed through an alien landscape of spouting geysers, red rocks, and cragged mesas, as if exploring a cabinet of geological wonders whose contents had been dumped alongside the tracks.

Frederick and May Rindge sat knee to knee in one of the first-class cabins, imagining their future together. The pair had been married for two weeks and had known each other for a grand total of only three, making conversation a stop-and-go pursuit. Each new topic represented another chance to plunge into the other's history, another search for a shared experience on which to build a lifelong connection. Few were successful, at least initially. Their life stories were so far apart from each other that only by chance had they been bound in the same book, much less placed on the same shelf. Luckily for them, they were speeding toward a place where the past didn't matter. At the end of the tracks, at the far edge of the continent, Los Angeles was waiting.

For as long as the place had had a name, the City of Angels had been little more than a backwater on the edge of anarchy. An 1850 census found no newspaper, college, library, public school, or Protestant church in the county. Two-thirds of its citizens could neither read nor write. What they could do, however, was kill. "There is no brighter sun, no milder climate, no more equable temperature, no scenes more picturesque, no greener valleys, no fairer plains in the wide world, than those you may now look upon," wrote the *Los Angeles Star* in 1853. "There is no country where nature is more lavish of her exuberant fullness; and yet with all our natural beauties and advantages, there is no country where human life is of so little account. Men hack one another to pieces with pistols and other cutlery, as if God's image were of no more worth than the life of one of the two or three thousand ownerless dogs that prowl about our streets and make night hideous."

All of California had once been like this. Under Spanish and then Mexican control, the state was an isolated, lonely place on the edge of nowhere. Few of those who were born elsewhere and yet called California home—mainly soldiers and their families—were there by choice. Living amid its brown valleys and long summers, trailed by stink of countless cattle, was thought to be such a hardship that three Spanish soldiers convicted of raping a Native American woman in San Diego were sentenced to remain in California for the rest of their careers, a punishment considered unduly harsh at the time. The transfer of the land to Mexico did little to fill in a landscape whose emptiness was frightening. In 1834, Richard Henry Dana Jr., who, like Frederick, was the heir of a prominent Cambridge family, left Harvard in his junior year to join the merchant marine and sailed on a trading ship to the Californian coast. There he found a hellish, barren region that seemed as if it had been given up for dead. "The Californians are an idle, thriftless people, and can make nothing for themselves. The country abounds in grapes, yet they buy, at a great price, bad wine made in Boston and brought round by us," he wrote in *Two Years Before the Mast*, which became a classic about California life before it was annexed into the United States. "The truth is, they have no credit system, no banks, and no way of investing money but in cattle. Besides silver, they have no circulating medium but hides, which the sailors call 'California bank-notes.' "

Dana spent more than a year shuffling hides and tallow along the lonely bays of Southern California, each blue harbor piercing a parched landscape seemingly more remote than the last. He passed months at San Pedro, a reedy inlet that in time would become the Port of Los Angeles but was then "entirely bare of trees and even shrubs; and there was no sign of a town,—not even a house to be seen." When Dana finally pushed off from the waterfront on his voyage back to Boston, he did so without hesitation. "Not even the last view could bring out one feeling of regret," he wrote. "No thanks, thought I, as we left the hated shores in the distance, for the hours I have walked over your stones barefooted, with hides on my head,—for the burdens I have carried up your steep, muddy hill,—for the ducklings in your surf; and for the long days and longer nights passed on your desolate hill, watching piles of hides, hearing the sharp bark of your eternal coyotes, and the dismal hooting of your owls."

The same scene repeated itself farther up the coast. Visiting Northern California in 1842, Commodore Charles Wilkes, the head of a four-year journey throughout the Pacific authorized by Congress and named the United States Exploring Expedition, found "a state of anarchy and confusion" and "a total absence" of all authority. Upon entering San Francisco Bay, where, Wilkes estimated, "all the navies of the world might ride in safety," he found a garrison of one barefoot private and one officer, who happened to be missing when Wilkes came ashore. That he even spotted the private should be considered an achievement; San Francisco's population at the time numbered just 196 people.

The discovery of gold six years later changed everything. Suddenly an ocean made of mostly young, unmarried men appeared from seemingly everywhere, overwhelming the small local population and creating a frenzy unlike any the world had ever seen. Across the country, storekeepers boarded up their shops; mechanics packed up their tools; even clergymen were said to resign from their pulpits, all to head west and chase their dreams. Boats full of men with gold fever swarmed the harbor, leaving some ships waiting for days for a slip to open up in order to discharge their passengers. When captains did find a place to dock, many still could not land, as each crew member who came ashore deserted and ran for the gold fields without taking the time to fulfill one last duty and fasten one of the ship's ropes to the wharf. Once their vessels finally were secured, skippers often abandoned their boats to charge into the mining camps alongside everyone else. By June 1850, a year and a half after President James Polk announced to the nation that gold had been found in the soon-to-be state of California, the masts of more than 630 discarded vessels stood sentry along San Francisco's shores.

Within three years of Polk's announcement, the city's population had swelled to more than a quarter million. Those who struck it rich in the Mother Lode, an immense vein of gold stretching nearly 120 miles through the Sierra Nevada, brought their wealth into what was starting to become known as "The City," and by 1880, San Francisco stood as a financial rival to New York and one of the major ports on the Pacific. A soup of languages could be heard along its foggy streets, teeming with men from as far away as China who were drawn to the place they called Gold Mountain. Lines of red-trimmed cable cars soon began shuffling men—and the few women who could be found amid such wildness—up its steep downtown hills, giving San Francisco, which now billed itself as the Paris of the West, one of its most lasting images.

South of Monterey, however, all of the excitement stopped. Few of the ships steaming north along the coast toward the Golden Gate made landfall in Southern California, leaving it a place so long marooned from the outside world that men seemed to forget that such a thing as laws existed. Over the course of 1850 and 1851, the murder rate in the city of Los Angeles spiked to 124 deaths per 10,000 inhabitants, the highest recorded in American history. Hunting other men turned into a sport in itself. An amazed—and frightened—J. Ross Browne, writing for *Harper's*, recalled, "You would sit at the breakfast table of the Queen of the Angels [hotel] and hear the question of going out to shoot men as commonly discussed as would be duck shooting in any other country. At dinner the question would be, 'Well, how many did they shoot today? Who was hanged?' "

Bloodshed became commonplace, a prospect all the more terrifying considering that fewer than ten thousand men and women lived in the six counties that then made up Southern California, an area that spanned more square mileage than several eastern states. If men weren't killing each other, then they wanted to watch something else die. Crowds gathered at bullfights and along the edges of bear-baiting rings, where a chained wild bear would fight a pack of dogs until only the winner survived. The few outsiders who ventured into the region came prepared for battle. William Brewer, a well-known Yale geologist and botanist who led one of the first extensive studies of the state, wrote to his brother near the end of 1860: "This Southern California is unsettled. We all continually wear arms—each wears both bowie knife and pistol, while we have always for game or otherwise, a Sharp's rifle, Sharp's carbine, and two double-barreled shotguns. Fifty to sixty mur-

ders per year have been common here in Los Angeles, and some think it
odd that there has been no violent deaths during the two weeks that we
have been here. . . . As I write this there are at least six heavily loaded
revolvers in the tent, besides bowie knives and other arms."

Murders frequently took on forms of barbarity that bordered on the
spectacular. In 1862, the body of John Raims, a prominent landowner,
was discovered in a cactus path about four hundred yards off a main
wagon trail. "The body gave evidence that the unfortunate gentleman
had been lassoed, dragged from his wagon by the right arm, which was
torn from the socket, and the flesh mangled from the elbow to the wrist;
he had been shot twice in the back, also in the left breast and in the
right side," the *Los Angeles Star* reported. "His clothes were torn off him,
and he lost one boot in the struggle. The body was not far from where
the wagon had been concealed. It had been mutilated from the depredations of wild animals."

Within a ten-year span, floods, drought, and massive swarms of
insects would devour crops from Ventura to San Diego and leave many
living there wondering whether Southern California had been cursed.
Abel Stearns, a New Englander who settled in Los Angeles before the
Civil War and became the owner of a ranch stretching over two hundred thousand acres through the present-day cities of Long Beach and
Garden Grove, gave up hope after losing more than a hundred thousand head of cattle in one season alone to drought. He instructed his
foreman to drive the rest of the animals, which had been whittled down
to little more than living skeletons, off the bluff at Point Fermin and
into the ocean, to prevent the odor of decaying flesh from spreading
farther.

Desperation soaked into the land as months went by without rain.
"Everybody in this town is broke, not a dollar to be seen, and God bless
everyone if things do not change," wrote one rancher in Santa Barbara
shortly before abandoning his property and heading up to San Francisco to recover. "Cattle can be bought at any price, real estate is not
worth anything. The grasshoppers have taken possession of this town,

they have eaten all the barley, wheat, there is not a thing left by them, they cleaned me entirely of everything and I expect if I do not move out of this town soon they will eat me also."

FREDERICK HAD ALREADY tasted the rough life in New Mexico and had no appetite to bring his new wife into such misery. Yet in towns throughout the West, the appearance of a railroad, its tracks trailing behind like bread crumbs, marked the end of chaos, and Los Angeles was no different. The Southern Pacific had finally entered the city in 1876 and had immediately produced a calming effect, brought on by the visible connection to civilization. But it wasn't until 1886, a year after the Santa Fe railroad arrived and broke the Southern Pacific's monopoly, that the region finally began to show life.

Redemption came as a result of capitalism at its most cutthroat. When the Santa Fe line entered the state, its officers offered an arrangement to the Big Four, a group of railroad barons who controlled almost all traffic going to and from California. The Santa Fe would give up its plans to continue its push toward Northern California in exchange for control of the southern half of the state. When the Big Four refused, an unprecedented rate war broke out. Within two months, the price of a ticket from Chicago to Los Angeles fell from $125 to $25. Prices would soon fall much further. On March 6, 1886, the Southern Pacific cut its rate from Kansas City to Los Angeles to $12. Within hours, the Santa Fe dropped its fare to $10 and then to $8 in response. In a flurry, the Southern Pacific not only met each new price but began underbidding itself, cutting its rate from $6 to $4 and then finally to a single dollar. Throughout the Midwest, men bought tickets to California on the spot, never to return.

Those who made it out to Southern California wrote back home with tales of an untapped paradise that seemed all the more glorious because it was suddenly in reach. Real estate men portrayed it as the promised land, open to anyone who could afford a train ticket. "Southern California is very like Palestine in natural features, resembling that country far more than it does Italy, to which it is often compared," wrote one guide to the region. "Like Palestine, it is a comparatively narrow strip of land facing a western sea; it is shut off from interior deserts by high mountains, snow-capped in winter; it has its dry and wet seasons; it is a land 'flowing with milk and honey' and in both countries flourish the olive, the fig, and the vine."

The religious imagery worked particularly well in attracting a new type of migrant: well-off, educated at the finest schools in the East, and lured to California by the prospect of building a new empire. Whereas the docks of San Francisco and New York City teemed with newcomers with little command of English and even less money, Los Angeles found itself importing a certain well-heeled Protestant sensibility. "Nowhere else in the world had such a class of settlers been seen," wrote T. S. Van Dyke, a Princeton graduate whose *Millionaires of a Day* chronicled the early days of Southern California. "Emigrants coming in palace-cars instead of 'prairie schooners,' and building fine houses instead of log shanties, and planting flowers and lawn-grass before they planted potatoes or corn." Companies like A. Phillips & Co. began running what became known as excursions every month, in which more than a hundred settlers from points along the eastern seaboard and the Midwest migrated as a group to Los Angeles and San Diego. Once there, each family would already have a home and, often, a job waiting for them. Farmers, sensing the shift, gave up trying to make money out of the soil and instead decided to profit on top of it by subdividing their sprawling ranchos into settlements, which in time became cities such as Anaheim, South Pasadena, and Long Beach. Hotels replaced alfalfa fields, and stately homes appeared where cattle had trod just a few months before.

Railroad agents paid writers to go on lecture tours of northeastern cities during the worst part of winter, describing the glories of Southern California. The very best of them, a German immigrant by the name of Charles Nordhoff, who left a post at the *New York Herald* to go west, assured packed audiences, "There are no dangers to travelers on the beaten track in California; there are no inconveniences which a child or a tenderly reared woman would not laugh at . . . when you have spent half a dozen weeks in the state, you will perhaps return with a notion that New York is the true frontier land, and that you have nowhere in the United States seen such so complete a civilization." His crowds, in a mood to listen, mobbed the ticket agents at the end of each lecture, leaving the dazzled railroads to credit him with selling more seats to Southern California than anything else ever written or said about the place. Men and women bought tickets without abandon, creating an avalanche of immigrants racing to secure their part of the golden land.

FREDERICK HELD MAY'S HAND as their train hissed into River Station, a squat two-story brick depot plunked in the middle of the Southern Pacific's freight yards. A crush of trains idled along the tracks, as their conductors grumbled about the line to unload at the undersized and overworked depot. Farther down the platform, men jostled each other for space in front of signs advertising lots for sale in developments that hadn't been fully mapped. Teenage boys who in New York or Chicago would be hawking newspapers instead cried out the names of the sixty new towns that had sprouted up along the Santa Fe line in 1887 alone, each appearing out of the wild landscape as if conjured by a genie's lamp. Behind it all roared a full brass band, hired by a wily real estate agent to lead a parade of fresh Californians toward a group of lots parked in the middle of a dry riverbed and get contracts on them signed before the newcomers had any sense to know better.

Los Angeles was full in the grips of one of the most manic real estate markets that ever flourished. All honest land values gave way to pure speculation, leaving every property with a price plucked out of the thinnest air. The city had no industries to support the thousands of immigrants whose trains pulled up daily into its two overwhelmed stations, no infrastructure to handle a boom that doubled the city's population twice within one year's time. That didn't seem to matter. With easy credit and few sellers requiring cash deposits, speculators shut down each other's doubts with the phrase "Nobody can make a mistake who buys land in Southern California," repeating it so often that it seemed to ring from a thousand tongues at once. Prices doubled upon themselves, then doubled again. A twenty-acre lot at the corner of Vernon and Central Avenues that sold for $8,500 in 1885 fetched a price of $40,000 just two years later. A man known as Mr. Luke bought eighty-eight acres in the center of what became Hollywood for $100 each in January 1886; by June of the next year, he had no problem unloading all of them at $600 apiece. His eye for property wasn't always right, however. The same year, he had to watch twenty-five acres at the corner of Seventh and Figueroa Streets that he'd refused to pay $11,000 for go for over $80,000.

Sellers whose land was located farther afield from the city center had to resort to more creative means to move their properties. In Orange County, hucksters planted their confidants in crowds with instructions to bid up prices and then slink away. When that didn't work, the auctioneer would point to a well-dressed onlooker and yell out the price of a bid as if the unknowing man had made one, just to spur some action. Colleges, libraries, schools, and hotels were all promised in developments throughout Los Angeles and San Diego, yet few materialized. If the property was in the desert, it was said to be full of natural healing properties; if it was in a swamp, as in the case of Ballona, developers heralded the coming of a harbor that existed only in their minds. Even the most undesirable lots were snatched up by buyers planning to sell them the very next day to the next flock of immigrants pouring out of River Station. Newspaper advertisements targeted this early form of house flipping directly. "Of all the booming booms in the booming city of San Bernardino, the boomiest boom is the boom in the Heart Tract, the garden spot of the Beautiful Base Line. Fourteen prizes aggregating $16,000. First 30 lots, $750; remainder $850. Buy now and make $100," an ad in the *San Bernardine Sun* screamed. Men desperate to unload their holdings were even known to hang oranges on the gnarled branches of century-old Joshua trees and pass off the desert lots as citrus groves to eastern newcomers fresh off the trains.

Frederick and May Rindge had little problem passing by the jostling crowds of real estate men yelling out their wares. Frederick, after all, was already rich, and not foolish enough to gamble his inheritance on the whims of the market. The pair had come to Los Angeles for another purpose. For all of his life, Frederick had measured himself against the mighty yardstick of his father's achievements, and often found himself lacking. Everywhere he went in Boston he was known first as Samuel Rindge's son, and he continued to live a life of luxury simply because of the luck of his birth. Here, in a boomtown erupting all around him, was a chance to make the Rindge name matter on a fresh coast because of his own skills and nothing else. Everywhere he turned, he could see opportunity. All of Southern California seemed like a blank slate, ready to be filled in.

And what better place to make one's name than a land where the sun always seemed to shine. With the sweet smell of gardenias and orange blossoms mingling with the ocean breeze, it seemed as if the entire city of Los Angeles was built in a garden. With this kind of weather, Frederick told himself, surely his illness would never return. He wasn't the only one who believed in the transformative power of sunshine. "The purity of the air of Los Angeles is remarkable," exalted Benjamin C. Truman, a journalist for the *New York Times* who came west and founded newspapers stretching from Los Angeles to San Diego. "Vegetation dries up before it dies, and hardly ever seems to decay. Meat suspended in the sun dries but never rots. The air, when inhaled, gives to the individual a stimulus and vital force which only an atmosphere so pure can ever communicate."

May voiced no objections to Frederick's ambition. In the span of just months, her life had already taken more turns than she could have ever seen coming, as if it were all part of some master plan to deposit her in a place where history was of no consequence and every morning promised better days ahead. She was a young woman in a young city, with a husband who seemed able to make any dream real. Yet no matter how sunny each new day dawned, the farm, and its harsh lessons of self-reliance, would never stray far from her mind.

Chapter Five

WHAT SHALL WE DO WITH THE MILLIONAIRES?

THE PAIR SETTLED INTO A VICTORIAN HOME ON South Bonnie Brae Street, then a part of one of Los Angeles's more fashionable neighborhoods. Shrubs of recently planted palm trees, each one no higher than a man's hips, lined the road, which crested a gentle hill just to the west of the city's core. During the day, soft breezes off the ocean cooled each room as the sun poured in through bay windows. At night, Frederick and May fell asleep to the scent of lemon blossoms and honeysuckle. If this wasn't paradise, it was close enough.

Though he now woke each dawn to another day of limitless sunshine, Frederick was still not at ease. Ambition knotted his stomach, challenging him to do more. Most mornings, as the sun rose over the city and painted orange strokes across the sky, he could be found in the living room with a cigarette in his hand, plotting a path toward a fortune he could call his own. The boom spilled trainloads of people onto the streets of Los Angeles every day, he realized, but that was about as far as it went. Banks, insurance companies, waterworks—all the elements of a proper city were few and far between. What this place needed was someone who could guide it through the rough transition from frontier town to respectability. People would come for the weather; he wanted to give them a reason to stay.

So began Frederick's conquest of Los Angeles. He hired a driver and spent long days touring the city nestled in the black leather seat of a horse-drawn buggy, taking notes on what he saw. He kept a bucket of cold water at his side, and as the heat rose in the valley and mixed with the pungent smell of horse manure and human sweat emanating from its streets, he would dip in a handkerchief and bring it to his forehead to give himself a small measure of relief. These lengthy work sessions would often sap his body of strength, forcing him to spend hours in bed the next day with one of Madam Preston's bottles of wine bitters at his side, going over the details in his mind. Cords of smoke rose from the cigarette curled between his fingers, then drifted away as the setting sun left pink clouds in its wake.

On these scouting expeditions to acquaint himself with his new home, Frederick could see that deep changes were already afoot. A wide plaza, surrounded by whitewashed adobe buildings facing a grand fountain, marked the spot where a group of forty-four Spanish settlers founded the pueblo of Los Angeles in September 1781. Ever since, it had stood as the heart of the Spanish and then Mexican city, the centerpiece from which all distances were measured and the terminal of the stage-coach line to Santa Fe, which stubbornly refused to go out of business even as the railroad starved it of customers. Any history of Los Angeles was mainly lost on the eastern boomers pouring out of the train stations three blocks away. The armada of immigrants, Frederick among them, instead gravitated toward the few hotels, bars, and churches then open in the wide, empty lots south of the plaza. It was a pocket of the city where a man just off the train from Des Moines or Atlanta didn't have to tie his tongue around Spanish words and could go about his business in English all day long without encountering anyone who was native to his new home. Even the "Los" in the city's name was too foreign for many to handle, giving rise to a mangled pronunciation that made the word sound like it rhymed with "toss" rather than "dose."

Sensing that the future of the city was in its English-speaking districts, Frederick purchased a dirt-filled lot several blocks south of the plaza on the northeast corner of Broadway and Third Street. There he sent a team of men to work at 254 South Broadway, intent on raising a modern commercial building that could hold the offices of the law firms and insurance companies he envisioned one day flourishing in Los Angeles. The building climbed brick by brick from the hard valley floor. When its three stories were complete, Frederick told his men to spell out the word "Rindge" in big iron letters out front, stamping his name on his new city. The building would prove to be a forerunner of more to come. Not long after the Rindge Building opened, in 1888, the mayor announced plans for the construction of a new city hall only a few doors down. With one move, Frederick had laid the cornerstone for what would become an empire.

May handled the transition to Los Angeles in her own, quieter way. As she paced the empty home after each of Frederick's morning strategy sessions, she felt grateful for the faint sound of horse-drawn carriages clopping down the street. For all her life, the cacophony of family had marked every moment of the day and many of the nights. The sensation of being alone was an utterly foreign experience, and the lingering hours of silence unnerved her. She wasn't quite ready to go back to Michigan, yet home had never felt so far away.

The arrival of Mary Lathrop at the Rindge home that fall lifted May's spirits when they were closest to sinking. Nationally known as the vice president of the National Woman's Christian Temperance Union, a forerunner to the Prohibition movement, Aunt Mary was a walking blast of thunder, eager to point out to anyone and everyone she encountered all the ways that alcohol was the first step on the road to hell. For May, whose religion was of the decidedly Old Testament variety, it was a welcome reminder of who she was. Her relatives in Michigan prided themselves on their willingness to fight to make something out of a land that could be so unforgiving. California, so unlike Trenton with its sunshine and palm trees, seemed too easy by comparison. Aunt Mary had planned on staying for but a week or two, but not long after she walked in the door she announced that her visit would be much longer. May, after all, was pregnant.

A LETTER BEARING a Cambridge postmark arrived at the home, addressed to Frederick Rindge. He opened it and read with delight that a classmate of his from Harvard, William E. Russell, had just been reelected mayor of Cambridge. Russell himself had written to share the good news. The two men had met as boys in Cambridge and remained friends throughout their adolescence, even as Frederick's long bouts of sickness prevented him from joining in Russell's adventures. Russell wrote now with more than the recent election on his mind. Appealing to the nostalgia he knew Frederick harbored for his hometown, Russell asked if Frederick would perhaps be willing to sell a plot of land his father had purchased years ago. Bounded by Broadway, and Cambridge, Trowbridge, and Irving Streets, it would be an ideal site for Cambridge's new public library.

The request stirred something inside Frederick beyond the wistfulness Russell counted on. Living in a place where it seemed like great wealth was there for the taking needled Frederick in ways he had never anticipated. His inheritance, long a source of comfort, seemed as if it were a dark cloud intent on casting long shadows over any of his own accomplishments. After all, he could hardly compare any success he mustered to that of a speculator in the boom who'd arrived with nothing, and much less to the triumphs of his own father, while he sat on a cushion of millions of dollars that he had played no part in acquiring. Intent on making his own fortune in Los Angeles, Frederick resolved to spend his father's in Cambridge.

His reply landed on Russell's desk a few days later. Frederick declined the invitation to sell his land and offered to donate it instead. That was not all. With a shock, Russell read that Frederick insisted on footing the construction of the building himself. His only condition was that the city include five tablets, either within or on the building itself, with inscriptions that reflected the power of faith in his life. One was to display the Ten Commandments, another an inscription that said that following God was the path to true happiness. On the last was a sentiment Frederick had penned that read, in part, "It is noble to be pure; it is right to be honest; it is necessary to be temperate; it is wise to be industrious; but to know God is best of all." Over the doorway to the building itself, Frederick envisioned an inscription that read, "Work is one of the greatest blessings; every one should have an honest occupation."

The aldermen of Cambridge accepted the gift with little delay, and in the following months Frederick surprised them with several more. He offered to furnish the city with a new city hall, as well as a manual training school that would prepare boys for work ranging from blacksmithing to carpentry. He insisted that neither his name nor his father's appear on any building he funded. Instead, he composed dedications to grace their exteriors, each one praising God. Over the entrance to city hall, Frederick instructed that metal or stone letters spell out, "God has given commandments unto men. From these commandments men have framed laws by which to be governed. It is honorable and praiseworthy faithfully to serve the people by helping to administer these laws. If the laws are not enforced, the people are not well governed."

Frederick's modesty was at odds not only with the times but with the traditions of Cambridge itself. All around the Harvard campus, grand red-brick libraries and dormitories bore the names of men who'd fancied themselves captains of industry and yearned for a way for their personal glory to carry on well after their own lives ended. Frederick admired these men for their accomplishments but thought little of their vanity. He pictured his gifts as a way to steer men and women toward a better path in this life and the next. "What I am aiming to do," he wrote in a personal letter to Russell, "is to establish certain didactic public buildings."

The final price tag of his generosity exceeded half a million dollars, a stunning figure at a time when the total number of millionaires in America was under four thousand. His donation attracted wide attention from

New York to Boston and thinly disguised jealousy from the West, where newspapermen now tracked his every move to see what was next from the eastern capitalist in their midst. The *New York Times* hailed him as "Cambridge's benefactor," while the *Hartford Courant* crowned Cambridge "a lucky town." Papers in San Francisco took the news as an opportunity to make note of the fact that, for all of the East's refinement, Rindge had ultimately decided to settle in California. "Mr. Rindge, it appears from facts learned, can hardly be classed in the lot with those moneyed men, who from time to time have expended in the East the money they have earned in this Western wonderland of rich resources," opined the *San Francisco Daily Bulletin* in an unsigned editorial. "He came to California a few years ago after a tour of Europe and much of the world in search of health. He found here what so many other New Englanders are now finding—a place where he could live in health and comfort."

Frederick was utterly baffled by the commotion surrounding his gifts. "It may be asked why so much has been given to one city," he wrote in a letter to Russell after he received an invitation to appear before the editorial board of the *Los Angeles Times* for the first time. "Cambridge was my father's and my mother's home and my own birthplace. The recollections of my boyhood center about it. On what is now the public library common I used to climb the hawthorn for its berries, which taste good to boys. Then, too, I believe that what is worth doing at all is worth doing well and thoroughly, and that concentration increases the power for good."

He didn't have much time to dwell on the attention, wanted or otherwise. On April 9, 1888, Frederick and May welcomed a plump baby boy into their home and gave him the name Samuel Knight Rindge, a move aimed at uniting their family histories, whose paths were so unalike, by adding a new chapter. Frederick, meanwhile, continued to put all of his efforts toward earning the first million of his own. He founded companies large and small, each one meant to further tame the wildness lurking amid the sunshine of Los Angeles. Sometimes, that wildness was literal, as in the case of the animal traps offered by his Cyclone Trap

Company. But more often than not, Frederick saw to it that Los Angeles would become more than a playground for real estate speculators. He started gas and electric companies in San Pedro, Long Beach, and San Bernardino; streetcar lines that took passengers up and down the glittery avenues of Santa Barbara; water companies that opened up thousands of acres of land in the San Fernando Valley that would become Los Angeles' first true suburbs. When, in 1888, the real estate boom collapsed under the weight of untenable prices, Frederick snapped up land throughout the west side of Los Angeles and sat on it, anticipating that the bust would be but a temporary pause in the city's expansion.

He was not content to contain his ambitions to Los Angeles. As he grew his business empire, Frederick frequently found himself in San Francisco, buying properties or opening new businesses in the city that was still then the largest and most important on the West Coast. Homesick and feeling out of place in his hotel abutting San Francisco's large Chinatown, he wrote letters to May daily, addressing her as "apple-blossom" and telling her to shower Samuel with a hundred kisses for him. "I would give so much to have you by my side. Your love and sympathy and presence and voice and eyes and laugh are worth so much. I am longing to get back to them," he wrote, each word crafted in his fine script.

Above all, Frederick tried to draw little attention to himself beyond what his gifts had already sparked. For the first time in the country's history, ordinary men and women could now amass fortunes once reserved for kings, and America was still grappling with the consequences. In Boston, Charles F. Dole, an influential minister from a long-established family, wrote a scathing article entitled "What Shall We Do with the Millionaires?" for *New England Magazine* that was republished throughout the country. "The increase of colossal fortunes threatens our civilization with serious problems," he wrote. "What shall we say . . . of the ordinary millionaire? Has he ever done for society anything to entitle him to command the unlimited services of the world? Indeed, too often he has speculated his way to fortune by gigantic methods of cheating and gambling; or he may have been made accidentally rich by the growth of the great town around his stupid grandfather's farm; or, very often his sole title to fortune is by the accident of birth."

Dole called for the rich to fund all the basics that made life decent—schoolhouses, hospitals, city halls, public parks—thereby sparing the taxes of men and women working to put food on their tables. As an example of the right kind of millionaire, he singled Frederick out by name. "We might cite the wise and generous gifts of Mr. Rindge in Cambridge . . . as among the signs which show that our rich men are not without conscience, generous ambition, and a healthy sensitiveness to the public opinion of their responsibility," Dole wrote.

In time Dole would have to confront an explosion of wealth in his own family. In 1899, nine years after his article appeared, his son James Dole began planting pineapple trees on a government homestead he had purchased on the island of Oahu. That small business would grow into the Dole Company, making Charles Dole the father of a millionaire many times over.

Frederick offered no public response to Dole's article, preferring to expand his footprint in the sun-drenched city he now called home instead of garnering additional attention. The Rindges brought home a second son, Frederick Jr., in September 1890 and soon moved into a mansion at the corner of Wilshire Boulevard and Ocean Avenue in Santa Monica, directly overlooking the water. Across the street stood the lush grounds of the Miramar, the fabled home of Senator John Percival Jones, an English immigrant who became a multimillionaire from the Nevada silver mines and later cofounded the city of Santa Monica. As his family expanded, Frederick happily noted that his life had taken on something of a routine. Each morning, he set off by horse-drawn carriage, accompanied by the sound of seagulls, on his way to the Rindge Building in downtown Los Angeles, and he returned home to see the sun setting over the palisades, just steps from his front door. Three years after their arrival in Southern California, the Rindge name had some weight to it. Frederick had little reason to think that his fortune would ever change.

———

THE CROWD FILLED the rooms of the stone library in Cambridge, leaving precious little space for a man to breathe. Outside, those not lucky or connected enough to have received an invitation milled about the library entrance, marveling at the craftsmanship of the arches framing its doorway and the sight of its tower, topped with red tile, jutting into the blue New England sky. A small speaker's platform stood in the spacious reading room, and gray-haired men, long accustomed to an audience hanging on their every word, waited their turn to speak. A choir of men and woman began to sing a rendition of the *Festival Te Deum* in E-flat, with a Miss Edith Torrey hitting the soprano notes. All of Cambridge's aldermen had turned out for the dedication of the town's new library, along with three ex-mayors and Dr. Charles W. Eliot, the president of Harvard, whose long muttonchops framed his face with a flurry of hair that few could match. There was only one man missing from the festivities: Frederick Rindge himself.

After an invocation prayer, Colonel Francis J. Parker stepped up to the platform holding an oversized gold key. He introduced himself as Mr. Rindge's representative, then presented the key to the city's mayor and aldermen, alongside an honorary deed to the building with the name "Frederick Hastings Rindge" written in large letters on the bottom. He unfurled a piece of paper and began reciting a message, he informed the crowd, from Mr. Rindge. "I regret that my father did not in his lifetime give more money for God's glory and for philanthropic purposes; and in saying this it must not be supposed that I am lacking in filial love and duty, for to my mind there are few men possessed of hearts kinder than my father's," Parker read aloud. "But if he who by years of toil, through seasons of deep anxiety, accumulated a fortune, had himself expended a moiety of it in good works, the satisfaction would have been a high reward to him, and the act would have been one of great generosity. It is easier for one who has inherited wealth to disburse it for public purposes than for one who has earned it by sweat of liver or brain; for the latter values it at what it has cost; that is, perhaps, at a lifetime of continuous exertion, and the mental habits incident to million-making are very engrossing, and therefore tend to the constant postponement of acts of duty and of liberal intention."

The crowd clapped approvingly. The ceremony moved on to the next in the line of distinguished guests. In light of his stature around town, Dr. Eliot spoke the longest. After a speech touching on the history of public libraries, he concluded by telling the assorted men and women, "Let no one hesitate to use this library, if only for fifteen minutes at a time. It is fifteen minutes' communion with the greatest intellects of the world."

While Eliot, Parker, and the other dignitaries filled the stage in Cambridge, Frederick Rindge was on the opposite side of the continent, struggling for air. The illness that had been his companion since birth had once again steered his life far off the tracks he had laid. A week earlier, he had boarded a train to Boston, intent on appearing at the ceremony, yet he soon found himself too weak to go farther. He headed north instead, toward San Francisco, where he again fell into the care of Madam Preston. Not wishing to draw attention to his illness and scare off any potential business partners, he holed himself up in a room at the grand Hotel Pendleton, just off the city's Union Square, and steadied himself for a weeklong battery of liniments and wine bitters that Preston brought to him and promised would restore his health. Letters from May sat stacked on a small wooden desk in his room, each one asking for him to return home to her and his young sons as quickly as possible.

His heart ached for home, yet he believed that Preston's treatments were his only chance at staving off another attack on his body. With liniment-soaked bandages tied around his body burning blisters into his skin, Frederick wandered among the clanging cable cars and the downtown buildings that towered fifteen stories overhead. The daily letters he wrote to May were his chief consolation. "May, I think this is the wickedest place I ever saw. I wouldn't live here for anything, but God has given me grace to keep better than I am at home, I think," he confided one night. "You don't know how lonesome and homesick I have been. When we are afar I begin to realize a <u>little</u> how deep my love is," he wrote, pressing the pen down so hard when he underlined the word that it left grooves in the paper.

Even as a young boy, Frederick had felt his faith the strongest when his body was the weakest, and he again turned toward God to sand the edges of his pain. He attended services at Methodist churches in the city and, departing from organized religion, sat in the audience as Madam Preston preached to a crowd in San Francisco from the messages she saw written in light. His thoughts kept returning to his wife and the two young boys now scurrying around his house in Santa Monica. "I am working to acquire the habit of thanking God for even the smallest things very frequently. I find it great wisdom," Frederick wrote to May one night from his hotel room.

Gradually, he regained his strength and, confident that he was not on the verge of another attack, returned to Santa Monica a chastened man. He had come to realize that Southern California, for all of the glories of its climate, could not prevent his illness from reappearing and wreaking havoc on his life's plans. Where he'd once thought only of making his name in business, he now looked to make the most of whatever life still held for him. He spoke of God frequently and wrote religious tracts with titles like *Thoughts of a Truth Seeker,* which he distributed among his business associates. He also resolved to allow some room for a little indulgence in his life. Scratching an itch he'd felt since childhood, he began amassing a collection of Native American artifacts, building a personal museum that included materials from Alaska to Central America.

But nothing appealed to him as much as finding a bit of unspoiled land far from the city to call his own. "I told a friend I wished to find a farm near the ocean, and under the lee of the mountains; with a trout brook, wild trees, a lake, good soil, and excellent climate, one not too hot in summer," he later wrote. "To this hope my good wife demurred, saying, 'You ask too much.' Such, however, was the picture of an ideal farm which came to my mind. But my friend said, 'I know such a place, I think, but I would like to refresh an old memory and see it again.' "

The site was about twenty miles away from the Rindge home in Santa Monica, and Frederick could make out the purple silhouette of its mountains on the far side of the bay each night as the sun dipped below the ocean. In early 1892, he eased into a saddle and set off up the coast to inspect it for himself. A modern city was rising in Los Angeles—much of it his doing—and Frederick yearned for a place where he could preserve the native paradise of Southern California for his own enjoyment. The towering Santa Monica Mountains all but blocked access to the ranch, offering a seclusion no other place could match. Its name alone tingled with romance: the Rancho Topanga Malibu Sequit.

Chapter Six

HAPPY DAYS IN SOUTHERN CALIFORNIA

THE SANTA MONICA MOUNTAINS ARE ONE OF nature's more peculiar accomplishments. Jutting up against the Pacific Ocean, they are built out of a flinty gray stone known as Santa Monica slate. Although its origins date back more than 165 million years, to the Jurassic period, it is a weak rock that breaks up easily, a quality that means that it is unlikely stay in one place for long. That a type of rock given to move formed at the junction of two of the shifting tectonic plates that compose the earth's crust is one of those accidents of geology that make it seem as if all of creation is nothing more than a boy playing with matches, waiting to see what happens.

Some twenty million years ago, the Pacific Plate, the tectonic plate that underlies much of the Pacific Ocean and abuts the North American Plate at the notorious San Andreas Fault, began pulling a two-hundred-mile long slab of Santa Monica slate sitting near present-day San Diego northward at a rate of about two inches a year. At some point, that slab slammed into a formation of harder rock propped on the North American Plate, which refused to budge. With nowhere left to go, the mass of stone, now miles away from where it formed, began rotating and spilled into the ocean, creating the southern portions of the Channel Islands, which dot the Southern California coast. What was left over became the Santa Monica Mountains. The peaks, which run from the Oxnard Valley to the Hollywood Hills, are part of the larger Transverse Ranges, the only stretch of mountains that run east to west in California, and one of only a handful of such formations in North America.

It is a place where peaks jutting up to three thousand feet high give way to deep and sudden canyons whose floors stand just above sea level. Clouds rushing in off the Pacific snag on the mountaintops, making each hour either bathed in sunshine or stuck under gloomy gray skies, but rarely anything in between. Freshwater creeks run along the bottoms of the canyons they carved and feed into some of the largest salt marshes left on the West Coast. A diverse array of animals—from deer to mountain lions to more than two hundred species of birds—make the area home, all despite a near absence of flat land. Caves pocket the mountainsides, holding bounties that, in its past, have ranged from hibernating grizzly bears to men trying to stay one step ahead of their fates. In some places, it is possible to come over a small ridge and find yourself face-to-face with a waterfall whose bubbling sounds like laughter, as if it derived great joy out of surprising you.

The ranch Frederick Rindge went to survey sat in the cradle of the range, at the point where the mountains meet the sea. The transition between the two is abrupt, giving the impression that the song of creation ended a half-measure early. Rock spills down to the coastline itself, where, left untouched, it can seal off the path onward from any visitor attempting to make a journey along the beach. With no means to clear the coastline of all its obstacles and a hilly landscape that offers few concessions for a farm, the first men and women who lived there and gave it its name depended on the sea for life.

The Chumash Indians called the area Maliwu, a word whose meaning is lost. They made their homes in a village that stood on the east side of what is now called Malibu Creek and became masters of the ocean, a skill that greatly impressed the Spanish explorers who first came into contact with them. "They are of good figure and disposition, active, industrious, and inventive," wrote Father Juan Crespí, the diarist of Gaspar de Portolá, a Catalonian noble who in 1769 led the first overland expedition into California and made the European discovery of San Francisco Bay. "They have surprising skill and ability in the construction of their canoes, which are made of good pine planks, well joined and of graceful shape, with two prows. They handle them with equal skill; three or four men go out into the open sea in them to fish, and they hold as many as ten men. They use long oars with two blades, and row with indescribable lightness and speed."

The success of the Portolá expedition brought more men northward from Mexico. Captain Juan Bautista de Anza, following Portolá's lead, guided 240 colonists, along with a stock of farm animals, to San Francisco Bay in 1775. Among them was a man named José Bartolomé Tapia, one of the eleven-strong Tapia family to make the journey. By 1789, Tapia, who called himself Bartolo, had moved south, to San Luis Obispo. There he worked as the majordomo, or manager, of a cattle ranch under the control of the local mission, one of the twenty-one Spanish outposts whose purpose was to systematically undo native life in California and replace it with a feudal system of wide farms under the control of the Catholic Church. Three to four thousand Indians lived under the control of each mission, where they worked on the surrounding farms for food, clothing, and shelter yet received no money or property to call their own. Tapia soon moved south again, to the tiny village of Los Angeles, which, as a pueblo, stood as one of the few secular settlements in Spanish California. He tended to a small farm in the foothills and brought produce to the market stalls of Los Angeles by way of an ox-driven cart. When he discovered an easier way through the San Gabriel Mountains, the sloping peaks that form the northern boundary of the Los Angeles basin, the route became known as El Paso del Bartolo in his honor. In time, it would be one of the last battlegrounds in the Mexican-American War.

In the late eighteenth century, the Spanish crown held the right to all land in California, yet few of its people were willing to uproot their lives in order to colonize a place sitting at the edge of the known world. Starting in 1784, governors began granting sweeping land grants on the far outskirts of pueblos and missions, hoping that these ranchos would encourage popular settlement. Mission-bound priests rightfully saw the development as a threat to their control of the local population. After touring the San Gabriel Valley while scouting a location for what would become the Mission San Fernando, Father Santa Maria described life on the nearby ranchos in disparaging terms: "Here we see nothing but pagans passing, clad in shoes, with sombreros and blankets, and serving as muleteers to the settlers and the rancheros, so that if it were not for the gentiles there would be neither pueblo nor rancho. . . . These pagan Indians care nothing for the mission nor the missionaries."

The sheer abundance of land made the chore of defining the exact boundaries of each rancho seem pointless even to the governors writing the grants. Rancho San Juan Cajón de Santa Ana, whose thirty-six thousand acres stretched across what became the present-day cities of Anaheim and Fullerton, was officially described as "beginning at the River Santa Ana and running out on to the hills where there is an oak, near the Valley of the Elders, which line is contiguous to the property of Bernardo Yorba, from the oak to a stone which is permanent and another one resting upon it. From the stone to the pillar which is now fallen, from the pillar to the sycamore tree, from the sycamore to the lake and from there to the river." In case of a dispute, the grant, and almost all others like it, ended with the words *más o menos*—more or less. The rancheros themselves cared little for the imaginary lines marking their territory and allowed their cattle and sheep to roam freely across the hills and valleys. Questions of ownership mostly concerned cattle and were settled during semiannual rodeos, during which vaqueros riding on horseback would rustle herds into wooden corrals, so that calves could be branded and older animals slaughtered for their hides.

As one of the earliest settlers of California, Tapia had little trouble acquiring one of the thirty ranchos granted during the Spanish era. In

1802, Don Felipe Goycoechea, the head of the military garrison stationed at Santa Barbara, offered Tapia a long splinter of land on the coast that he called the Rancho Topanga Malibu Sequit. The grant proclaimed that Tapia now had full ownership of the terrain "bounded on the North by the Sierra Mayor, on the South by the Pacific Ocean, on the East by the Rancho Santa Monica, where it joins the Canada de Topanga, and on the West by the mouth of the San Buenaventura River." There, on one of the largest and most isolated ranchos in Southern California, Tapia planted vineyards and cornfields, built a small wooden house for his family, and lorded over a herd of more than six thousand cattle. With no roads leading to his property, Tapia approached by boat or by horseback through the mountains, leading a train of mules bearing supplies over a rough trail along the rim of the Santa Monica Mountains where one misstep could send a man plunging a thousand feet into the canyon below. He soon found that the seclusion of the Malibu rancho served as a lure to men on the run from the law. Bandits roosted high above the mountain passes and robbed anyone foolish enough to make their way through. The shoreline, with its hidden coves just a day's horseback ride to Los Angeles, became known as a choice spot for American traders eager to find ways around Spain's stiff tariffs. Sailors would drop anchor a hundred yards off the beach and smuggle out leather hides and jugs of wine under the light of the moon.

The place gave every indication that it was untamable. John Muir, a Scottish immigrant who introduced the world to the glories of Yosemite and became the country's foremost naturalist, called it a land where "Mother Nature is most ruggedly, thornily savage. Not even in the Sierra have I ever made the acquaintance of mountains more rigidly inaccessible. The slopes are exceptionally steep and insecure to the foot of the explorer, however great his strength or skill may be, but thorny chaparral constitutes their chief defense. With the exception of little park and garden spots not visible in comprehensive views, the entire surface is covered with it, from the highest peaks to the plain. It swoops into every hollow and swells over every ridge, gracefully complying with the varied topography, in shaggy, ungovernable exuberance, fairly dwarfing the utmost efforts of human culture out of sight and mind."

Those shrubs engulfing the mountainsides were also virtual matchsticks, waiting for a chance to burn. At the end of every summer, wildfires sparked by lightning or the actions of a careless settler whipped across the rancho. Fueled by the hot Santa Ana winds, the fires sent up clouds of black smoke thick enough to choke a man and scatter his livestock in every direction. When the rains finally did come, mudslides washed out any newly planted crops and sent rocks tumbling down the canyons and onto the shore. A weaker person might have given up after experiencing the yearly cycle of fires and floods. Yet Tapia lived there for the rest of his life, locked in a battle to subdue paradise.

ON JANUARY 24, 1848, James W. Marshall noticed glimmering flakes of gold in the American River east of Sacramento while building a sawmill for James Sutter along its banks, setting in motion the Gold Rush. On the same day, four hundred miles south, a twenty-six-year-old Frenchman by the name of Leon Victor Prudhomme agreed to pay Tapia's widow four hundred pesos for the Malibu ranch. He envisioned it as a coastal complement to his Rancho Cucamonga, which ran along the desert foothills in what became San Bernardino County. It was a purchase that he would soon regret.

Ten days after Prudhomme bought Malibu, a garrison of American troops occupying Mexico City prompted the United States and Mexico to come to terms on what became known as the Treaty of Guadalupe Hidalgo and formally end the nearly two-year-long Mexican-American War. The pact gave the United States control of what was then known as the Republic of California and all or part of what became nine other states. In return, the United States government agreed to recognize private-property claims considered valid under Spanish or Mexican law. Even so, there was soon chaos. Within weeks of the signing ceremony, the office of the U.S. secretary of state filed a report questioning the legitimacy of many land grants. Gold-crazed settlers outside Sacramento, meanwhile, ignored all property claims from the Mexican era and began staking out choice spots owned by Sutter along the river. When the local sheriff attempted to evict the squatters, in August 1850, a two-day riot broke out that left the sheriff, the city assessor, several deputies, and many claim jumpers dead, and the mayor seriously wounded.

The problem was even greater along the shore. More than thirteen million acres of prime coastal land sat in the hands of just a few hundred farmers, many of whom had received questionable grants during the last anarchic days of the Mexican era and had little initiative to turn their rolling farms, home to thousands of long-horned cattle, into anything that could be put to better use in a suddenly land-hungry state. In order to settle the broiling questions of ownership, Congress established the Board of Land Commissioners in March 1851. Based in San Francisco, this three-member board was given the job of assessing the legality of every title issued in Spanish and Mexican California. The task would occupy officials for two decades and spawn 813 cases.

Prudhomme, the nominal owner of Malibu, was one of the first men to seek the new commission's recognition of his claims. The board saw no issues with his stake to the Rancho Cucamonga and granted him the title in 1852. Yet a search through old leather trunks containing yellowing handwritten deeds in the Surveyor General's Office in Sacramento produced nothing that backed up the original grant to Bartolo Tapia. Prudhomme immediately filed an appeal and paid Tapia's friends and relatives to testify to the family's long presence in Malibu, yet he was turned down in 1852 and again two years later. When he had a chance to sell the land during the Panic of 1857, as a run on the nation's banks pushed the economy into a free fall, he took it.

Matthew Keller became the owner of Malibu, all of it for the price of ten cents an acre. An Irishman who had once studied to become a priest, Keller traveled to Mexico and then California to seek his earthly fortune. He settled in Los Angeles, where he raised cotton and tobacco, ran a general store, organized the city's first volunteer fire brigade, and tended to more than a hundred thousand grapevines, which produced bottles of white wine, claret, and Madeira. In a place more frontier than city, he soon earned a reputation as a hard-driving businessman. Each week, he would run an advertisement in the *Los Angeles Star* that read, "Mr. Keller to his customers. You are hereby notified that the time has at last arrived when you must pay up, without further delay or I shall be obliged to invoke the aid of the law and the lawyers. Your most ob't servant, M. Keller." He built a brick house in the center of the city and surrounded it with an orchard that included scores of apple, cherry, and peach trees alongside more than 550 orange trees. It was a barbarous place, yet Keller found a way to make himself quite comfortable and eased into a cozy life among the city's elite.

Not long after purchasing the Malibu rancho, he filed a request to the Board of Land Commissioners, seeking the legal claim to the land. Whether it was due to his standing in Los Angeles or simply persistence, Keller succeeded where Prudhomme could not. The state confirmed his ownership of the Rancho Malibu on October 24, 1864. Surveyors climbed over its rocks and through its steep ravines and gave it an official size of 13,315.70 acres, an area roughly half the size of the island of Manhattan. Though he spent seven years securing the deed to the land, Keller did not do much more with it once it was officially his than build a squat stone house for himself high in Solstice Canyon and bring in flocks of sheep to roam the canyons. He lived there with his wife and a team of ranch hands, whom he instructed to drive away any hunters or fishermen attracted by tales of the abundant deer and trout found in the Malibu hills.

In 1875, Keller filed a petition with the county to request that a proper wagon road be cleared along the beach westward from Santa Monica to the ranch. The trail at the time was full of "projecting points and rocks that make said highway impassable at high water," Keller stated, adding that "the necessity for such a road for the convenience of public travel will be quite obvious." Yet with no one living on the sprawling ranch or in the Santa Monica Mountains except for Keller and the men working on his estate, the county board of supervisors had little reason to undertake the cost of blasting rocks to clear a path along the coast and offered no official response. Henry Keller took control of the land after his father's death, in 1881, and after years passed with few signs that a road to the ranch would ever be built, he began looking for buyers. He found one in Frederick Rindge, who in 1892 agreed to pay ten dollars an acre for the still-wild estate.

NONE OF FREDERICK'S previous adventures could compare to this. In Malibu, he had stumbled upon a place where he could escape the metropolis that he was in the process of building. "Oh! to be free from assailing care; to see no envious faces, no saddened eyes; to see or hear no unkind look or word!" he would later write. "To absorb the peace the hills have, to drink in the charm of the brook, and to receive the strength of the mountains, by dwelling in their company,—this is living! To lose one's self by the side of the sea! Free indeed am I!"

Within days of acquiring the Malibu rancho, Frederick and May climbed into a horse-drawn wagon in Santa Monica stacked with enough provisions to last them a week. The carriage plodded westward along the bay. With each clop of the horses' hooves, the sounds of the city evaporated further, replacing by a whipping ocean breeze that threatened to blow the hats off their heads. After they rounded the curve toward Topanga Canyon and left Santa Monica behind, Frederick and May soon passed under Arch Rock, a natural twenty-foot-high bend carved by the erosion of the bluffs. The otherworldly spot, which in time would become a favorite of tourists, stood as if it were a grand doorway to the Malibu kingdom, which Frederick and May now called their own.

The route along the beach was passable only at low tide, but even after taking that into consideration the wagon still stumbled along the rocky path. At one point their driver lost his way to the Keller house, forcing Frederick and May to get out and help lead the horses by hand. Hundreds of holes dug by squirrels pocked the hills, each one a threat to swallow the horses' hooves whole. The party eventually reached the Keller house, which they would later rename Oak Cottage. Frederick and May spent days on the ranch, looking for a site on which to build their country retreat. They found one in a valley on the edge of Malibu Creek, a place where Frederick would later say that it seemed as "if the mountains had stepped back to give us space for our home."

Over the next year, as workers began raising a new Rindge mansion amid the wilderness, Frederick and May frequently traveled up the coast to check on its progress, always by the rhythm of the ocean. A tide book May kept in a drawer in the family library functioned as if a train schedule. They would leave Santa Monica early in the morning as the tide went out, and would travel back from Malibu later in the afternoon as the tide came in. Getting off that rhythm could have grave consequences, as the couple learned one afternoon when they took a team of horses and a carriage and ventured alone toward the western end of the ranch to explore. An unexpected storm came in from the sea, sending waves that May would later estimate were more than ten feet high crashing onto the shore. With little daylight left, they decided to try to race through the rising tide. Frederick led the horses one by one across the rocks spilling out from the mouth of a canyon while May waited. Once each horse was secure, Frederick and May then grabbed the reins of the carriage and pulled it along the shore, all the while straining to avoid the jumble of sharp edges and holes along the rocky path.

The family, which now included a daughter, Rhoda May Rindge, put their first stamp on Malibu in the fall of 1893 with the completion of an immense three-story Victorian mansion on the edge of Malibu Creek. Ranch hands planted orange groves and vegetable fields, turning the home into the center of a self-sustaining kingdom. For Frederick, a man who saw God in every living thing, it was as if he'd stumbled upon a cathedral of the sun. He spent long days tracking deer through thick sycamore groves atop horses he named Columbia and Geronimo, pausing only to drink cool water from mountain springs. At night, he huddled with Samuel and Frederick Jr. around a campfire on the beach, watching the moon glimmer across the breaking waves. During the bright days of early spring, the spout of a passing whale would bring Frederick and his children out of the house at a gallop, each one racing to the shore to be the first to see it surface. At the house itself, May would laugh with them about the antics of the mule they called Don Quixote; the name, when said aloud as Donkey-o-ti, never failed to get them giggling. The family took turns naming the coves, lakes, and valleys of their new domain. "That high ridge up there, from which the view is surpassing, we call the Wunderschon Vista Ridge," Frederick wrote. "You smile. Why should we not? In this polyglot country of ours, why not have such a title? It will appeal to three nationalities. And there is no one word in English that will express what wunderschon does in German. You see we please by that name the Germans, Mexicans, and Anglo-Saxons who come to see us," he wrote in *Happy Days in Southern California*, his description of life on the rancho, which in time would be seen as a classic of Old California.

He was now living out a fantasy he'd harbored as a little boy, and he wasted no time in letting everyone back home know about it. "'I do not like Southern California, because the seasons are not distinctly marked,' said an eastern misanthrope one day. 'There is too much sameness in your climate,' the same party continued," Frederick wrote in *Happy Days*. "'True,' I replied; 'we have no frozen water pipes, no March slush, no interruptions from elementary causes to travel, to telegraphing, or to commerce, save a few wash outs of a day; we have no Oklahoma cyclones, our barns are not commonly struck by lightning, our citizens are not prostrated by sunstroke in August, our hats are not smashed in by falling ice from high buildings in winter thaws; but all the same we have a very reasonable climate.'"

The splendors of Malibu were so much that Frederick began imagining the pleasure God himself must have felt while designing it. "Our Father in Heaven must love color, for behold its variety in His creations;

and, in the Apocalypse, the glimpses of the Heavenly City abound with mention of various hues. So, in the creation of this earth paradise, God must have entered deeply into the joy of its making and beauty," he wrote. He escaped Los Angeles as often as he could to spend long hours exploring the trails, climbing higher and higher into the mountains. Upon reaching a peak, he stood and gazed out over the wide blue sea swallowing the horizon. "There was nothing human about that vista; it was divine," he recalled.

After a lifetime of searching, Frederick had at long last found peace. When he felt his body weakening, he would camp on the beach at Point Dume, believing that the air there was so fresh that it alone could rebuild a man's strength. "It is delightful to live in such a place that, when the prevailing winds blow, one can send one's mind in the direction whence the wind comes, and realize that it sweeps over a pure expanse of ocean, or over righteous aromatic mountains; and not to be obliged to breathe the air that is blown over an iniquitous city or over some malodorous low-lands. In this good country you need not fear to take a deep, long breath," he wrote.

As he snuggled next to May each night in bed, with their three children snoring in rooms next door, he finally felt at home.

Chapter Seven

FILLING THE MOUNTAINS WITH MEN

MARION DECKER WAS ONE OF THOSE MEN WHO liked nothing more than telling the world to get out of his way. A gruff, wire-limbed midwesterner with tanned skin and sharp eyes, Decker had little money and even less desire for it. He centered his life instead on a compass of self-reliance: if he could do something with his hands, then it was good. And if he had to answer to no boss but himself, then it was even better.

Fate smiled on Marion Decker and allowed him to live in an era when those skills were rewarded as at no other time in history. A year into the Civil War, President Abraham Lincoln signed the twice-delayed Homestead Act in order to propel the westward expansion of a country whose citizens still lived chiefly along the East Coast. Nearly all government land west of the Mississippi was suddenly there for the taking. All a settler had to do was find an open claim and file an application. If he built a small house, planted some crops, and lived on the spot for five years, he would have 160 acres to call his own, no money required. Homesteaders fanned out across the country, trampling into deserts and scaling up mountaintops to stake out their piece of the continent. Once a family found a lot, it was up to them to turn it into something liv-able. Settlers on the plains with no access to timber built houses out of sod, while those in the deserts rigged up makeshift irrigation systems to preserve every drop of rain. The government made few efforts to build roads out to the homesteads, leaving it up to each settler to find his way there and back. It was rough living, but the very idea of free land made a man half crazed with excitement. Between 1861 and 1930, more than 270 million acres—about 15 percent of the land that makes up the continental United States—passed into the hands of those willing to chance it on the frontier, the largest giveaway of land ever recorded.

Decker wasn't the first person to stake a claim in the canyons abut-ting Malibu, but even amid a group of settlers that could be charita-bly described as ornery, he was the orneriest. The rancho's boundary line ran to the southern peaks of the Santa Monica Mountains, giving Henry Keller, its owner at the time, access to all of the choice val-leys that sloped down to the sea. What was left over on the other side of the peaks was an unforgiving hellscape, all rocks and canyons and danger. That did little to deter Decker. Sometime in 1885, he crossed over a mountain pass on horseback by way of Ventura and settled on a near-vertical plot of land high in Encinal Canyon where the morning breeze brought the smell of the ocean. There he built a low wooden shack for his family, standing not more than twelve feet wide and four-teen feet long, topped with a slanting roof made out of tin and anchored by a stone chimney in one corner. He lined knee-high stacks of sand-bags around the house to give it a fighting chance against the inevitable mudslides and then got to work clearing trees and shrubs to give himself some room to plant beans.

But mostly, he shot things. Decker attacked quail, mountain lions, and bears in equal measure, using the barrel of his gun to provide what the ground under his feet could not. Antlers from the deer he killed piled up outside his door until he made one of his monthly trips down from the mountains and set off for either Ventura or, more often, along the beach to a general store in Santa Monica, where he could trade horns, skins, and whatever meat he had left over for milk, butter, and more bullets. During these trips he would stop by Sutz's butcher shop, the closest thing he had to a post office, and pick up any letters waiting for him and a stack of newspapers, to get some idea of what was happening in the outside world. Then he would mount his horse again and brave the steep climb toward the mountaintops, not to be seen again for another four weeks. The Malibu hills were a lonely, lawless place where a man who knew how to take care of himself had nothing to worry about, and that suited Marion Decker just fine.

There were only two other homesteading families in the hills at the time, giving each person plenty of space to go about their business without interruption. Every so often, other hopeful settlers would make their way in, intent on beating back nature to create their own paradise. But more often than not they couldn't handle the perennial threats of fires and floods and would abandon their claims, leaving Decker with another plot of land to take over. He eked out a comfortable enough life that family members from Texas and points throughout the Midwest followed him out there, all settling in an area on the western fringe of Malibu which everyone got to calling Decker Canyon.

It wasn't long before Marion Decker began acting like he owned the whole mountain range. If he wanted to cut the time to get to Santa Monica, he would simply ride his small buckskin horse across the Malibu rancho and onto the beach itself, all with a mule-driven wagon in tow. No one lived on the sprawling estate at the time except a man named Pedro, Henry Keller's ranch hand, whose main job was to shoo hunters away so that they wouldn't accidentally shoot one of Keller's cattle or start a campfire that could get out of control and set the whole ranch ablaze. Only seventeen people in all called the Santa Monica Mountains home, generating an amount of traffic so light that Keller could tell who had traveled along the beach just from the shape of the tracks they left in the sand.

The beach was the main outlet to the outside world and, without it, the prospects of long-term survival in the hills were dim. Though

Decker and the other men and women living along the mountaintops had mastered trails through the canyons that few others would brave, it was hell on a horse's back the whole way through. It would take a day and a half of riding along cliffs just to get to the far side of range, and from there it would be another half day's ride to Los Angeles or Ventura. Then a settler would have to turn around and do it again, this time stocked with a month's worth of provisions, which would slow him down even more. One misstep could send him—and everything he needed to keep his family alive—tumbling down the mountainside. The ride along the beach, with its loose sand deep enough to break a horse's leg if it was pulling too much weight and the threat of the shifting tide, wasn't much better, yet it cut the time to Santa Monica and then on to Los Angeles down to hours instead of days. Even then settlers would carry a pick and shovel as insurance against boulders that might have crashed down onto the coast, blocking the trail. Remedies for snake-bites, medicine to soothe a child's fever, oil for a lantern—everything people might need for survival but couldn't furnish for themselves could be found at the general stores in Santa Monica, just beyond Arch Rock. Take that away, and a family would be left with two options: fight back or wither and die.

THEIR FORTUNE notwithstanding, Frederick and May Rindge initially saw little difference between themselves and the homesteaders whose claims edged up against the borders of the Malibu ranch. In a place so far removed from the contours of the city, the act of survival took precedence over social status. Most of the time they didn't even realize anyone was out there. Frederick could ride for hours in the mountains without seeing another soul. When he did come across someone, he was more inclined to strike up a friendship than anything else. A man named Harris, the first settler to ever stake a claim in the mountain range, supported himself on just two hundred dollars a year by keeping hundreds of beehives on his property and selling the honey in Santa Monica for food and clothing. Shortly after Frederick wandered into his clearing high in the mountains, Harris began keeping the Rindge pantry stocked as well.

Life in the Rindge household revolved around the twin centers of Frederick and May's lives: their growing business empire and their children. With each new success at his ever-expanding stable of companies, Frederick climbed a little higher up Los Angeles' social hierarchy, just as his own father had once scaled Boston's invisible heights. With the tentacles of his businesses reaching as far as Oregon, Boston, and Colombia, he became a regular on the trains chattering between Los Angeles and all points north. Once he reached San Francisco, he could board a steamer that would take him anywhere in the world, or jump on an express train on a direct route to Chicago, New York, or the other prosperous cities of the East.

It was an echo of his itinerant wandering after leaving Harvard, and yet on each of his travels he now felt the weight of the distance from his family. "May, I would give so much to have you by my side," he wrote to her on one such voyage. "Your love and sympathy and presence and voice and eyes and laugh are worth so much. I am longing to get back to them." Instead of adventure, the world outside of Malibu seemed to offer only the opportunity for stress. It took just one look at Frederick to notice that money seemed to seek him out, rather than the other way around. People lined up to try to get him to point a little in their direction. "I thought to avoid all people I know but on the train were several who knew us," Frederick wrote to May after arriving in his room at the Hotel Pendleton in San Francisco one evening. "One man asked me if I did not live in Santa Monica. I shall go up in a balloon the next time."

May adapted to every turn in Frederick's success and forced herself to become comfortable in more refined company. She ate the finest foods, sat for fittings with the best dressmakers in Los Angeles and San Francisco, and attended grand parties with senators and congressmen at the Miramar in which overflowing bouquets of roses, poppies, and geraniums hung from dangling baskets in every room. In the summers, she herded her children into a first-class train cabin for a cross-country journey to Marblehead, Massachusetts, the tony seaside town where Frederick had spent his summers as a child and where he continued to own property that had once been his father's.

It was a place where bloodlines and fortunes ran deep, and as far from the farm in Trenton as she could imagine. Growing up, she had wondered each morning whether there would be food at the dinner table that night, and now every meal was a several-course affair prepared by hired help. At her lowest points, overwhelmed by the customs of a culture she never fully felt a part of, May would pen letters to her aunt Emily in Preston. "I am very homesick tonight to see you, you are such a comfort to me," she wrote one evening on her first trip to Marblehead. She turned her energy toward Frederick, who, despite his strictly maintained appearance of vigor, still struggled to keep his body from failing him. The return to Boston, where he had spent the worst days of his life, amplified the anxiety that had become a constant companion. "The doctor has just called and says of Mr. Rindge that he ought to be out of bed in two days anyway, but as he is very nervous he does not know what this nervous condition may bring on," May wrote. "He is trying now in every way to get things to please him and if he succeeds I think he will be the first one. He does not want the front stairs used, not the children to make a noise, and as long as they are alive I don't see how we can keep them from it."

The next day, she wrote to Preston again, at Frederick's urging. "Mr. Rindge was not satisfied with the letter I wrote yesterday and wanted me to write again and say he was feeling very weak and if there was anything he could do. He has no fever, but just lies there and frets as he always does. I am not strong enough to wait on him, but the nurse waits on him hand and foot. His bowels are all right again, but of course he will feel weak until he gets to eating strong food. Will you send 2 gallons of wine bitters, I think that will do us until we start [back to California]."

Frederick soon recovered, and he boarded a train to California with his two sons in tow. With Rhoda fighting an illness that made it hard for her to travel, May remained in Marblehead for another week, acutely aware of the absence of her husband.

THE LIVES OF THE homesteaders and Rindges on the Malibu ranch couldn't remain separate for long. In the summer of 1892, only a few months after he had purchased the rancho, Frederick sent word to Decker and the other homesteaders that he wanted to see them. Decker, Harris, and a man by the name of Swinney soon made the trek down to Santa Monica. The three men, who looked and smelled like they were fresh out of the mountains, were easy to spot among the well-to-do women pushing baby carriages along the boardwalk. They made their way to the Rindge mansion on Ocean Avenue, tied their horses up to a post outside, and listened in the living room as Frederick laid out an idea.

He had more money than they did, he said, and they had more muscle than he did. Together, they could combine forces and get to work on taming the wagon trail hugging the high-tide line along the beach. It would take some dynamite and some digging, but within a few weeks' time they could make the path a lot less risky to men and horses alike. As for payment, Frederick told the men that he would simply start counting, and it was up to them to say when to stop. "Five hundred dollars . . . six hundred . . . seven hundred," Frederick began. Once he reached a thousand—a sum greater than a homesteading family would see in years—the three men yelled "Stop!" in unison. "Now," Frederick said, "before I put in a dollar of this money I want you three men to take charge of it. You are interested in it, and you will do more with the money than any outsider. If you won't take charge of it and take hold of it to use to the best advantage, I don't want to spend my money." The men agreed, and they set off to buy the hammers, shovels, and powder they would need to blast open the path.

It was an unlikely alliance between solitary homesteaders and one of the richest men in the country, united in their goal to bring some order to the wild coast. At least one person from every homestead gathered on the beach the next day. The Hippolytes—a French family whose last name was inevitably mangled into "the Polites"—sent three. The only homesteader who didn't show up personally was Marion Decker, who claimed to anyone who would listen that he was too busy building a barn and had to hire a man to go in his place. The rest of the settlers whispered that the true reason for his absence was that his feelings had been bruised when Rindge didn't put him in charge of the project, and everyone knew that Marion could hold a grudge better than anyone.

For the next eighteen days, a makeshift party of homesteaders huddled near a point just past Arch Rock, where the coastal path was the most treacherous. There, they widened the trail along the beach, blasting boulders that were too large to move by hand. The leftover rock was stacked high into carts, later to be used to fill in gullies so steep that they forced anyone traveling through to get off his horse and walk. The settlers fixed planks of wood along the approach to and from Arch Rock, creating a platform above the high-tide line, and slid supports under the arch itself to ensure that it wouldn't come crashing down on some unlucky person's head. This wasn't enough to make the trip along the beach easy, but it was now possible to pull a wagon across the most ferocious spots most of the time. When the wind kicked up, the trail would be overcome by the shifting sands, forcing anyone passing through to select his own course and hope for the best.

The route along the coast held until winter, when a procession of heavy storms and pounding waves destroyed every last bit of the trail they had cleared. The following spring, nine men reconvened at the mouth of Las Flores Canyon and got to work. Instead of Rindge, a collection of shop owners from Santa Monica—H. A. Winslow, who ran a grocery; R. C. Gillis, who ran the drugstore; and E. H. Carpenter, a lumber salesman resigned to forever hearing puns on his last name—furnished the men with supplies, guided by the self-interest of removing any obstacles that kept their best customers from them. Marion Decker appointed himself in charge this time around. The homesteaders worked for eight days, once again grading a path along the beach just past Arch Rock. Once they finished on the beach, Decker took the tools and began clearing a path from the beach up to his place in the hills, and other settlers soon followed suit. More than fifteen trails in all snaked down from the canyon rims and across the Rindge property to the coast itself. The settlers considered the beach a natural road built out of sand and thought nothing of asking the Rindges for permission to cross their property to reach it. The lonesome hills of Malibu had long been a place where a man did what he had to in order to survive, and what could be more important than making a way to get to and from your own home?

FREDERICK SAID NOTHING when he came across the dirt paths trampling through the hills. Malibu was still a big, isolated place, and there seemed to be little harm in letting his few neighbors cross his property as they went about their business. Yet as the booming population of Los Angeles brought more potential homesteaders west, Frederick decided to prevent their numbers in the hills from swelling much further. With one of his ranch hands in tow, he rode his horse up toward cabins along the canyon tops, intending to offer to buy out each family's claims for a price so high they wouldn't give it a second thought.

One of the first he targeted was a man by the name of Novarino, whose main preoccupation in life, as far as Frederick could tell, was finding a way to guzzle as much of his homemade moonshine as he possibly could, then occasionally selling what he had left over to his neighbors. Novarino took the money without hesitation and cleared out. Frederick repeated the same approach with Novarino's closest neighbor, and then the next. Most sold happily. Bit by bit, Frederick expanded the boundary of his ranch deeper and deeper into the mountains, tightening his grip on the Malibu coastline in the process. Though he never admitted it to the homesteaders, Frederick planned to purchase every claim on the southern side of the mountain range close enough to Malibu that a settler would think to cut across his property to reach the coast. The land itself was useless to him except as a buffer. He would let the Santa Monica Mountains do what they had always done until the Homestead Act, and protect Malibu from the reach of the outside world.

Malibu wasn't the only place where the old ways were quickly changing. Frederick noticed it each time he traveled up to San Francisco. While in the city, he attended revival meetings held on Market Street, part of a wave of religious fervor that was sweeping the country as booming factories pulled more and more men off their farms and into the city, where they would drift for days, unmoored in a sea of strange faces. Singing a familiar hymn in an alien city helped ease the homesickness and the sting of an uprooted life. Frederick spent his nights in the Palace Hotel, writing letters home complaining of his loneliness. "I was so happy in knowing Frederick Jr. complained of my absence," he wrote to May one spring night in 1893. "Tell the boys I have been to the toy store. Tell M. K. R. I have been to Shreves," he added, hinting that he had purchased a gift for her at the city's finest jeweler.

On every trip back home, it seemed as if the population of Southern California had doubled in his absence. All of his efforts to turn Los Angeles into a real city were paying off, and he was now staring at a place whose prospects made his own natural optimism look timid. The city was a paradise where dreams were just there for the taking, and everyone wanted in. Clanging streetcars hustled along the downtown blocks around the Rindge Building, each one crowded with men and women who'd had their fill of East Coast winters and were not going back if they could help it. Eucalyptus trees, their seeds imported from Australia, materialized on just about every street corner thanks to the zealotry of Abbot Kinney, a former tobacco businessman who would go on to found and develop the beach city of Venice. Kinney believed that a eucalyptus alone could turn any patch of dusty brown dirt in Los Angeles into a slice of Eden, and his single-minded devotion to planting saplings spurred a mania that would be eclipsed only by one for the palm tree a few years later.

Los Angeles first grew up, and then it grew out. The city line crept out of downtown, with its huddle of three- and four-story buildings, and raced toward the mountains, spilling into the San Fernando Valley and on from there. Before long, the Malibu ranch was no longer in the middle of nowhere but an untouched island amid a bustling harbor. Tourists and newcomers alike began making treks along the beach to get a picture of themselves standing under Arch Rock, which they would send to their families back home as proof that they had arrived at the California wonderland. So many tourists made the journey up from Santa Monica that the rock became one of the defining images of the Southern California coast in the late nineteenth century, evidence that all of the stories of Los Angeles' splendor were true. The bravest tourists continued exploring up the coast and onto the Malibu ranch itself, where one of the Rindge ranch hands would politely but firmly tell them to turn around.

FREDERICK FOUND HIMSELF faced with a problem of his own creation. He had done everything in his power to make life in Southern California irresistible, and with the population on a path to double to more than a hundred thousand by the end of the decade, he had clearly done a very good job. There was only one part of this promised land that he couldn't bring himself to share. The newcomers could have everything Los Angeles offered, yet he would keep Malibu for himself.

In March 1895, he instructed his foreman to buy enough lumber, steel, and wire to build a gate at the mouth of Las Flores Canyon, at the eastern property line of the Malibu ranch, and another one at Point Dume, near the ranch's western edge. Within days a rough barrier stood at each end of the beach, wedged between the surf and the rocks in a way that prevented anyone on a horse from simply going around it. To ensure that no one would tear the gates out of the ground, Frederick posted a guard at each one and told him to stand watch. Frederick then had a ranch hand by the name of Joe Dubriel, whom everyone called French Joe, ride out to every homestead in the hills and deliver a message, along with a key: from now on, Rindge would keep the gates to Malibu locked. If a settler needed to occasionally pass through the ranch on the way to or from Santa Monica, he had better not lose his key.

The families living in the hills bristled at the thought of a gate standing between them and their property. They had moved out west, to where the hills rolled endlessly and a man was free to come and go as he pleased. Passing through another person's locked gate just to get to your own land? That was out of the question. One settler by the name of Chauncey Hubble came across the gate at Las Flores Canyon before French Joe had made it out to his homestead, and he reacted about as well any other would in the same situation. He first argued with Frank, the ranch hand manning the gate, when he insisted that Hubble go to the Rindge mansion in Santa Monica and ask for a pass. When words wouldn't do the trick, Hubble took out his revolver and butted it against Frank's head. That changed Frank's mind, and Hubble was allowed to pass without any more questions asked. Marion Decker, meanwhile, wouldn't let French Joe leave his house until he had wrung three keys out of his hands, insisting that he needed an extra two to be sure that all of his visitors could get to him whenever they liked. He left two of them at Sutz's butcher shop and let it be known that anyone was free to grab one whenever he wanted, so long as he put it back when he was done.

Something about those gates didn't sit well with Decker, no matter how many keys he held in his hand. He rode to Santa Monica to meet with James Hay, the local representative to the county board of supervisors. The two men had formed a quick bond, as each recognized in the other a version of himself. Tall, with a flowing white beard and thick hair despite his advancing age, Hay had sailed to America from his native Scotland as an eight-year-old, and he still retained the accent of his youth. He'd bought a ranch in what became the city of Artesia in 1875, a year before the railroads made it to Los Angeles, and ran a blacksmith shop at the corner of Pioneer and Artesia Boulevards.

When Decker showed him the key he was now forced to carry to pass along the beach, Hay's mouth fell open. "Don't you know," he asked, "that if you carry it for five years Mr. Rindge can lock that gate and keep you out of there?" Hay wasn't any more of a lawyer than Decker was, so Decker next went to the district attorney's office, where he was told the same thing. By locking the gate, the lawyers told Decker, Rindge had essentially made a public declaration that the path along the beach was private property and that he could close it at any time. If the gates stood for five years, the settlers would have no right to claim that the coast offered a natural right-of-way, or easement, that would allow them to reach their homes. Braving the mountain passes would then become the only legal way to get to their land. Decker recoiled at the realization that those gates weren't just keeping tourists out of Malibu, they were penning him in.

He rode to the Rindge mansion at once, where Frederick tried to set Decker's mind at ease. The gates certainly weren't there to prevent homesteaders from reaching their property, he told Decker. He considered them friends and neighbors, he said, and on the spot he offered Decker a deal: if he would go into town and get a lawyer to draw up an agreement stating that the settlers in the mountains could make their way across his ranch at will, then he would sign it.

Even with a tentative peace brokered, each man left the encounter wary of the other. Neither was used to being hemmed in by another person's prerogatives, and the first taste of capitulation was enough to send both spinning. Their personalities and wealth were about as far apart as one could imagine, yet Frederick and Decker shared the same essential traits. Where Frederick had always relied on his money to open any door in life, Decker had leaned on his own willpower. Both now owned land in the closest place they could get to heaven in this life, and had no plan to back down.

While Decker set off to find a lawyer, Frederick began nursing a grudge against all the homesteaders, replaying in his mind the countless times he had allowed men to cross his property even while they built fences around their own. He prided himself on forgiving easily, yet taking the high road did not come readily this time. When Decker returned with the paper in hand, Frederick told him he needed some time to look it over and waved him on.

Frederick was still hot a few days later as he rode with May in a horse-drawn buggy along the mouth of Latigo Canyon, just above the beach. The deep blue of the ocean stretched out all around him until it merged with the sky, but he couldn't focus on anything but the gates. He owned every bit of land he could see, but what good were his millions if they couldn't do something as simple as allow him to keep people off his own ranch? Just then, Marion Decker, Swinney, and a man named Reeves came galloping in their direction.

"Mr. Rindge, we want to have a talk with you about the road," Decker called out.

"All right," Frederick muttered. He halted the horse, got out of the buggy, and walked toward the three homesteaders. May stood back, holding the reins, and listened.

Decker was the first to speak. The homesteaders wanted Rindge to take the locks off the gates at once, he said. If he wouldn't, then they would go to Hay and demand a more permanent solution: a road, built by the county, that would pass along the Malibu ranch and lead up to each of the homesteads. Not only would all of the settlers be able to pass whenever they wanted, but so could any person who could get on the back of a horse. The beautiful isolation of the Malibu ranch would be ruined, crisscrossed with public roads.

Frederick erupted with a ferocity that none of the men would have ever guessed he had in him.

"I will spend twenty-five thousand, fifty thousand dollars before I have those locks taken off and throw my ranch open to the public," he bellowed.

Swinney stammered out something to the effect that Rindge's money could do a great deal, but it could not do everything. Decker cut him off, having already passed well beyond his own boiling point. He had seen enough during his two decades of roughing it in Southern California to know that only one thing was certain: tomorrow would always bring another train full of people, each one ready to step out into the sunshine and into their dreams. And with a number of homesteads still unclaimed in the canyons behind the Malibu ranch, some of them would surely find their way there, if only given a little encouragement.

"I'm going to fill these mountains with men," he threatened. So many, he added, that the county would have no choice but to build a road across the Malibu ranch for them.

It was a standoff that flipped everything each man had stood for all his life. Frederick found himself desperate to wall off part of the golden land he'd staked his life and reputation on bolstering; Decker, a man most comfortable in no one's company but his own, was suddenly in the position of marshaling an army of settlers who would inevitably get in his way. The battle for Malibu had begun.

Chapter Eight

CALIFORNIA SHALL BE OURS AS LONG AS THE STARS REMAIN

SOONER OR LATER, THE LAW WAS GOING TO MAKE its way to the Malibu frontier. In November 1895, the Los Angeles County Board of Supervisors called a hearing to investigate whether a public right-of-way ran along a patch of coast everyone knew to be some of the roughest land in the state.

At the heart of the matter was a bit of property law confusing enough that it often tripped up lawyers paid to argue it for a living. The law holds that, generally speaking, a person has the right to cross a portion of someone else's land in order to get to his or her own. Known as an easement, this right-of-way is typically established by some written document, court decision, or verbal contract, though not always. Simply acting as if one were already in place can be enough to establish what is known as a prescriptive easement, granted that the property owner must have been aware that someone was crossing his land and let it go on for at least five years without putting a stop to it. Once a prescriptive easement is established, there are only a handful of ways for a property owner to get it reversed. Chief among them are proving either that the easement was misused in a way that caused harm to the landowner or that the path itself was not used for at least five years. Moreover, letting someone cross your land, even repeatedly, typically isn't enough to formally create an easement, provided that the owner makes an effort to regulate traffic by requiring anyone passing by to carry a permit, pass, or the equivalent—such as a key to a locked gate.

Everything about the Malibu frontier confused the situation further. While the homesteaders were considered the owners of their lots in the eyes of their neighbors, technically many of them were squatting on land that had yet to be surveyed by the government—a kind of legal limbo that meant their claims received no formal recognition in the eyes of the law. Because a right-of-way is meant to provide a remedy for landlocked owners or their tenants to come and go from their property, this muted the homesteaders' contention that the path along the Malibu coast was necessary. Frederick and May Rindge, meanwhile, testified that Keller had attempted to prevent use of the rancho as a shortcut to the homesteads in the mountains. Yet they had seen settlers cross their land many times and even paid them to improve the path and, until now, had done nothing to interfere with them.

In early November, Decker found a letter waiting for him at Sutz's butcher shop. At Hay's suggestion, the county board of supervisors had scheduled a hearing that it hoped would settle the matter. A week later, Decker rounded up Swinney, along with a group of settlers by the names of Reeves, Pritchard, Pusey, and Newton, and set off on horseback down the coast and into Santa Monica. The men, every bit the image of the region's rough past, clopped along the city's wide boulevards past bright Victorian homes framed by orange and lemon trees, and then headed on toward Los Angeles, dodging clanging streetcars and rumbling trains as they neared their destination. They hitched their horses in the shadow of city hall's imposing red-tiled tower and trudged through the arches spanning its entrance before making their way to a cramped courtroom.

Frederick was already there in a twill suit, seated next to his lawyer, having walked over from the nearby Rindge Building. He wore the terse expression of a man who knew that he had already lost. With Hay, the man who'd cautioned Decker against accepting a key to the gate, sitting in judgment of him, Frederick had resigned himself to the fact that the courtroom proceedings were little more than show. Yet he clung to a reason to believe that the solace he had found in Malibu would not be taken away from him by this assortment of penniless men he saw as little more than a nuisance. It would take some time to pull off, but the solution was simple: delay, and let his millions resolve the problem for him. As long as there was no formal judgment that established a right-of-way through his property, Frederick could buy out all of the families causing him so much trouble. With no one left to petition the county to build a road, the issue would become moot, and paradise would be his alone. All he had to do was offer as few facts as possible to the board, ensuring that nothing he did or said could be used against him, and smother anything that undermined his cause.

Shortly after eleven, the proceedings began. Rindge's attorney, a man by the name of John D. Bicknell, stood before the board and argued that the hearing was a waste of each man's precious time. Nearly all of the families who called themselves settlers were in fact mere squatters on land owned by the state, he said, leaving the board with no reason to grant them a right-of-way across the property of a tax-paying landowner. Frederick next testified that he had never given the settlers the right to use the path along the beach without his permission. But even with his plan to settle the problem outside the courtroom in mind, Frederick proved that he was not as good an actor as he'd hoped. Frustration seeped into his voice as he told the court that he had spent more than $1,300 to improve the coastal route for the benefit of his neighbors, and in return he had been threatened with this very hearing by men too proud to carry a key.

Decker couldn't let the insult stand. After Rindge finished his testimony, he rushed over to the multimillionaire and asked if Rindge didn't think that he had contributed just as much to improve the road as Rindge had, given the difference in each man's wealth. Decker, still indignant from Frederick's testimony, then took the stand and told the board that he had traveled along the coastal route to reach his property for more than ten years without interruption until Rindge built his gates.

Though they didn't have much money, the settlers did have a fine legal mind in their corner: Walter Haas, a native of the tiny town of California, Missouri, who would later go on to serve a term as the city attorney for the city of Los Angeles before becoming a senior partner at one of the more prominent law firms downtown. Yet all of those accolades were still far ahead of him. As he stood before the board of supervisors, Haas was twenty-six, fresh out of law school, and willing to take any case he could to support his struggling private practice. After Decker finished his testimony, Haas pulled out a map that supposedly showed the path of a road the county had authorized, but never built, that snaked along the coast before ending at Malibou Lake, high in the mountains.

It was just the thing that Frederick had feared most. After he looked at the map, which he told the board of supervisors he had never seen until that day, Frederick walked over to Haas and asked to speak with him privately. Out of earshot of the board members, he suggested a solution: he would take the locks off the gates by the end of the day and even pay the settlers' legal fees, provided they let the matter drop. Everything would go back to how it was. He asked only that the settlers allow him to leave the gates themselves standing, and latch them after each time they passed, so that his cattle would not get out. Haas talked it over with Decker, who voiced no objections, and announced to the board of supervisors that the parties had come to a settlement.

As far as Decker knew, the matter was over. Frederick, however, prolonged his fight outside of public view. A month later, he sent a private letter to each member of the board of supervisors. Regardless of the agreement he'd reached with the settlers, he hoped to ensure that no formal right-of-way across his property remained up for consideration. His land was simply too vast for him to police the entire thing effectively, he argued, and the board should not misconstrue the wildness of the Malibu ranch for lawlessness.

"Now, during the past four years, notwithstanding the fact that my men have politely refused to allow campers to pass through the ranch, there have come secretly onto my ranch parties who have fed their stock on my range, built fires on my land, endangering my business, and no one said them 'nay' for the reason that their trespassing was not discovered until after they had left," he wrote. "I doubt not that ten men could be found who would bear witness that they passed through the road in question during the last few years. That does not prove I have abandoned it. The violation of the rule does not annul the rule. It is just as if ten motormen bore witness that they frequently ran their cars at a rate of speed greater than allowed by law. Yet that fact does not make the law void."

While he worked to sway the law in his favor, Frederick redoubled his effort to buy out as many settlers as he could. Some took the money without question. Others sold on the condition that they could remain on the land until they found another homestead nearby, a stipulation Frederick agreed to readily. Word soon got around that the Rindges were paying top dollar to settlers, no matter how rocky the land underneath their feet. When a family wouldn't listen to an offer because they didn't want to be seen taking Rindge's money, Frederick would arrange a sale through an intermediary, all the while keeping the true nature of the exchange secret.

Only one family refused to even hear him out: the Deckers. As soon as Frederick rode his horse up Decker Canyon, Marion was there waiting for him with a big grin on his face. He spat out a figure so high that Frederick turned right around and never attempted to buy him out again. Decker wouldn't sell, and he soon turned on anyone who would. "He changed over—he used to be a very good friend of mine as long as he could use me," said Pritchard, one of the settlers who rode with Decker to the hearing in Los Angeles. The men had a falling out after he sold his land to Rindge. "When he found he could not use me he told me he had a right to choose, that he was working for his own interest, for bread and butter."

———

A TEAM OF GOVERNMENT surveyors made their way into the mountains in the spring of 1897, unsure of what they would find. With armed United States marshals riding along for their protection, they set out to mark the county line separating Los Angeles from Ventura, as well as to draw the borders of what became known as the Malibu School District— grandly named, considering that it was then a one-room schoolhouse sitting on the bottom of a canyon floor that could fit fewer than twenty students.

But they were on the lookout for more. As they climbed along the canyons, the surveyors kept an eye out for tar or other hints that oil flowed beneath unclaimed land; such a discovery would preempt any homesteader's chance to file for its deed. Five years earlier, the life of a thirty-six-year-old prospector named Edward L. Doheny had forever changed when he jerry-rigged the trunk of a eucalyptus tree into a make- shift drill and set about boring a well down into earth's surface on an empty lot near the corner of Patton and West State streets. When a gush of oil spurted out, a new industry was born. Doheny, who at the time was behind on his rent for the cramped room in a boardinghouse he shared with his wife and daughter, was the first person to tap into what became known as the Los Angeles City Oil Field, a vast reservoir lying just a few hundred feet beneath the city's streets. Within a year, hundreds of towering oil wells rose across the valley and along the coast. Los Angeles had always been a place that attracted men who wanted a do-over in life; now the promise of millions of barrels of oil flowing under their feet had lured even more of them out west to follow their dreams of striking it rich. In a city where there was no such thing as old money, the prospect of a sudden fortune seemed all the more within reach.

The presence of the government's agents did little to alter the lives of the men and women in the mountains. They still considered that rugged landscape the frontier, and the rules of the frontier held sway, even if the clutch of buildings climbing skyward in Santa Monica were close enough that you could almost see them on a clear day. At the age of sixty-eight, J. W. Hilton had lived by those rules for nearly his entire life. After finding an open claim only a few hours' ride into the mountains from the village of Calabasas, he'd settled with his wife on a lonesome spot where passersby were few and far between. He built a tiny house in a clearing just off the trail that led deeper into the hills. As the years passed, his advancing age made the chore of plowing his land that much harder. Yet on the whole he had a simple existence that ran neatly along the contours of his expectations for what life could offer.

That peaceful life more or less ended in January 1898. It began with a fence. Hilton, recognizing that he no longer had the energy or ability of youth, made up his mind to build a barrier around his land to slow the coyotes and other scavengers from ruining each day's toil. The route he planned for it would block the mountain trail that passed by his house, so he rode his horse up to the home of Ike Harris, his only neighbor. At thirty-three years old, Harris was the son of the first settler to venture into the hills above Malibu and had grown up with the open canyons as his playground. Hilton promised Harris he would build a new path around his property to make up for what he planned to fence in, and after Harris made no objections, Hilton went ahead with it. Once it was complete, though, Harris told Hilton he needed to cut the fence down because the new path wasn't as level as the old one. Hilton thought otherwise and refused to do so, and for good measure, he posted a written notice warning trespassers to give way.

From an early age, Ike Harris had been taught that, as much as pampered city men might claim otherwise, the only true laws a man had to follow were those laid down by the barrel of a gun. On a sunny blue Saturday, he rode down to the Hilton place with a rifle slung over his shoulder and a pistol at his side. George Cardwell, one of his few friends in the mountains, trailed a few steps behind. When they reached the clearing, they saw Hilton on the far side of his house, plowing a field of alfalfa. Without a word to him, Harris and Cardwell began snapping the wire fence blocking the old trail. Hilton caught on to what they were doing and yelled for them to stop, and when they didn't, he charged into his house and emerged with a rifle in his hands. He'd made a few strides toward the men when Cardwell blasted two rounds of buckshot into his chest. Shots from Harris's rifle ran out half a second later, sending a bullet through his temple. Hilton's lifeless body fell to the ground.

Readers of the *Los Angeles Times* would pick up an interview with Hilton's widow a week later, describing how Harris wouldn't put his gun down until she went over to her husband's body and checked that he was dead. "Be sure about it," Harris yelled, before lowering his weapon. While Hilton's widow wiped the blood from her husband's body, Harris rode off with Cardwell, cutting another hole in the fence for their exit.

It was the kind of story of vengeance and blood that made the mountains, and the secrets they held, seem all the more foreboding. Los Angeles still had its rough edges, but nothing compared with this. A person standing on the beach in Venice could watch the setting sun behind Malibu at the far side of the bay and wonder just what was happening in that lawless place.

THE ONLY HARM THAT came to the Rindge family in their kingdom of Malibu was the self-inflicted kind. Cuts, bumps, and bruises were standard for all five members of the family as they roamed the ranch, and nothing more serious came than the day when Frederick Jr. fell out of a tree, forcing May to send word for the family physician in Santa Monica to come up at once to set his broken arm. Not long after, the children came across a mountain lion while exploring on their own, frightening them enough that they did not sleep for two days afterward.

In the universe of wealth in Los Angeles, where each man loved nothing more than recounting how poor he had once been, Frederick's inheritance had long set him apart. He was one of the few millionaires in the inchoate city whose wealth had been with him from the start, or, for that matter, to have attended college, much less one as elite as Harvard. He carried with him a worldliness and deep connections to the East Coast that few others in his orbit possessed, and he soon developed a reputation as a man comfortable in the presence of money new and old. One night he could be found entertaining scions of eastern wealth such as Cornelius Vanderbilt II, the grandson of Commodore Cornelius Vanderbilt and heir to the family's fortune, who sought Rindge out while on his first visit to Los Angeles. On another night, Frederick and May mingled among the guests at the fiftieth wedding anniversary celebration of the self-made millionaire Myron H. Kimball, a photographer and Civil War veteran who'd sold his New York City gallery and set off for the West Coast for a fresh start. In 1878, he opened a hotel known as the Kimball Mansion in Los Angeles, which soon attracted a clientele of wealthy artists to its halls. Helen Hunt Jackson would later write much of *Ramona*, a novel that romanticized the region's Mexican past, while a guest there. The book's immense popularity would lead to more than three hundred printings and would spur an annual Ramona Pageant in the nearby desert city of Hemet.

Men sometimes remarked that Rindge seemed to live on both coasts at once, given how often he traveled back to Boston to check on his interests, sometimes with his family in tow. On those occasions he would set them up in a home just off the water in Marblehead, where yacht clubs ringed the harbor, and tell them to soak in the fresh New England summers he remembered from his youth. Like so many other aspects of life on the East Coast, May found the experience foreign, but she pushed on anyway. "This is certainly a strange climate and I do not wonder that the people are tough here," she wrote to Madam Preston that summer.

Frederick set off on a trip alone in the late spring of 1898, intent on making stops on Philadelphia, New York, and Washington to tend to his business interests. He reached as far as Philadelphia before his body gave way. Stricken by fever and chills, he lay in a hotel room shaking uncontrollably, tended to only by a nurse. Throughout his life, Frederick had carried with him an illness that pushed his body to the very edge of death, and he had come to accept that his plans could unravel at any moment. Yet for every time he had fallen down, he had found just as many ways to recover, giving him the feeling that he was unsinkable. He slowly regained his strength, and once well enough, he boarded a train for Boston as if little had happened. "My merry May: I am myself again," he wrote to his wife. "An illness overcame me in Philadelphia, and as I had nearly 30 operations [applications of liniment], I became very weak. . . . This is my first letter—to you of course. I have been pursued by invitations. Have no fears, I am all right now."

Frederick made his way to Cambridge, where he spoke before an audience of the mayor and city council in the gleaming city hall he had furnished. He next toured the Cambridge Manual Training School, where he listened to a performance by the orchestra and the glee club and then readied himself to give a speech. The auditorium was packed with the sort of boys whose physical health he'd envied when he was a young man of their age. Standing before them, he felt overcome with wistfulness for the rough-and-tumble boyhood that was forever outside of his grasp. "I built the school largely to prove the principle that to make the highest type of man, a boy must learn to work with his hands," Frederick told them, unconsciously describing the man he had wished to become when he was a sickly child, stuck in a drafty mansion haunted by the empty rooms of his departed siblings. He had gone on to make his own fortune and name on a new coast thanks to the strength of his mind rather than his body, yet the pain of those lonesome days would never fully recede.

ONCE AGAIN, Frederick returned to Los Angeles to forget. Already, the ethos of jettisoning one's origins was beginning to define the city. As Los Angeles neared the turn of the century, the number of large-scale projects then under way seemed to be part of an aggressive campaign to erase its frontier past from memory. In San Pedro, the steamer *J. C. Elliott* unloaded 600,000 feet of lumber straight from Everett, Washington, to feed a plan hatched by Horace Dobbins, the mayor of Pasadena, to craft a new type of city in which the bicycle reigned supreme. Dobbins envisioned an elevated highway, fifty feet high and built entirely of wood, atop which bicycles could zip along the ten miles to and from Los Angeles. The first mile-long section of the California Cycleway, wide enough to hold four cyclists side by side, opened on New Year's Day in 1900 and was hailed by the local press as "a wheelman's dream." In downtown Los Angeles, Henry E. Huntington, the nephew of one of the men instrumental in building the Southern Pacific Railroad, was at work designing a streetcar system connecting the city with nearby suburbs. Known as the Red Car line, the system at its peak would be the largest electric railway system in the world and would bring passengers from as far as the orange groves of Riverside some fifty miles away into the city for just a nickel.

Frederick felt that another boom was afoot, and though his seat atop the city was unchallenged, he wanted more. He built a boardwalk in the nearby city of Long Beach and opened up bathhouses along the shore, which soon teemed with women clad in billowing bathing suits that hung down to their ankles. On the corner of Hill and Third Streets in the sleepy Bunker Hill neighborhood in downtown Los Angeles, he began work on a five-story stone building to serve as the headquarters of the Conservative Life Insurance Company, an outfit he had founded and still ran as its president. The simple fact that Rindge was buying in the neighborhood was enough to increase its status. The purchase "by one of the coolest-headed business men in the city, indicates that the situation has been carefully analyzed," hailed the *Los Angeles Herald,* "[and] shows the foresight and good business judgment that have characterized all the investments of Frederick H. Rindge." When completed, the building, crafted of polished sandstone and ornamented with stone antlers over its arched entranceway, would be lauded as one of the most beautiful ever constructed in the city.

More than anything, Frederick refused to indulge in any outward show of weakness, as if, like his college friend Theodore Roosevelt, he could will himself into fine health. On Conservative Life Insurance Company letterhead, he wrote a series of maxims titled "Learn to Laugh" that offered a window into the extent to which he denied the precarious state of his body. "Learn to laugh," it began. "A good laugh is better than medicine. Learn how to tell a story. A well-told story is as welcome as a sunbeam in a sick room. Learn to keep your own troubles to yourself. The world is too busy to care for your ills and sorrows. Learn to stop croaking. If you cannot see any good in the world, keep the bad to yourself. Learn to hide your pains and aches under pleasant smiles. No one cares to hear whether you have the earache, headache, or rheumatism. Don't cry. Tears do well in novels, but are out of place in real life. . . . Above all, give pleasure. Lose no chance of giving pleasure. You will pass through this world but once. Any good thing, therefore, that you can do, or any kindness that you can show to any human being, you had better do it now; do not defer or neglect it, for you will not pass this way again."

Frederick soon expanded his physical mark on the city. Henry Huntington was the only other person in Los Angeles whose business empire rivaled his, and with his well-traveled streetcar lines, Huntington owned an asset that Frederick could not easily replicate. Frederick met with Huntington and proposed that they work together: Frederick owned several thousand acres south of downtown that were just waiting to be developed, and Huntington had the means to get people there. The result was the West Adams District, a tony residential neighborhood that quickly filled with elaborate Queen Anne, Mission-, and Craftsman-style mansions. Doheny, then well on his way to becoming one of the richest men in America, put down $120,000 in gold coins for a French Gothic chateau at 8 Chester Place, cementing the new neighborhood as the best in Los Angeles. In time, he would be joined by the likes of Fatty Arbuckle, Buster Keaton, Wyatt Earp, and W. C. Fields, each one drawn toward a place that soon became synonymous with the city's most powerful men.

Two miles away from Doheny, Frederick began work on his own baronial estate on a street he named Harvard Boulevard. There, a short walk away from the high stone pillars that marked the gate of the neighborhood, he built a twenty-five-room French Château mansion crafted out of golden yellow bricks and topped by four chimneys. Four arches spanned

its front entryway, and flowers and vines hung from its second-floor balconies. He planted young palm trees throughout the grounds, content
that he could watch them grow to tower above the mansion in his lifetime. Inside the home, its redwood halls were filled with a collection of
furniture that was said to be the largest single shipment the city had
ever received from New York. Just as he had in the buildings he'd constructed in Cambridge, Frederick covered the walls with maxims and
poems, offering a constant reminder of the path toward a higher life.
Above the largest mantle in the home, he instructed workers to paint
what had become his motto toward his adopted home: "California Shall
Remain Ours as Long as the Stars Remain."

WHILE BY ALL outside appearances Frederick met every challenge
of life, in private he continued to suffer. His body continually perched
on the edge of illness, and when it tipped over the edge, its descent
could be sudden and deadly. Nurses and doctors became a constant
presence in the Rindge household, each trying to restore calm to a body
that raged against its earthly shackles. May wrote long letters to Madam
Preston, asking her if she could use her gifts to help Frederick from afar.
"Fred wished me to write you and tell you that he is feeling very weak,"
she wrote in one letter. "He would like to know if his trouble is caused
by healing the sore that was on his leg and if that went up into his stomach and is making all this trouble for him? He would like you to send
him one yard of the old fashioned oiled silk," May wrote in another,
underlining "old fashioned" for emphasis. Soon, no letter to Preston
passed without an update on Frederick's condition. "I think Mr. Rindge
is much better, yet he has his days of feeling poorly. He has started the
blister on the back of his neck and it is almost ready to break," May
wrote that summer.

The constant care for her husband, along with the responsibility
of raising her three children, pushed May near her breaking point.
No amount of fine foods or grand homes could compensate as she

watched the man she loved struggle to force air into his lungs. "I have given up the thought of ever having any peace on this earth, which is so full of everything horrid, and hereafter will take the knocks that come just like any dog that has grown used to it," she wrote in a bitter letter to Madam Preston. "The two doctors that Mr. Rindge called in to see me say that I must stop taking so much responsibility or I will be dead."

The family made another trek to Marblehead that summer. With Frederick occupied by his business in Boston, May resolved to enjoy her life despite its challenges. She wrote a letter to Madam Preston congratulating her on learning to use a typewriter and, for the first time, did not focus on Frederick's health. "I am worrying less this summer than I ever have at least for some years before and I am learning to think of the male creatures like the Boston women—to feel so glad that you have one of that particular gender that you will love them faults and all—at least to put up with them and think them indispensable," she wrote to Madam Preston. "To begin on the same basis I have bought some of the real Boston shoes and they are the funniest things that ever peeped out from under skirts. I will carry some with me and since having the shoes in my possession I feel that I have taken quite a step in the right direction. Boston is a great place for character study."

Later that summer May consoled Preston after the growth of the commune attracted unfavorable attention. The *Sonoma Democrat* sent a reporter to Cloverdale and came away with an article that described the wealth Preston had acquired from the free labor of men and women who were convinced that she had saved their lives. "What a shameful thing for anyone to do to one who has done as much good as you have," May wrote to her. "You may be sure they will not profit by it. The children all feel so sorry for you and want to do several things to that reporter and send you a little note expressing their sympathy."

More than most men, Frederick understood that his wealth gave him the power to change the world as he saw fit, even as his own time left on earth was unassured. The same year he began work on the West Adams home, he dipped his hand into politics for the first time in his life. Santa Monica, then on the verge of banning the sale of alcohol, was enmeshed in one of the early battles in what would culminate in Prohibition two decades later. Frederick stepped in and offered to personally replenish the city for all of the lost tax revenue from alcohol sales. With the millionaire's backing, Santa Monica voted to become a dry city.

On April 8, 1901, Frederick strode up to a makeshift stage in Santa Monica to celebrate. By then he had been in Los Angeles for nearly fifteen years. His body was wider and his hairline was higher, but his youthful lust for life was still contagious. No matter how many times his failing body sent him to seek out another one of Madam Preston's cures, he seemed to have an unwavering conviction that he would bounce back again, and that all men could share the same optimism if they tried.

"If a man wants to succeed in life, he has got to rule himself," he told his audience. "He must cultivate the mind, soul and body. A successful man is the one who makes the most of his opportunities in the fear and love of God. We must remember that there are many men in the world who have had very few opportunities. Take, for instance, the man who is a bootblack who cleans the streets. If he makes the most of his opportunities I say he is a successful man."

Frederick had no way of knowing it then, but his belief in the fundamental goodness of men would soon be tested to its core.

Chapter Nine

THE FIRE

FOR SIXTEEN YEARS, FREDERICK RINDGE HAD WORKED to establish his name in Los Angeles. As the calendar turned to 1903, he decided to let himself finally enjoy the life he had made.

Everything seemed to be falling into place. The Rindge family had spent the previous summer in Marblehead, Massachusetts, part of Frederick and May's plan to ensure that their children would make the proper connections to the eastern families that still loomed large in Frederick's eyes, even while his own success surpassed them all. The summer was the coolest in memory, sparing the Rindge children from humid, sleepless nights spent broiling in their beds. Not all connections to home were severed, of course. A man by the name of Scotton made the trip alongside the family to serve as the children's tutor, just as he had every time they decamped for Malibu. Before the family returned to Los Angeles at the summer's end, Frederick ushered them all onto a train bound for Washington, D.C., where he had an appointment with the Harvard classmate who'd inadvertently sparked the adventure that had launched him far from Boston and the world he had once known.

When Frederick returned to Los Angeles, all everyone wanted to hear was what Theodore Roosevelt thought of the growing metropolis in the West. "California and its attractions may be old stories to those who live here, but they are ever new to the people of the East," Frederick told the local press. "It is surprising to one who has lived here for some time to note the interest that the Easterners display in the Pacific Coast and especially in Southern California. They seem to be just awakening to the fact that this is the promised land, and that the country is alive with vast possibilities for development. On all sides I have heard inquiries about California, and it was apparent that the movement hither will be greater than in any previous year. While in the East I had the pleasure of meeting President Roosevelt, and he, too, was intensely interested in hearing of this State and its growth. From the tenor of his conversation there seems to be no doubt that he will pay us a visit next spring."

The people of Los Angeles had ample reason to wonder about their status in the eyes of the president. At a time when California as a whole still had about as many residents as the state of Kansas, the rapid growth of the Los Angeles region was a nationwide curiosity, leaving the country unable to decide whether there was a major city rising in its lower left-hand corner or if it was all a mirage, as ephemeral as the Gold Rush mining camps, which had vanished and left only ghost towns behind. *Out West*—whose subtitle touted that it was *A Magazine of the Old Pacific and the New*—attempted to build up the city's confidence with the unwavering logic of numbers. "Since 1880, not a single city in the Union has overtaken Los Angeles in rank by population. But in these two decades, Los Angeles has outstripped ninety nine American cities which were numerically larger in 1880, and in one decade has passed nineteen cities that were numerically larger in 1890," the magazine noted. It continued: "In this last decade, the city of Los Angeles has gained over five thousand more people than the whole states of Maine, Vermont, Nebraska and Nevada put together gained in the same period."

The *Los Angeles Times* followed up with an editorial that argued it would be reasonable to assume that the city would have 250,000 people living in it by 1910, and by 1920 over half a million—all in a city that held just 12,500 in 1880. "The man who talks about the probability of Los Angeles becoming a larger city than San Francisco within twenty years may no longer be justly regarded as a candidate for a lunatic asylum as he certainly would have been twenty, or even ten years ago," the paper noted, hinting at the ambition that many in the city had to one day trump San Francisco in terms of clout.

Its two decades of uninterrupted growth made Los Angeles not only anxious about its status in the eyes of the rest of the country but nostalgic about its past. Builders across Southern California picked up on the yearning for simpler times and began mimicking the architecture of the decaying Spanish missions and other relics of what was now widely known as Old California. In Los Angeles, elaborate Queen Anne and Victorian homes were gradually replaced with unassuming structures marked by red tile roofs, wide arches, and shaded courtyards, giving birth to the Mission Revival style, which would define the city's look for decades to come. Farther away, in the suburb of Riverside, an engineer's son by the name of Frank Miller was in the middle of what would become a thirty-year project that would transform a city block into a maze of courtyards, bell towers, chapels, and catacombs that he called the Mission Inn. Miller rarely left the premises, and he would often roam the grounds dressed like a friar, handing out fresh oranges to guests of the hotel.

Frederick and May were not immune to the widespread yearning for the California they had first encountered, which was now just a memory. As the city grew around it, the untouched hills of the Malibu ranch seemed more and more like an artifact from a more romantic time. In April 1903, the Rindges invited more than a hundred members of the city's elite up to the Malibu ranch for what the papers would later describe as a "genuinely western incident." As the sun fell over the ocean, the stiff-collared crowd of real estate developers, bankers, and railroad men watched a team of cowboys round up more than twelve hundred cattle roaming the ranch's hills and corral them into a green meadow in the shadow of the Rindge mansion, where each one was pinned down and branded. If the men and women attending the party were aware of the irony of celebrating a past they had played a large part in undoing, they didn't show it. Instead, under a banner of stars, they raised toasts in the cool night air to Frederick, to themselves, and to Los Angeles, content that their growing city would only rise higher.

THE OPTIMISM FREDERICK carried into the new year had its first real test a month later. Once again he fell ill, and his condition grew serious enough that it attracted the kind of attention he went to great efforts to avoid. Whispers that Frederick was near death soon reached the ears of journalists, who were keen to investigate the health of the man who controlled much of Southern California. "Frederick H. Rindge, the capitalist, has been ill for several days at his home on Ocean Avenue," the *Los Angeles Times* noted in mid-May. "At the house today it was reported that, although Mr. Rindge is not sitting up much as yet, his condition is improving." Like he had countless times before, Frederick turned to Madam Preston's liniments as a solution to his pain, and in time he was able to rouse himself and resume the upward arc along which his life only seemed to travel.

The puzzle pieces of his life, long scattered by his ambition and his fickle body, were coming together. His two sons, now young men of fifteen and twelve, seemed to embody the twin sides of his personality. Samuel, the oldest, was headstrong and exacting and yearned to follow Frederick into the world of business. His future acceptance at Harvard had already been secured, and Frederick often took the time to counsel Samuel on the details of each transaction he entered into, just as his own father had once tutored him. Frederick Jr., on the other hand, often shrank in his older brother's shadow and preferred spending days outside on the Malibu rancho to submitting to the dreariness of numbers or a stiff collar. He seemed to have an innate understanding of the earth, and he found his confidence in the open expanse of land. Frederick recognized his son's talent and gave him a patch of the Malibu rancho to oversee. Soon the boy was growing vegetables and raising hogs whose size far outstripped those tended to by the professional ranch hands.

The family moved into the estate on Harvard Boulevard in West Adams in early August. The home was situated atop the crest of a small hill, allowing Frederick and May to sit on the front portico and glance down upon the cluster of buildings rising in the center of Los Angeles, a few miles away. They could see a city shaped by their desires. The frontier town where they had once arrived as shy newlyweds was now but a memory, a place whose rapid growth into a respectable metropolis—largely as a result of Frederick's hand—made it all but unrecognizable. At the end of the mountains framing the backdrop of the city sat Malibu, where Frederick had quietly consolidated his grip on paradise. Nearly every homesteader had proved willing to sell, and those who remained seemed lulled into an uneasy quiet. He had not come across Decker for months, and while he was unable to tell whether that was by accident or design, he cheered it as a mark of progress nonetheless.

The only hint of trouble at the Malibu ranch had come at a time when the Rindges were not there. On a warm late-summer afternoon, two sheriff's deputies on a dove-hunting expedition came across a Dutch drifter by the name of Rene Meyers riding a mule along the Malibu coast. A fat bundle was balanced precariously in the saddle behind him, yet that was not what drew the sheriffs' attention. The sheriffs instead locked eyes on Meyers's fine white shirt, where the stitched name "Frederick Hastings Rindge" gleamed atop the breast pocket. Meyers told the men that he was lost and asked for directions into Los Angeles. With only a raised eyebrow between them, the deputies hitched the lead rope of the man's mule to their wagon and proceeded to lead him straight to the Santa Monica jail. Inside his bag they found several other shirts from the Rindge mansion and a collection of Frederick's toiletries. A later search of the home showed that tins of food were the only other items missing.

Frederick found the story hilarious and retold it at any chance he got. His mirth did not translate so readily to May, however. She often wondered aloud why they were paying men to guard their home if a stranger could so easily find his way inside. To her, the robbery was an open wound, and it seemed that nothing short of building a fortress in the mansion's place could suture it to her satisfaction.

EVER SINCE THE FIRST person found his way into Malibu, fire has been the price of living in paradise. The hillsides turn green with the first drop of rain each fall, but by spring the sun has whittled the dense thicket of brush and shrubs down to little more than brown kindling. The annual cycle is so well established that Malibu is said to have three seasons: winter, summer, and fire. From October to December, hot, dry Santa Ana winds howl from the desert through mountain passes and on to the coast, threatening to transform the smallest flicker into a wildfire capable of consuming miles of land. Fire season is a time of sleepless nights and long hours spent staring out into the wilderness, hoping that no unseen person passing through will be careless enough to drop a cigarette, or that an ember floating up from a campfire will not set off a firestorm.

The Rindges had come across charred trees and other evidence of past wildfires while exploring their ranch, but they had experienced nothing more serious than a flare-up that engulfed a thousand acres of grain. The summer of 1903 passed without incident, and as the final days of November ticked by, Frederick and May finally allowed themselves to relax, confident that their ranch had been spared for another year. They fell asleep at their home on Harvard Boulevard on the night of December 3 without any hint of what was to come.

By seven the next morning, thick black smoke was rippling across the Santa Monica Bay. The Rindges awoke to the distant smell of singed wood and charred earth, not knowing its source. Twenty miles away, a wildfire raged across the Malibu ranch with a ferocity that seemed as if it could consume all of creation. The fire had started at the southeastern end of the ranch, not far from the Rindge mansion, and barreled its way up the coast. As the sun began to rise, flames engulfed the rows of fan palms lining the entrance to the home. Embers carried by the wind rained down onto the roof of the house itself, and before long it, too, was swallowed by the fire.

Ira Graham, the foreman of the ranch, ran into the burning building in a foolhardy attempt to salvage Frederick's collection of antiques and any family photographs. He emerged sputtering a few minutes later, unable to withstand the smoke and flames. Suddenly aware that the fire would soon circle him, Graham ran to the nearest horse and jumped on its back, praying that the animal would be strong enough to escape. He directed it toward the last opening in the wall of flames and charged forward. The horse's tail caught fire as it jumped through the blaze. Graham abandoned the dying animal and scampered on foot toward the ocean, tripping every time his charred boots caught on the rocks. He ran fully clothed into the waves and kept going until he was safely up to his neck. Only then did he turn around to face the true scale of destruction. Graham watched as the blaze continued westward through a grove of eucalyptus trees, building a heat so intense that the trunks of trees not touched by flames crackled from its intensity. Within an hour, over thirty miles of the coast was burning, a line of destruction spanning from Santa Monica past the Ventura county line.

Graham, his face raw and blackened by the fire, reached the Rindge home in West Adams that afternoon. It would take three days for the blaze to burn itself out before Frederick and May could tour the damage. Once there, they found a scorched moonscape that seemed unlikely to support life ever again. Where Frederick had once worshipped the glories of nature, he now saw only desolation. Deer spooked by the flames huddled along the lip of the ocean, unsure of what to do or where to go now that all the plant life had been extinguished by the blaze. Sheep,

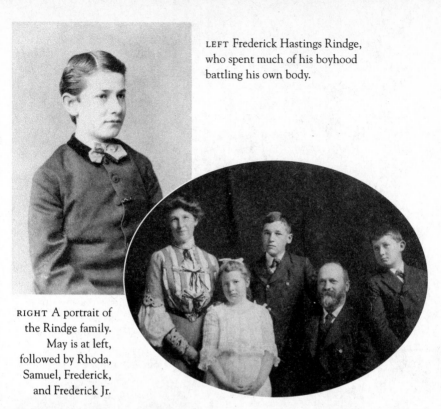

LEFT Frederick Hastings Rindge, who spent much of his boyhood battling his own body.

RIGHT A portrait of the Rindge family. May is at left, followed by Rhoda, Samuel, Frederick, and Frederick Jr.

ABOVE The Rindge family on the beach at Malibu. Samuel is at left, followed by Frederick Jr., May, and Rhoda.

LEFT Frederick Rindge, taken near the time he met and married May, all within the span of a week.

BELOW When the Rindges first moved to Malibu, the only way to reach the rancho was by horse-drawn carriage along the coast. Poor conditions often forced anyone traveling that route to get out and walk.

TOP AND ABOVE Arch Rock, pictured here circa 1900, was once a natural doorway into the Malibu kingdom.

RIGHT May Rindge, left, walking with one of Rhoda's friends at Point Dume. Half a century later, the final scene of the original *Planet of the Apes* would be filmed at this spot.

ABOVE At the time it was completed, the Rindge mansion in West Adams was one of the largest private homes in Los Angeles.

LEFT The original Rindge mansion in Malibu; it burned to the ground in 1903. May suspected that homesteaders were behind the blaze, fueling her animosity toward them.

BELOW Frederick Rindge saw his Malibu ranch as his escape from the world. Here, he herds sheep with his daughter, Rhoda.

ABOVE Frederick and May Rindge erected gates like this one, which reads, "Malibu Rancho: Trespassing Strictly Prohibited," to prevent homesteaders from crossing the rancho, sparking the call for a public highway along the coastline.

LEFT May Rindge's railway to nowhere along the Malibu coast, seen here in 1908, prevented the Southern Pacific from moving in.

RIGHT This trestle of the Malibu railway spanned Ramirez Canyon. Today, the same spot is known as Paradise Cove and features a trailer park favored by celebrities where a single lot can go for more than $3 million.

RIGHT The Los Angeles branch of the American Automobile Association held one of its first car rallies in Malibu. The thrill of driving along the coast was so novel that those who did it rarely grew tired of recounting their adventures.

LEFT May began construction on a fifty-four-room mansion that she hoped would serve as a symbol that the Rindge family would never leave Malibu. Unfinished in her lifetime, it was purchased by a sect of Franciscan friars and is now known as the Serra Retreat.

RIGHT The Malibu Rancho, which Frederick Rindge called his "country home." Four decades later, May Rindge would begin construction on her own mansion on the hill in the center of this photo.

Bird's-eye View of Rancho Malibu, Showing Improvements Made by Frederick H. Rindge.

ABOVE May built the home now known as Adamson House as a present for her daughter, Rhoda. Tucked against the side of what is now known as Surfrider Beach, the home overlooks the break where Gidget was said to catch her first wave.

ABOVE The Malibu Potteries factory turned out ornate tiles that were soon found in the mansions of Beverly Hills and in Los Angeles City Hall. Rufus Keeler, the genius behind the glazing process, lived in the tent pictured to the left, in order to better guard his secrets.

LEFT This sixty-foot-long simulated Persian rug, constructed entirely out of tile, was meant for May Rindge's mansion. A fire destroyed the tile factory, taking away one of May's last sources of income.

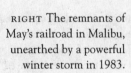

ABOVE AND LEFT The Malibu Movie Colony, pictured here in 1932, became Hollywood's most exclusive getaway.

RIGHT The remnants of May's railroad in Malibu, unearthed by a powerful winter storm in 1983.

some with their legs blackened by the flames, huddled around a single stack of hay left miraculously untouched. Ashes covered the ground, leading Graham to guess that it would be at least three years before anything green grew again. The mansion where the family had spent some of their favorite times was now a scorched ruin, stripped of any semblance of a home. Its seared chimney was the only thing left standing. Everything inside—their furniture, Frederick's collection of native art, their mementos of life in a spot they considered almost holy—had been reduced to nothing but ash and soot.

As she toured the damage with her husband, May mulled over its cause. While they did not know what had sparked the fire, everything about it raised her suspicions. It was well known that the homesteaders in the mountains still lived by a code of frontier justice, and that fire was a part of their arsenal of revenge. Tales, many of them based in reality, floated across the hills and into the city: homesteaders, it was said, would sometimes settle a score by lighting a fire that they expected to burn their rival out. Most families living in the hills had no recourse to turn to after a fire enveloped their home, forcing them to abandon their plot for another go at life.

No name in Malibu evoked as much resentment among the homesteaders as Rindge. The blaze appeared to have started near the Rindge mansion, an area that held few places a man would stop to light a campfire. And at the end of the fire season, it seemed unlikely that a small flame might accidentally get out of control and take flight. Reports trickling in from higher up in the mountains further raised May's ire. Decker, the Rindges learned, had been able to save his home, as had three other settlers in the hills. The only other homes destroyed beyond their own had once belonged to Pritchard and Nickerson, both of which Frederick had purchased as part of his effort to clear all of the Malibu backcountry of settlers.

May saw a conspiracy, a plan on the part of men she viewed as barely able to survive their squalid existence to rob her own family of its happiness. The years of refining herself to Frederick's expectations melted away, and the resentment and anger at the larger world nurtured during her childhood on the Trenton farm flooded back in. The change in her countenance came as if a dark mask had fallen over her, and through it she could see only future harm. She began considering anyone outside of the family a threat, convinced that the world was working in tandem to ruin her.

In the months after the fire, her outlook hardened further. Whereas she would once exchange pleasantries with her cooks or servants, she had only ridicule. She insisted that Frederick build more gates along the coast of Malibu and hire an ever-larger army of men to patrol the ranch in their absence. In the late spring of 1904, Frederick readied May and their children to embark for Marblehead. Still unable to accept the loss of their Malibu home, she began to filter the world into only sources of happiness or sources of trouble, with no ground in between. Anyone outside of her family was immediately suspect, as if they were part of a grand plot to shatter her life.

The only solace she found was in writing letters, sometimes two or three a day, to her aunt Emily. Together, the missives amounted to a daily chronicle of slights, both perceived and real, as May could barely contain the invective she harbored against a world that could never promise her a cushion from further heartache. "Everything has gone along about the same as usual since writing you last except the California servants refused to do some cleaning I asked them to," she wrote that summer. "I never will bring any more East, they are not worth it, and it is impossible to get any comfort out of any of them. They are all scrubs from beginning to end and there is no use trying to make anything out of them."

Their time in Marblehead passed without incident, and the family boarded a train for Los Angeles a few weeks later. As May settled into the first-class cabin, she hoped that her life would return to normal once they returned to their home in West Adams. Little did she know that her pain was just beginning.

Chapter Ten

ONE LAST ADVENTURE

FOR THE FIRST TIME IN HIS LIFE, THE SIGHT OF LOS
Angeles did not make Frederick happy. He had taken countless trips to the East Coast since grafting his life onto the bustle of
California, and spotting his adopted hometown growing taller across
the horizon on the return trip had never before failed to send pulses
of excitement and pride through his body. This time, however, he
approached it with dread.

The fire in Malibu had not just destroyed his favorite home and his
collection of relics but had extinguished his conviction that, while God
would test him, life would ultimately bend in his favor as recompense
for a childhood spent lurking in the shadow of his siblings' deaths. He
felt the optimism that had carried him since he was a teenager waning
in the face of the first setback in his adult life that neither his money nor
his energy could easily overcome. His place of refuge was a charred ruin,
and there was little he could do but wait for it to recover.

In early February 1905, he took the first step to rebuild. After a heavy
storm washed out most of the trail along the beach, he hired a brigade
of men, two hundred strong, to carve out a serviceable trail running

from Santa Monica to the Malibu ranch that would not stop until it
hit the rancho's western edge. The men attacked the hillsides, blasting
away any rocks that presented obstacles to the creation of a smooth,
graded path sitting high enough up on the shore that a powerful wave
could not destroy it. All the while, Frederick consoled himself by imagining tarp-covered wagons, laden with bricks and timber, lining the
road as they delivered the materials to rebuild the family mansion.

The burst of road construction led to speculation that Rindge was
using the reconstruction of his mansion as cover to clear a path for
a long-rumored railroad line that would run across the Malibu ranch
and up the coast, all the way to San Francisco. A few years earlier,
the Southern Pacific had completed construction of a pier at the tip of
Santa Monica that snaked nearly a mile out to sea. Dubbed the Long
Wharf, it was the railroad's attempt to claim the bay as the chief port
of Los Angeles and control all of the traffic of goods flowing from its
harbor. Rindge, while clearing a path along the coast, seemed to be
outflanking the railroad, making space along a coastal path that it had
never considered possible. He had hatched the plan in secret two years
before, when he'd incorporated a company he called the Port Hueneme
and Port Los Angeles Railway, then doled out nearly all of its shares to
himself and May. Yet at the time he considered it a form of insurance,
leaving it in his back pocket in case the railroads attempted to force
their way into Malibu. Now, to tamp down the talk of his plans, he
directed N. D. Darlington, his chief assistant who managed the day-to-
day business of the Rindge empire, to dispel it through the press. "Mr.
Rindge looks upon Malibu as his real home, and he has missed keenly
the comfort and pleasure he took in the big ranch-house that the flames
swept away," Darlington told a gathering of newsmen in the Rindge
Building downtown.

May never knew her husband to stay unhappy for long, and when
his spirits did not liven after months back in Los Angeles, she arranged
for the family to head up to the commune at Cloverdale. There, she
believed, Frederick could regain his passion, while she could spend long

afternoons with her children and Aunt Emily, far from the faceless hordes that made living in Los Angeles intolerable. Preston's followers were soon called on to lug more than a dozen trunks filled with clothes that the Rindges brought north with them. Frederick was ushered into a private cabin, where all talk of business and rebuilding were kept far from him.

Years before, doctors had identified his bouts of fatigue, often marked by an unquenchable thirst and blurred vision, as a likely sign of diabetes, but they were powerless to offer any lasting remedy. The array of ailments he suffered overwhelmed the understanding doctors had of the body at the time, leaving Madam Preston's so-called cures nearly as good as anything a properly trained physician could provide. If his blood sugar wasn't failing him, then his weak heart valves, damaged by the bouts of rheumatic fever he suffered as a child, would often leave him light-headed, pale, and prone to fever and chills. On his worst days, he was apt to faint, causing doctors and nurses to puzzle over whether this was the result of his frail heart losing its place in the circulatory system's choreographed rhythms or if his blood sugar had crashed and sent his body into a tailspin.

As he spent the spring of 1905 with a succession of Madam Preston's blister-therapy liniment bandages tied around his body, Frederick had no way of knowing that the development of commercial insulin in 1923, and of penicillin in 1928, would soon offer the lasting remedies he so desperately sought. Instead, he remained in the care of the person he believed had saved his life countless times before, and who he expected to do so again, simply as a matter of faith. He ate frequent, small meals that kept his blood sugar in check, while the pastoral location of the commune, far from the stress of managing each strand of his empire, gave his heart time to regain its strength.

Unable to keep still, he sat with a pen in hand, letting his words venture where his body could not. He wrote several long poems to May, one of which opened with a play on her name:

Born in May, queen of May. Mayflower fair
Light as the note of a musical air
Fostered by pansies, nurtured by rose
Destined for happiness, child of repose.

The breeze stops blowing as you pass
To wish you well, my merry lass
The birdies in the garden walk
Cease their chatter to hear you talk
The blossoms bend their stems and say
Ever welcome winsome May.

Within weeks, he was himself again, and true to his character, he began chafing at the restrictions of any form of confinement. He went on long horseback rides across the hills, stopping at farms and ranches nearby to inquire about everything from the production of their vineyards to the latest gossip from San Francisco, some eighty miles south. He soon heard stories of untapped gold mines in the far reaches of Northern California where miners had recently emerged with nuggets the size of a man's thumb. On the face of it, these sounded like the sorts of tall tales intended to separate gullible men from their money. It had been more than fifty years since the Gold Rush brought waves of prospectors to California, a collection of men so hungry to strike it rich that they seemed to have overturned every rock between San Francisco and Oregon. Yet the stories intrigued Frederick as much as for the promise of adventure as for the potential for profit. Here was his chance to live out the last of his unfulfilled boyhood fantasies, descending into the earth and reemerging with gold, the metal that gave his new home of California a luster like no other. He penned letters to trusted friends in San Francisco, informing them that he was looking for someone who had experience with gold mines, all the while begging everyone involved to remain discreet. He soon settled on a man named Thomas Miller, who was touted as one of the state's foremost experts in unearthing its riches.

Just weeks after he was thought to be on his deathbed, Frederick hopped aboard a train heading north, with Miller in tow. They were bound for the Siskiyou Trail, an ancient pathway that weaved between the snowcapped mountains dividing California and Oregon. The journey would take them over and through some of the most remote and rugged terrain in the state, far from anyone who could recognize Frederick or give away his intentions. Unlike others who had once been lured into Northern California by the scent of gold, Frederick did not need to strike it rich. Instead, he carried himself with the desperation of a man who wanted to prove that he was still the master of his body, despite his advancing age and the weight of disappointment. On a brilliant late August day, Frederick waved good-bye to May and his children, intent on claiming one more adventure.

The men were bound for Yreka, a virtual ghost town that had once been the heart of gold country. In 1851, a mule-train driver by the name of Abraham Thompson rested his team by the banks of a stream running along the bottom of a ravine called Black Gulch. While the animals fed, Thompson noticed something shimmering in the water. He went over to inspect it and discovered countless gold flakes clouding the streambed. His interest piqued, Thompson pulled up the grass his animals were eating and found thick gold flakes glinting off the roots. Without realizing it, he had stumbled upon what would soon be called the richest square mile on earth. As rumors of a place where gold was just sitting there for the taking got out, a stampede of more than a thousand miners rolled in over the next few weeks and began laying claims at a spot that became known as Thompson's Dry Diggings.

The instant city attracted men from San Francisco, and then all over the world. That it was far from any train station and nestled among jagged cliffs in the shadow of the snowcapped peak of Mount Shasta, an active volcano climbing fourteen thousand feet above the valley floor, was no matter to men in the grips of gold fever. It became a bustling place where "a tide of people poured up and down, and across from other streets, as strong as if in New York," noted the poet Joaquin Miller, who lived there in 1853 and 1854. "The white people on the sidewalks, then the Chinese and mules in the main street. Not a woman in sight, not a child, not a boy. . . . All this city had been built, all this country opened up, in less than two years."

Tents and cabins lined every stream and pond, filled with miners who emerged each morning with their beards still carrying flecks of rock and rubble from the day before. "They stretched themselves in the sweet frosty air," Miller wrote, "shouted to each other in a sort of savage banter, washed their hands and faces in the gold pans that stood by the door, and then entered their cabins again, to partake of the eternal beans and bacon and coffee, and coffee and bacon and beans. The whole face of the earth was perforated with holes, shafts sunk and being sunk by these men in search of gold, down to the bedrock. Windlasses stretched across these shafts, where great buckets hung, in which men hoisted the earth to the light of the sun by sheer force of muscle."

The city soon took the name of Yreka, from the native Shasta Indian word for "white mountain." Yet the origin of the name was often lost among the ragged men who roamed its streets. One San Francisco newspaper reporter who ventured into the camp in the years after its founding, struggling to find something to write about, created a backstory all his own. The place "acquired its mysterious name—when in its first days it much needed a name—through an accident. There was a bakeshop with a canvas sign which had not yet been put up but had been painted and stretched to dry in such a way that the word bakery, all but the b, showed through and was reversed. A stranger read it wrong end first, yreka, and supposed that that was the name of the camp. The campers were satisfied with it and adopted it," wrote the man who had only recently begun calling himself Mark Twain.

The fortunes of the place rose and fell with the production of its mines. As gold became harder to find, Yreka's population dwindled to less than a thousand. What little life the town had left in it was extinguished on July 4, 1871, when a fire burned down most of its business district. By the time Frederick and Miller stepped off a train in 1905, Yreka was little more than a collection of dilapidated Victorian buildings and empty streets, saved from complete abandonment only by its role as the seat of government in one of the state's least populated counties.

Men still trickled in every so often with gold on their minds. The latest were a collection of recent Chinese immigrants, working off the memories of their fathers and grandfathers who had been a part of the Gold Rush fifty years before. The men formed a company and began buying up the rights to those abandoned mines that seemed the most promising. It seemed a foolhardy enterprise; that is, until one man emerged with a nugget that would be worth more than $1.1 million today. The story swept across the lightly populated countryside, gathering momentum until it drifted into the ears of Frederick Rindge.

While Miller fashioned a list of mines for the pair to inspect, Frederick was content simply with the thrill of movement. Just as he had as a young man, he once again found himself chasing the horizon to soothe his pain. He already owned gold mines in Colombia, and he had recently signed on to a syndicate that planned to drill for oil along the Southern California coastline. Even if he found a productive mine, it would simply become just another asset stashed among his collection.

Miller ushered Frederick up a rocky path outside town. All of the gold that could be found in the streambeds was long since recovered, leaving the mountains themselves as the only viable option left. The pair soon arrived at the mouth of a mine, no bigger than a doorway, blasted into the hillside. They stopped for Frederick to catch his breath, then began their descent. The light from their hand-held lanterns glistened off the jagged stone walls of the mine as the men made their way deeper into the earth. All the while, Miller scanned the rock walls for a telltale streak of amber that had somehow been passed over amid the madness of the Gold Rush.

They were still underground when Frederick collapsed. Miller attempted to revive him with cold water. It wasn't out of the ordinary for men even half Frederick's age to succumb when faced for the first time with the stagnant air and tight quarters of a mine. As the minutes passed, however, Miller began to worry. All the color drained from Frederick's face, and each breath in his lungs seemed to come only as the result of a hard-won struggle. Miller lifted Frederick off the floor and raced toward the sunlight with one of the country's richest men on his back.

Temporarily blinded by the daylight after emerging above ground, Miller somehow managed to get Frederick up on a saddle. He jumped behind him and galloped into town. He rushed Frederick into their hotel and urged its owner to call the first doctor he could find. A man named O. B. Spalding soon arrived and began trying to diagnose the illness of an unresponsive man he had never before seen. Spalding worked throughout the night, and all of the next day, yet was unable to revive Frederick or stop his heart rate from racing. Running out of options, Spalding sent word to every physician in the area for help, hoping that one of them would have an answer. He then pulled Miller aside and told him that the outlook was grim. If he had a way to reach Frederick's wife, he should do so at once so as to give her time to reach her husband before it was too late.

MAY STEPPED ONTO the Yreka train platform at noon on Monday, just three days after her husband had walked the same path. She hustled across Miner Street, the main street in town, and into the hotel where Frederick lay unresponsive. There, she discovered that his room had become a makeshift hospital. A team of rural doctors surrounded him, filling the narrow space to its edges. She began listing each of Frederick's many health conditions, at last giving the doctors a few useful clues to work with. An hour later, Frederick regained consciousness for the first time since he'd fainted inside the mine. He cast a dazed look around the room, his eyes unfocused until they came to rest on May's face and glimmered in recognition. The spell was soon broken, however, and Frederick lapsed back into unconsciousness and never recovered. He was pronounced dead a few hours later. Unsure to the end of how to ease his pain, the doctors treating Frederick told May that the immediate cause of death was a diabetic coma, complicated by stomach and gallbladder troubles they could not resolve.

For forty-eight years, Frederick had been able to outrun the illness that had taken all of his siblings from him at an early age. He had lived a life full of adventure, never bowing to the limits of his physical frame, even until the end. The boyhood he'd spent staring out the window of an empty mansion had fostered a fire within that had pushed him throughout his life and had directly led him here, intent on fulfilling one more of his childhood fantasies. That he would eventually yield to the inherent flaws of his body was a given; doing so in the pursuit of gold was only fitting for a man who still had much of the boy inside him. Frederick had always lived for the future, and yet he had never been able to fully escape the scars the past had left on him.

May had often tried to prepare herself for this moment. She'd known that it was only a matter of time before Frederick would lose his fight, no matter how strong his will. But as she sat next to her husband's lifeless body in the hotel room, wondering what would come next, every option seemed overwhelming. The man her life had revolved around was gone, leaving her a widow at the age of forty. She knew that while Frederick had often talked of writing a will that would give her direct instructions on how he wanted her to disburse the fortune he had built up, the only one he had ever signed was a handwritten document that left a sum that would today be worth nearly $700 million to her and their three children. At that moment, May wanted nothing more than to use every last dollar to stop time and retreat back to the long afternoons she'd spent with Frederick and the children on the Malibu shore, far from anyone or anything that could do them harm.

LATER THAT AFTERNOON, a private train carrying only a few cars edged into the Yreka train station. Agents from the Southern Pacific Railroad draped the railcars in black bunting as a mark of respect for the cargo they would soon be carrying. Men bearing a simple wooden coffin holding Frederick's body soon emerged from the hotel and placed it in a horse-drawn wagon, which slowly made its way down Miner Street. After the coffin was loaded onto the train, May boarded as well. She would go back to Preston and deliver the news to her children, then head down to Los Angeles, the place where Frederick had come closest to realizing all of his dreams.

As the train crawled its way south, May felt more alone than she had in any moment in the past. Her only comfort was the fortune Frederick had left her, a sum so staggering that it ensured that she would never again have to depend on anyone. The train chugged throughout the night, bringing her closer to Los Angeles, where she would have to begin life again on her own terms. She would never remarry.

Chapter Eleven

ARCH ROCK

NEVER BEFORE HAD SO MANY MEMBERS OF LOS Angeles' elite gathered in one place. The more than twenty rooms of the Rindge home on Harvard Boulevard overflowed with powerful men, each one accustomed to commanding the attention of any gathering he happened to be a part of. The sheer number of attendees crammed into the mansion made its grand spaces seem small, stuffed to the edges with the overlapping spheres of influence around which daily life in Los Angeles swayed. In life, Frederick had had no equal in terms of his grasp, which spanned from the city's pulpits to its banks; in death, representatives of each tentacle of his empire came to pay their respects.

His death had "left a gap such as is seldom caused by the passing of a citizen to a higher life," the *Los Angeles Times* wrote the day of his funeral. "As a business man, as a church leader, as a YMCA president, as a consistent worker for the development for the city and state, Mr. Rindge made himself so useful that no other man can readily take his place." Even those in the city who had never before heard the name Frederick Rindge felt his absence. On the day of the funeral, the offices of Conservative Life, Edison Electric, Union Oil, and more than twenty other local companies Frederick had either founded or been a board member of closed their doors, a unified symbol of grief that nearly ground the city's economy to a halt.

The service began shortly after three in the afternoon. A parade of speakers came forward and, standing in front of a lectern nearly lost among the sea of orchids and birds-of-paradise surrounding the bier, touched on the life of a man at home among both the country's greatest wealth and its most fervent believers. Reverend W. H. Rider, the pastor of Westlake Methodist Church, led the mourners in a rendition of "Nearer, My God, to Thee." Holdridge Ozro Collins, the governor of the Society of Colonial Wars, recounted how Frederick could trace his lineage to Robert Kinsman of England, a Puritan who was born in 1629 and came to the Massachusetts Bay Colony in search of an earthly paradise. Reverend John L. Pitner, whom Frederick had first met years before, while recovering in St. Augustine, and who was now considered one of the favorites to become the next mayor of Los Angeles, told the mourners that Frederick had burned with a religious conviction that bordered on the mystic. "He was one of the men who touch barren places and make them blossom; one of the men who work with nature and God to bring about the eternal fulfillment of the possibilities of the long ago," Pitner said, his voice echoing in the cavernous space. A message was read from the mayor of Cambridge, General Edgar Champlin: "I personally feel his loss, for not only was he my fellow townsman, but also my childhood playmate. Mr. Rindge has done more for Cambridge than everybody else combined."

After an hour-long ceremony, the congregants made their way to the nearby Rosedale Cemetery, which Frederick had helped establish during the boom of the 1880s and was the final resting place for several of the city's early mayors. There, a group of pallbearers who collectively ruled Los Angeles carried the coffin to a grave site marked only by a modest headstone. Leading the men was Senator Frank P. Flint, a real estate developer then in just the fifth month of a six-year term in Washington. He was flanked by J. C. Drake, the head of the Los Angeles

Trust Company, and Arthur Letts, a man whose department store, the Broadway, was already on its way to becoming one of Southern California's most popular chains. Trailing behind were a collection of honorary pallbearers, men too old or infirm to lift the coffin themselves but whose power nevertheless went unquestioned. The streetcar magnate Henry E. Huntington stood next to General M. H. Sherman, a land developer and the namesake of the nearby city of Sherman Oaks, while General Harrison Gray Otis, the publisher of the *Los Angeles Times*, marched alongside J. Ross Clark, a successful miner and banker who just three months before had convinced his brother, Senator William A. Clark, one of the richest men in the world, to build a railroad from Los Angeles to Salt Lake City. The project would lead the pair to found the city of Las Vegas, the hub of what became Nevada's Clark County.

May took a seat next to the grave site, draped in black. Under a clear early September sky reminiscent of the day she'd first arrived in the small town called Los Angeles, she placed a wreath of flowers on Frederick's coffin and said good-bye to him for the final time.

As May headed back toward her home, she knew that the hardest part was yet to come. The unspoken question among the formidable men milling around after the ceremony was what May would do with the sweeping kingdom over which she now presided. Seldom had any person, much less one with no training or experience in business, been asked to step in and oversee an enterprise so sprawling. That May was a woman at a time when suffragettes in the United States and Britain were only taking the first steps in what would become the movement for women's voting rights made her situation all the more puzzling in the eyes of Frederick's former business partners and competitors. Few women held positions of authority in California at the time, and those who did often came to inglorious ends. Only months before, May's distant cousin Jane Lathrop Stanford, whose squabbles with Stanford University's president in the decade since her husband's death had intensified as she struggled to keep the institution afloat, had fled to Hawaii after a servant in her Nob Hill mansion attempted to poison her. While in

Honolulu, Stanford requested a solution of baking powder to settle her stomach one evening before bed. Within minutes of drinking the mixture, poured from a bottle packed in San Francisco and placed within her luggage, she was overcome by violent full-body spasms and fell lifeless to the floor, killed by strychnine poisoning at the hands of a person whose identity was never discovered.

That gruesome end was surely on May's mind as she contemplated her future. All of Los Angeles expected her to hire a man to preside over the Rindge empire if she was inclined to keep it—or, more likely, to sell it in bits and pieces and live off the proceeds for the rest of her life. Leaving the cemetery, the collection of businessmen—some titans, and some still hoping to become one—mourned not only the man who had been their friend but what they considered the end of a Californian empire they had all looked at with a mixture of jealousy and awe. With Frederick's death, a gaping hole had opened at the top of the city's hierarchy, and they all quietly hatched plans to fill it.

FOR YEARS, May had been content to live in Frederick's shadow, where she'd focused on the responsibilities of family and home while her husband chased his dreams. Now, with his death, she was forced to step into the light and reveal herself to a city that had long overlooked her presence. She knew that she barely registered in the eyes of the men who coveted Frederick's businesses and his property, that she was merely an afterthought to their grand designs who could easily be disregarded. For all the money she had at her disposal, it still felt as if she was once again a child on that Michigan farm so far away, told to stand by while her father pleaded his way into higher prices for his crops. Those haunting days had left her with a stone resolve that no act of man or God could sway. She refused to entertain the notion that Frederick's death would force her to give up any part of the life to which she had grown accustomed. There would be no man to tell her what to do, no abandonment of the places where she had spent long happy days with her husband and children. If Los Angeles had other plans, well, it would soon find out whom it was dealing with.

Within days of Frederick's death, May rode a horse-drawn carriage to the offices of O'Melveny and Myers, one of the most elite law firms in the city. Once there, she directed the attorneys to set up a corporation she called the Rindge Company, with her at its head, that would claim official ownership of each strand of Frederick's empire. It was a step that would allow her to limit what she would be obliged to pay in taxes as well as provide a layer of protection for any claims against her assets, but that was not what struck the attorneys who worked with her. The decision to form a corporation demonstrated a level of financial sophistication that few expected in the wife of a business titan, much less one whose husband had died without giving her any instructions in how to manage his estate. May awarded herself the majority of the new company's shares and allotted a small percentage to each of her three children.

She quickly saw that Malibu was the most vulnerable asset in her control. Real estate developers and officials in the county public works department responsible for building a road that could reach Malibu had long shied away from its hidden hills, largely out of respect for Frederick's influence. That detente seemed unlikely to hold now that he was gone. Homesteaders continued to pour into Los Angeles, leaving spots high in the Santa Monica Mountains above the rancho as some of the last unclaimed land in the county. Still bitter at the homesteaders she blamed for setting the blaze that had destroyed the family's mansion two years earlier, May ordered her foreman to construct five heavy gates along the private coastal wagon trail nearing completion between Santa Monica and the Ventura County line. It wouldn't be enough to clear the hills of men, but it could deter any would-be settlers from traveling across her kingdom.

In October, she made her next move. Horse-drawn heavy wagons, their contents draped in canvas, clomped through the streets of Santa Monica, trailed by dozens of men. Few in the city paid any attention, and those who did assumed that it was all connected to the annual bean harvest at the Malibu ranch. It wasn't until a week later that May revealed her true intentions. On October 5, she announced plans to build a new railroad, called the Hueneme, Malibu and Port Los Angeles Railway, whose construction was already under way. When completed, the line would reach far into Ventura County, where a connection to existing railways in Santa Barbara and parts farther north was presumed likely. May named herself executive president of the operation, making her the first woman ever to head a railroad in California, and the only one in the country at large.

Nothing like the railroad had ever threatened to upend the power dynamics of Los Angeles—or the state—so suddenly. The black veins of rails crisscrossing the city were its lifeblood, a network of thousands of tiny arteries behind its beating economy that allowed it to expand beyond the confines of the former pueblo and sprawl from the mountains to the sea. The simple act of laying down a track could transform an empty brown clearing into a small city of lush homes and fragrant gardens—or make ghost towns out of those developments the railroads decided to circumvent. Los Angeles was a city built on movement, and those who mastered that concept would go far. The so-called robber barons who opened California up to the rest of the country had known that fact early on, and they continued to get fat off the dollars they skimmed from every ticket sold to the countless people jumping on and off trains as they went about their daily business.

The Malibu line seemed to spring fully formed from the ether. Just three days before, H. W. Lemcke, Frederick's personal secretary, had opened a telegram and learned the astonishing news that he was now a railroad man. "Dear Sir," he read. "This is to notify you that you have been appointed General Manager of the Hueneme, Malibu and Port Los Angeles Railway, with present headquarters at Santa Monica, said appointment having becoming effective of this date, Oct. 2, 1905. Signed May K. Rindge, Executive President." He then discovered that a hundred yards of its track had already been laid, spanning a flat patch of beach fifteen miles from the Santa Monica end of the ranch. The steel rails and ties had been brought up by covered wagons whose path through Santa Monica had been overlooked a week before.

Lemcke, still trying to steady his feet from the news, soon found himself describing the railway's ambitions in detail to a group of reporters who'd assembled in Santa Monica to chase what was now the biggest story in the city. "Especial pains have been taken to select a route that will at once command by reason of its picturesqueness," he told the men. When further questioned why the railroad was being built now, he offered up the idea that May was simply fulfilling a dream held by her late husband, who would have done the same thing if his life had continued just a few months longer.

Anyone could broadcast their intention to build a railroad; it was the existence of those hundred yards of track that threw some of the most powerful interests in the state into chaos. The Southern Pacific Railroad had long controlled the route through the state's Central Valley that was the only link between Los Angeles and San Francisco, and had grown accustomed to the enormous profits it brought in. Its directors, paranoid that the company would lose its most important monopoly left in the state, had pursued a strategy of quietly purchasing a right-of-way through every conceivable mountain pass, effectively quarantining the Los Angeles basin from Northern California. The only untouched route left was along the Malibu coast, a place long thought to be too rugged to hold a railroad and that, until two months earlier, had been controlled by one of the few men whose influence rivaled that of the Southern Pacific. With May's decision to build, the last bottleneck preventing a long-speculated coastal train route spouted open, and three men—Henry E. Huntington, the baron of the city's streetcar system, E. H. Harriman, the New York–based director of the mighty Southern Pacific, and George Gould, the Oakland-based son of the original train baron, Jay Gould, who intended to build his own railroad to rival that of his father's—began a feverish contest to guess at her intentions.

Each man dispatched intermediaries off to every beachfront landowner south of the Malibu ranch with instructions to pay any sum requested for a right-of-way across the property. Franchise rights soon began selling for twenty times what they would have fetched before word of the new Malibu railroad leaked out. Over the next few weeks, teams of surveyors carrying tripods and telescopes worked their way up the coast, plotting the tracks of grand train lines whose existence depended on the outcome of the ownership of a few hundred feet of sand.

The battle between the railroad giants, a group of men whose names were widely known throughout the state, quickly overshadowed any assumption that May could still be a factor in its outcome. "There is no longer any doubt that if this line, which has created so much specula-tion for several months past, was a private enterprise of Mrs. Rindge's, at its inception, it has now been turned over to larger and more pow-erful interests in the railroad world," the *Los Angeles Times* reported. "Hung, as it will be, fairly upon the precipitous sides of the cliffs and bluffs running directly to the water's edge, this line will be in a way to attract tourist travel from all over the world. Once under operation, its fame would quickly spread, and no one would think of visiting South-ern California without making this trip, suspending in a high-speed, luxurious electric palace car, fairly above the blue waters of the Pacific," the newspaper added.

What the speculators and railroad men alike did not know was that all of it, from the railroad ties to the hiring of Lemcke, was all part of a plan whose scope would not become widely known for years. Despite rumors of the grand hotels she intended to build above the coves of Malibu, May had no desire to see her estate overrun by trains freighting in the very sort of outsiders she considered nothing more than vandals. It was all a charade, yet one built firmly on the law. In consultations with her attorneys, May had come to realize that the only way to prevent a railroad from one day obtaining a court-ordered right-of-way across her land was to enter the business herself. Regulations at the time prevented the construction of a competing line along the same corridor as existing tracks; going ahead with work on a private railroad across her land was enough for her to claim an undisputed right to the franchise. It was an option never before available to a landowner who stood in the way of the Southern Pacific, yet for May, now one of the wealthiest women in the country, money was no consideration. "I almost have to kill myself with work, Frederick left so many things unfinished," May wrote in a letter to Madam Preston. "I am only laying enough tracks to keep the other companies out."

May began pouring millions into the railroad, all the while aware that it was not designed to carry anyone or connect with anything. One contractor on the job built more than ten miles of path, including a grand fifty-foot-high trestle spanning an oceanfront gulch, without ever knowing where either end of the line would terminate. N. D. Darlington, Frederick's former assistant whom she placed in charge of the railroad's construction, drew up sketches in which the train lines ran far inland. She ordered him to move them onto the beach itself. Over time, her reasons became clear: heavy storms inevitably sent violent waves crashing onto the coast, destroying what work had been done. May would then direct Darlington to rebuild the tracks along the same spot, fully aware that the next major storm would once again spoil any notion of progress.

The Sisyphean nature of the railroad would not become clear to outsiders for several years. Harriman, the head of the Southern Pacific, considered May an imminent threat and directed his men to do anything possible to prevent the Malibu line from reaching Santa Monica. The company filed a lawsuit alleging that the wagon trail then under construction to the ranch was merely a front behind which the proposed Malibu railway was already engaged in grading along the coast, all on a right-of-way the Southern Pacific had obtained from a Santa Monica landowner as early as 1892. Lemcke, as general manager of the Malibu line, dismissed the charge as frivolous. A few weeks later, after he learned the true purpose of the railroad, he quietly resigned his position. Darlington took over. He told the men to continue with their work, all the while knowing that he was overseeing the construction of a line never meant to be finished. But as long as there was evidence that work was still ongoing, it would do its job of protecting paradise.

DURING HIS LIFETIME, Frederick depended on Malibu as a retreat from the pressures of overseeing his empire. Now that she had stepped into her husband's former role, May, too, began escaping to the ranch as often as she could. She passed long afternoons on the empty sun-drenched shoreline with her children, often bringing a maid and cook along to supply a picnic on the beach or by the banks of Malibu Creek. She chased those fleeting moments of calm, determined to hold on to the anchors of her life when everything seemed poised to slip out of her fingers.

Frederick's presence could be felt everywhere in Malibu, from its coves to the top of Laudamus Hill, the promontory that had overlooked the family's former mansion. May could sense Frederick as soon as she rode beneath Arch Rock; the graceful bend of stone falling into the ocean had been his favorite spot on the entire ranch. He'd often joked that it seemed as if God had built a door into Malibu just for him, and he went to lengths to protect it, even when it presented an obstacle to his other plans. He commanded the men grading the wagon trail up the coast to neither deface nor disturb Arch Rock in any way, a stipulation that slowed the progress of engineers who took pleasure in blasting anything that stood in their path. The span was the one aspect of the Malibu ranch he freely shared with the outside world, and Los Angeles seemed to reciprocate his joy. "Its natural beauty and historic association with the early settlement of the country" so charmed tourists and locals alike that "nobody would listen to any development plans that contemplated its destruction," noted the *Los Angeles Times*. The preservation of its natural heritage was one more way Los Angeles attempted to prove that it was different, and perhaps better, than San Francisco, which had demolished its own Arch Rock just a few years before. There, a few hundred yards from the island of Alcatraz and directly in front of the Golden Gate, had stood a thirty-foot-tall slab; in its center curved a small arch visible at low tide that everyone likened to the eye of a giant stone needle. Though beautiful, the rock was ultimately damned by its location, smack in the middle of ferry lines running toward Sausalito and next to the spot where ships waited while in quarantine, and was dynamited by the city to clear a path across the bay.

Nearly seven months to the day after Frederick collapsed in Yreka, the site in Malibu that brought him the most pleasure vanished. Sometime during the night, Arch Rock collapsed, leaving only a pile of rubble in its place. The loss resonated far beyond May. Men and women throughout Los Angeles mourned its passing, even though it "had no historic significance other than its natural beauty and romantic surroundings," one paper reported. "It was a familiar landmark to all tourists, and talli-ho parties to this post were included in all itineraries of the sightseers."

There was no immediate cause that could account for its destruction, leaving rumors to fill in the gaps. Suspicions that the Southern Pacific had something to do with the leveling of Arch Rock were never confirmed, yet they only grew in the following weeks, after the railroad dispatched a team of surveyors to begin grading northward from Santa Monica along a shoestring path that led directly to the rock's ruins. Not long after, May toured the remnants of the archway Frederick had loved, which she had come to see as a symbol of his company. One of the last reminders of his time in Malibu had been erased, and with it went any hope that Frederick's reputation would continue to protect her. She knew now that she was in a fight all on her own, and she vowed to not let the world take anything more away.

Chapter Twelve

TO FORCE HER GATES OPEN

THE IDEA CAME TO HER SUDDENLY. SHE WOULD never be sure if it was a moment of clarity born of desperation or if an offhand remark Frederick had once uttered had lodged itself deep in her mind and only now rose to the surface. Yet whatever its source, it was, she thought, perfect.

In early 1907, May instructed her attorneys to draw up a proposal that she could send to the White House, where the college classmate whose influence had once propelled Frederick to California was spending his sixth year in office. Every aspect of the scheme was designed to appeal to the sympathies of a man already becoming known as America's greatest conservationist. By the end of his presidency, Theodore Roosevelt would double the country's number of national parks, unilaterally decide to designate the Grand Canyon and seventeen other sites as national monuments that could not be touched by development, and set aside over 100 million acres' worth of national forests. May hoped he wouldn't blanch at adding another seventy thousand more. In the letter to Washington, she suggested that the unforgiving terrain behind the Malibu ranch was more suited for a national reserve than for human habitation. The proper thing to do, she argued, was to preserve the land before it was too late.

It was a suggestion deeply at odds with the spirit of the conservation movement. Roosevelt and the members of the recently created U.S. Forest Service focused on protecting the nation's natural wonders not only for their beauty but to maximize the resources they contained. Roosevelt's men considered conservation a national duty whose greatest aim was, in the words of the head of the forest service, to "make the forest produce the largest amount of whatever crop or service will be most useful, and keep on producing it for generation after generation of men and trees." Simply stripping an area of men, much less homesteaders scraping by on government land, for no good economic reason, was not something they did lightly.

Yet May had her reasons to hope. Untouched land among the golden coastal hills of Southern California, once so abundant, was now scarce. The local General Land Office had recently announced that nearly all the plots designated for homesteads within the county of Los Angeles were claimed and suggested to men and women still straggling in with paperwork in their hands that they would be better served looking elsewhere. Everywhere a person turned was the sight of a city expanding beyond its natural limits, propelled by nothing more than the feverish hope that the boom times would last forever. Amid such a fever, it would be only a matter of time before every trace of the region's forests would be erased, with a phalanx of oil derricks and apartment buildings growing in their place. The Santa Monica Mountains, May suggested, offered the last cushion from the meteoric whirl of development that had birthed a major city in less than twenty years' time. Without unveiling her idea to anyone in Los Angeles outside of her attorneys and her immediate family, May sent the plan to Washington and hoped that gazing upon his old friend's name would sway the president in her favor.

When word of the proposal leaked out, it shattered the illusion that May was nothing more than a widow waiting to be guided by someone or something more powerful. Whereas Frederick had accepted that he could not clear every homesteader from the mountains behind his property, May now proved her intentions to rid the area of settlers for all time, and to get the federal government's assistance in the process. Homesteaders and some of the most influential men in Los Angeles soon formed an unlikely union against the widow they now considered their common enemy. All of the reasons May had counted on to convince the government to declare a new national forest were the very ones that turned everyone from the publisher of the city's largest paper to Marion Decker cardinal with rage. "How would you like to be the owners of a principality composed of rich, fertile valleys and rugged, picturesque mountains, stretching along the shores of the balmy Pacific Ocean for a distance of from twenty to thirty miles? And after having maintained this principality in all the exclusiveness to be obtained by padlocked gates and boundaries patrolled by hired agents . . . would it not be balm to your soul for Uncle Sam to create at your request a forest reserve extending along the back of this magnificent land-holding, thus adding to your exclusiveness and practically doubling your domain, as well as guarding it with his stalwart forest rangers?" sneered the *Los Angeles Times* in an incredulous editorial.

The promise of easy travel to the long-forbidding coast along railroad tracks then under construction down the Malibu coastline only inflamed the city's ire. Once those tracks were connected with existing lines in Santa Monica, "these beautiful canyons will be within two hours' ride of Los Angeles," the *Times* noted. "One can easily realize how popular they might become, as the city grows, for suburban homes such as now dot the canyons in the mountains back of San Francisco and the northern bay cities."

In Marion Decker's eyes, a man wearing a suit and tie sitting in a fancy downtown office could carry on about how the proposal was an affront to progress for as long as he wished and it wouldn't do much good. Decker had once put his faith in the men from the city, and he was still waiting for it to pay off. For years, he had passed through one of Rindge's gates every time he left his home and every time he came back, an insult to his pride that hadn't dulled with time. Resorting to other measures to compensate gave him some satisfaction, however fleeting. It wasn't at all out of the ordinary for someone who had an appointment with Decker to reach the first gate of the Malibu ranch and find it torn open, its chains broken in half and pieces of wood scattered along the rocks. The ranch foreman never caught him in the act, but he knew that Decker was the chief reason why he needed to build new gates at least once a month.

Until now, destroying the literal obstacles placed in his path had been enough for Decker to get by, albeit grudgingly. Yet if May's plan was successful, he knew, there would be no way he could outmaneuver the federal government. He had scraped out a living in the hills far longer than any other man, and never once had he contemplated taking the Rindges' money, even as he saw his neighbors pack up and move on. His deep belief in the righteousness of his decisions allowed him to withstand hardships that would send others scurrying. If May was now successful, the rewards of all of those lean years would be lost. The government would likely pay him a small fee for his land, but with the open spaces of Los Angeles virtually filled in, where would he go? Each night, Decker stared for hours into his campfire, the only light in the mountains save the stars, searching for a solution that would block May's plan. Finally, one evening, he found one.

THE GRANDSTANDING BY the *Los Angeles Times* had its desired effect. Days after the paper condemned May's plan, L. E. Aubrey, the state mineralogist, wrote from San Francisco to join in the cause. Aubrey had once been part of a government survey that pored over the Santa Monica Mountains in search of untapped natural resources and came home empty-handed. "No good reason could be found for this district being converted into a reserve," he wrote to the *Times*, and he vowed to take the matter up personally with Gifford Pinchot, the man Roosevelt had appointed as the first ever chief of the United States Forest Service, the next time he was in Washington.

The proposal soon reached the desk of James R. Garfield, whose position as secretary of the interior granted him sway over the management of more than 200 million acres of federally owned land stretching from the coast of Maine to the unseen hinterlands of Alaska. He shared the same philosophy of guarding the nation's resources as President Roosevelt, the man who had appointed him to the task. Yet that wasn't the chief reason why Garfield had become one of Roosevelt's most trusted advisers. On the morning of July 2, 1881, he had been standing next to his father, President James A. Garfield, in the waiting room of the Baltimore and Potomac Railroad Station when a deranged man pulled out a gun and shot the president twice at close range. He died eleven weeks later. Roosevelt originally saw working with James R. Garfield, who at the time of his father's death had been just fifteen years old, as a tribute to his late father's memory, and over the years he grew impressed by the determination of this young man who'd had every reason to shy away from a public life and yet continued to believe in the virtues of service.

Garfield, in his role as the secretary of the interior, had shown himself to be comfortable with the mixture of ideology and practicality that a functioning government required. His ability to take seemingly incongruent positions mirrored that of Roosevelt himself, who praised self-reliance at the same time he expanded the reach of government and lined up protections for the common man.

Garfield prided himself on the defense of untouched lands, yet proved that his resolve could be bent by circumstance. The year before, he had signed off on a bill to divert water some four hundred miles down the state from the rural Owens Valley and into Los Angeles, a mammoth undertaking that promised to finally solve the water problems that had long threatened to stall the city's growth. Settlers in Owens Valley railed against the move, which had the potential to transform a snowcapped area once called the Switzerland of California into arid badlands. Yet Garfield readily agreed with Senator Frank P. Flint of California, who argued that the project would provide Los Angeles with water for more than a century, to strike a provision that would have

prevented the city from using any water from Owens Valley for irrigation. When it was completed, fifteen years later, the water gurgling out
of the Los Angeles Aqueduct allowed green suburbs to sweep across the
San Fernando Valley and beyond. Before he finished his term, Garfield
would go on to back numerous projects opposed by preservationists,
most notably his decision to build a dam that flooded Hetch Hetchy, a
valley whose beauty was often compared to that of the nearby Yosemite
National Park, in order to create a reservoir filled with drinking water
for San Francisco.

The guiding principle in each of those decisions was shepherding the natural resources of the land in such a way as to benefit the
maximum number of people. When he looked at the proposal to turn
the land behind the Malibu ranch into a national preserve, however,
Garfield saw little for him to protect. The ground held few minerals of
any value, the quality of the timber paled in comparison to that found
in the ancient redwood groves in the northern half of the state, and
the streams and waterfalls, while beautiful, were so small as to hardly
matter; as far as Garfield was concerned, any settler who braved such
harsh conditions deserved a title to his land. As he prepared to deny
the proposal, however, one detail unnerved him. The government had
provided no conceivable roads for the settlers to reach their land. He
considered such oversight an assault on their right to make something
out of the natural resources available, no matter how poor, and resolved
to do something about it as soon as he could.

May offered no public reaction when the proposal was dismissed, nor
made any attempt to salvage her reputation as she faced a blitz of criti-
cism unlike anything she had experienced before. While Frederick was
alive, the papers had printed nothing but glowing reports of his generosity and business acumen, never once questioning his hold on Malibu
or his right to protect his interests as he saw fit. Now she began each
day by scanning rounds of newspaper editorials, each one arguing that
the ranch should have been developed long ago. None swayed her. She
responded to the calls to open up Malibu by adding additional guards to

patrol the property. Each man was issued a shotgun and told to do what was necessary to keep outsiders from coming onto her land.

SHY AND RECLUSIVE by nature, May had little aptitude for trying to sway the public in her favor. Her attention instead turned toward another emerging threat to her empire: the automobile. The horseless carriage was just arriving in the city, and Los Angeles was already proving itself car crazy. One in every eighty Angelenos was the proud owner of an automobile, a rate 25 percent higher than that of comparably sized cities in the East. The feat was all the more impressive considering that most cars at the time cost twice the average person's annual salary and, despite that price tag, were little more than an engine with a set of wheels, the whole shaky contraption prone to breaking down at any moment. No matter: Los Angeles was becoming, in the eyes of the local press, "without exception, the banner automobile city of the world." That January, a crowd of more than three thousand people waited in the rain to enter Morley's Grand Avenue Skating Rink, home of the first ever Los Angeles Auto Show. Ninety-seven gasoline-powered cars glimmered inside, arranged among overflowing baskets of flowers. Two electric vehicles sat off to one side, ringed by banners calling them the perfect choice for lady drivers. Henry Ford was among those who walked through the doors, ticket in hand. Mostly unknown at the time, Ford paced the floor, sizing up each model. His Model T, designed to bring automobiles within reach of the average family, was then in its final planning stages. Production would start the following year, forever changing the car business.

Elsewhere in the country, the appearance of cars on city streets had been met with derision by local officials who considered them nothing but smoke-belching toys of the wealthy that, when they weren't spooking nearby horses, were conking out in the middle of intersections or running over pedestrians. The number of fatal accidents grew so high in large cities on the East Coast that the *New York Times* ran editorials arguing for fewer cars on the streets, quoting one local traffic court official as saying, "The slaughter cannot go on. The mangling and crushing cannot continue." Not so in Los Angeles. The geography of the city, where homes spread out across smooth hills and along oceanfronts, seemed to have been built with cars in mind. A driver behind the wheel of a car could experience something never before thought possible: the thrill of going wherever he wanted, at whatever time he wanted, at a speed no horse could ever hope to match. Those fortunate enough to have access to an automobile took off on some of the first road trips, seeking out adventure where trains could not take them.

Malibu proved an enticing prize. On an early Sunday morning in late April 1907, a party of eight men clambered into two spartan automobiles equipped with neither windows nor roofs to protect them from the elements and set off north along the coast from Santa Monica. They carried chisels, chains, and charts with them, the arsenal of what their leader, a man by the name of W. H. Seely, happily called an invasion. They were motivated by what had always motivated men in Los Angeles: the promise of free land. With maps highlighting unclaimed government plots in the Santa Monica Mountains in tow, they timed their journey in the hope that both the Rindge family and the guards protecting them would be asleep or at church. They reached the first gate without incident. Seely jumped out of the car and filed off the lock that held it closed. With the gate now open wide, the men continued across the ranch on a path toward the mountains, following the trails that homesteaders on horseback had built to their remote homes.

They were the first outsiders in years to venture so deep into the ranch. Driving along the empty paths with a soft ocean breeze at their backs, the men felt as if they had fallen into a dreamscape, surrounded by beauty on a scale they had never before seen. That the unclaimed land that had brought them here was ultimately unsuitable for development would later seem of no consequence. "If you were to keep mountain goats on the land that remains open for settlement you would have to fasten climbing irons on them," Seely would go on to say.

Instead, the men returned to Los Angeles with tales of perfect beaches and hidden coves, heightening the mystique built up by Malibu's seclusion. Stories had long floated down to Los Angeles about what lay beyond its gates, every so often compelling the press to address them. "There really is no mystery" to Malibu, one paper argued. "The talk of mystery is built on the fact that no one is allowed on the property on any pretext, and that a railroad is underway there. Even a school teacher employed in one of the mountain districts was chased off when she thoughtlessly went on the ranch to pick wild flowers, it is claimed." Seely and his men had traveled along parts of the coastline others in Los Angeles had only imagined, and the true stories they brought back of its beauty compelled the curious to take a look for themselves. A string of copycats would soon attempt similar journeys up to Malibu, each seeking their own little kingdom amid the mountains that Garfield had ruled would not become a forest reserve.

May learned of the broken locks and tire tracks later that evening. Without wasting time on the question of how her guards could have missed something as obvious as two cars sputtering up the mountainside, she ordered Darlington to go to Los Angeles with a demand that the district attorney secure warrants to arrest each man who'd dared to cross onto her land. The police brought Seely in the next day and released him hours later, after he deposited twenty-five dollars in cash as bail. May waited for word that he would receive a jail sentence that would serve as a warning to anyone else contemplating a similar act.

It wouldn't be the last time her expectations would clash violently with reality. Los Angeles was running out of room at the very time when automobiles made it easy to go wherever their drivers wished. With the question of whether a public road crossed the Malibu ranch still unresolved, Seely's case offered the government just the sort of test case it had pined for. A verdict that forced open the Malibu gates would not only be a victory for the settlers in the hills but, more importantly, would inevitably open its unsullied valleys and canyons up for development.

Seely hired a man named M. C. McLemore as his attorney. Seven years before, McLemore had held a position as a U.S. district attorney for the eastern part of Texas, until the hurricane that destroyed his hometown of Galveston forced him to flee to Los Angeles with his family. That unusually high qualification for a lawyer brought in to defend a simple misdemeanor was the first sign that the case was not going to be as simple as May expected it to be. She soon learned that interest in the outcome spilled up to the highest reaches of government. During a brief appearance in Los Angeles that spring, reporters probed Secretary Garfield for his thoughts on the Malibu deadlock. Standing in front of the group of men, he declared that not only should the rights of settlers to reach government lands be protected but that over the previous few days he had held several meetings with local officials concerning that very subject.

FOR MONTHS, Marion Decker had secretly worked on his own plan to force the county to build a road along the coast. He had long ago resigned himself to the fact that neither the government nor a millionaire like May Rindge would ever go out of their way to do anything to make the life of an aging settler like him any easier. What really mattered, he realized, was money. It took a while, but he finally had a way to get some of it flowing into his corner. While on one of his trips to Santa Monica to refresh his supplies, he struck up a conversation with a man named I. S. Colyer, the son of bank president in Brooklyn, New York, who had come west for his health. It wasn't long before they realized that they could solve each other's problems. Decker had land; Colyer had both funding and the benefit of an East Coast pedigree. Together, they erected eight large tents near a sulfur spring bubbling on the corner of Decker's place. It was the start of what both men expected to blossom into a health resort that would draw thousands into the mountains.

As soon as he heard of Decker's plan, Darlington ordered the ranch guards to prevent anyone from making the trek along the Malibu coast to reach the springs. It was just the sort of reaction that Decker wanted. Along with Colyer, he vowed to bring in resort guests via the coast by any means necessary. Another standoff along the coast, this time with a banker's money involved, would surely add to the pressure mounting on May to open the ranch.

What Decker didn't anticipate was that Colyer's father had no intention of seeing his son get dragged into a fight he might not win. The elder Colyer came out to California just as the controversy began to percolate and quietly requested a meeting with May, aiming to soften her stance. Over lunch in the Rindge mansion, he regaled her with tales of his days as a pioneer in California in the 1850s. Whether it was the fact that the man had the same eastern habits of her late husband or the realization that the last thing she needed was to give the government another reason to pry open a path across Malibu, May relented. She thanked Colyer for coming, then sent a letter to Decker and his young partner informing them that their guests would be allowed to cross the ranch. Just as Frederick had done in the past, she'd correctly anticipated that giving him just enough to placate his immediate desires would quiet Decker, preventing him from spilling his frustration out in the open.

Yet the meeting with Colyer left May sullen. Since her husband's death, she had found herself ostracized from the world of society teas and formal dinners that his money and prestige had opened up to her. That it was a group in which she'd never truly felt comfortable softened the blow, but only somewhat. With Samuel nearly ready to leave for Harvard and Frederick Jr. and Rhoda both teenagers with lives of their own, she often passed hours in the mansion on Harvard Boulevard alone, pondering how life would be different if Frederick were still there. Her greatest solace was the fortune she controlled, which, no matter how far from her former heights she might fall, still served as a bulwark against any outside designs on her property.

She readied herself for the courtroom fight that Frederick had made every effort to avoid. Malibu had grown to represent not only the husband she had lost less than two years before but the proof that she, too, was capable of bending others to her wishes. With her former life slipping further into the past, her focus turned to defending what she had left.

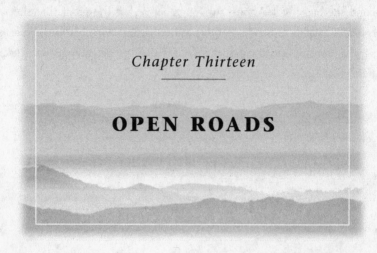

Chapter Thirteen

OPEN ROADS

I N OCTOBER 1888, A THIRTEEN-YEAR-OLD BOY BY THE name of Oscar Lawler picked up from the family onion farm in Marshalltown, Iowa, and set off west, along with his parents and nine siblings, to Los Angeles. Even then, the young man seemed uninterested in the possibilities that could spring from the potent combination of adolescence and independence waiting on the sunbaked streets of his new home. He wore a stern look constantly, as if his face had never realized that it had been granted other options. Strangers often took this as evidence of character, a fact that in time helped him find a job as a bellboy at the California Club, one of the city's oldest social organizations and perhaps its chief den of influence.

His gift for carrying himself with a certain humorlessness was a natural fit for the law, and he thought about little else. During afternoon lulls at the club, Lawler often passed the time reading Sir William Blackstone's *Commentaries on the Laws of England*, a nearly 150-year-old tract that was then among the required study for most first-year law students. Henry O'Melveny, a noted attorney in the city and a club member, noticed Oscar's reading material and, impressed by the young man's focus, soon brought him in as an apprentice. With his new mentor's help, Lawler was admitted to the California bar in 1896, and he centered every minute of his life on the profession that consumed him. He "lived and breathed the law . . . spending little time in conventional family and social activities," his son would later say without rancor, as if describing the color of the sky. Nine years into his career, Lawler received word that President Roosevelt had appointed him to serve as a United States attorney for Southern California. Still in his early thirties, he settled in behind his new desk and started looking for a case that would help make his name.

He eventually found one in the newspaper. Like nearly everyone else who climbed to the higher reaches of Los Angeles social life, Oscar had been familiar with Frederick Rindge during his lifetime, and now, given Secretary Garfield's well-known position that the roads through Malibu should be opened, he closely followed the trespassing case against Seely. For Seely to win, Lawler surmised, he would have to prove that there was some compelling reason why the government should provide a road to unclaimed land, a prospect that seemed altogether unlikely. What would truly seal the case against May Rindge, he reasoned, would be to argue on behalf of the settlers already making their homes there that the paths across her property were in fact public roads that were illegally blocked by her guardsmen and strands of barbed wire. His professional interest piqued, Lawler resolved to further investigate the matter himself.

He set off on horseback along the coast toward Malibu on a cloudy December morning in 1907, flanked by two armed deputies. The trio reached their destination a few hours later. As soon as he saw them coming, a guard by the name of H. J. Marsh scrambled out of a hut by the side of the gate and demanded that the men turn back. Lawler's reply that they were on their way to the government land in the mountains behind the ranch did little to change Marsh's mind. He again denied them access and, for good measure, defied them to break down the gate so that he would have a good reason to shoot them. When told that the men were agents of the government, Marsh answered, "I don't care a damn who you are, you can't pass through this gate." To ensure that his point was clear, he pulled out a pistol and aimed it squarely at Lawler's head.

Thus far in his life, nothing had come between him and what he saw as the proper execution of the law, and Lawler saw no reason why a gun should stop him now. He again told Marsh who he was and, with Marsh's finger still on the trigger, produced an identification card signed by Secretary Garfield. Marsh slowly withdrew his weapon. He notified the men that he was under strict instructions to not allow anyone whose name did not appear on the list approved by Darlington to pass through. Lawler, by now a master at marshaling facts and logic to sway an opinion, soon convinced him otherwise. Lawler continued on toward the mountains in relative peace, though not without struggle. Overmatched by the steep inclines, his horse gave out, forcing him to walk the final seven miles up the mountainside to reach the homesteaders.

Darlington was waiting for Lawler when he came back down, and he apologized extensively for what he called his overzealous guard. It did him little good. The following day, Lawler filed federal charges accusing May Rindge of blocking public roads running both along the coast and through the Malibu ranch, all by way of a system in which guards were instructed to shoot and kill any person who should force his way through the gates. The suit demanded that May immediately tear down all obstructions and allow open travel across her property. Lawler included with his filings his own affidavit that detailed the standoff with Marsh, in which he warned that the clash between the homesteaders and Rindge would soon devolve into a "bloody feud" if the government did not step in to intervene.

The charges were far graver than May had anticipated. The Seely case, which had been her focus, concerned the simple matter of trespassing. Even if the court ruled that she could not prevent anyone from traveling along the coast, she would retain the right to keep people off the ranch itself. That now seemed wholly inconsequential. Lawler's suit asserted not only that there was a public road along the coast but that all nine paths the homesteaders had built across the ranch leading up into the mountains were unrestricted roads as well. The county followed with its own suit the same day, piggybacking on Lawler's contentions and adding criminal nuisance charges against May on top. Within twenty-four hours of the filing, a U.S. circuit court judge granted a temporary injunction that forbade May from blocking any of the allegedly public roads identified by Lawler and threatened her with contempt of court if her guards were found harassing anyone traveling upon the paths in question. A higher judge affirmed the injunction a week later, ordering that the roads remain open until the conclusion of the trial.

With a few words, all of the barriers against the outside world that the Rindges had built crumbled. Suddenly, anyone who wanted to could come into Malibu, and there wasn't anything May could do to stop them. As she watched strangers tramp into the paradise she had long called her own, the injustice of it all gnawed at her. Men and women on horseback, barely able to provide for themselves, were now free to move about on roads on the ranch that she and Frederick had paid for. No doubt they would light fires, or kill her cattle, or destroy what was by no right their own. May had already spent millions building her railroad to nowhere. She steeled herself to continue the fight, undaunted by the list of charges against her. The unsullied span of Malibu was her last connection to her late husband, and she planned to spend whatever it took to preserve the feeling that she was in control of life, not the other way around. Henry O'Melveny, Lawler's onetime mentor, counseled her that the work of gathering evidence and taking depositions from settlers could require months, or even years. With few options left, she hardened herself for what was to come.

A YEAR PASSED without any obvious progress on the case. As the calendar turned to 1909, May had no way of knowing that her life was about to darken yet again. On January 22, Madam Preston, May's first connection to Frederick and the only person she truly trusted in his absence, suffered a fatal heart attack while washing dishes in the mansion overlooking her commune. Her death left her followers adrift, unable to reconcile the fact that someone who they'd believed could see beyond this temporary world and heal any ailment had failed to use those supernatural gifts to prevent her own demise. They "had such faith in her, that nothing could happen to her. I really believe that all those people thought she was immortal," one resident of Cloverdale would later say.

May rode north to Preston, where the funeral service was held in the church constructed by Frederick during his first summer under her care. No preacher spoke at the service, following the Madam's final orders. She was buried in a lavender casket on the commune grounds. In her handwritten will, she left everything to her church, with the stipulation that should any of her heirs claim anything from her property they should be awarded a dollar each. With its leader gone, the commune lost its reason for being. A few families with no other options lingered on, relying on the Russian River for sustenance. Those that could, however, left the remote spot, their belief finally shattered by reality.

For May, it was the final schism from the life she had once known. The person she'd most relied upon after Frederick's death was now gone, leaving only memories behind. Now fully on her own, she steeled herself to fight back against a world that seemed to revel in finding new ways to cause her pain. When she returned with her children to Los Angeles, May bought a .32-caliber Smith & Wesson revolver for Rhoda and extracted a promise from the girl that she would take the weapon, along with a holster and cartridge belt, with her each time she ventured out alone. After Rhoda began spending more time in the company of a friend from school named Jessie, May bought a pistol for her, too. For herself, she hung a revolver prominently on her hip, and in the coming years she rarely went on the Malibu ranch without it, even when in the company of armed guards.

Rather than bow to the pressure closing in on her, May only hardened. A month after Preston's death, she left her children under the care of their tutor, Fred Scotton, and boarded a train alone, headed toward

Boston. Mirroring the numerous cross-country trips Frederick had made during his lifetime, she, too, crossed the continent with business on her mind. Yet where Frederick sought to expand his holdings, May now planned to sell her stake in the many companies and factories he owned in New England, as part of a push to free up cash for her stand in Malibu. "Now that I have this extra burden added to mine already so heavy you and Frederick [Jr.] must help me all you can," she confided to Rhoda one evening. The only question was whether the men she had arranged to meet to broker the sales would be comfortable doing business with a woman. She arrived in Boston and checked into a room at the Hotel Touraine, an eleven-story building made of brick limestone that towered over Boston Common. Samuel, then in his second year at Harvard, met her for dinner, as he would each night he was in town for the remainder of her stay.

She soon grew frustrated by the slow pace of the negotiations. "I have tried my best to get business completed so as to go home . . . but I cannot and if I should try to hurry things I might do a great deal of damage to the business and things are now going along very nicely with some hope of coming to a settlement next Monday but of course it may run along until the last of the week or maybe into next week," she wrote to Rhoda one March evening. "Oh my, oh me! I get tired staying here but there cannot be more than a week of it any way. And then it will be settled forever."

Even on the other side of the country, her thoughts never strayed far from Malibu. "I know you dislike business so I have not written you any but I want to say this much—I heard of the decision in the Malibu case reading it in the Times," she wrote to Rhoda in early March, referring to a judge's order that extended the injunction keeping the ranch roads open. "Not one word from Mr. Scotton. I wonder if you can tell me why he did not telegraph me at the time. Then I telegraphed him for particulars and he waited almost 48 hours before he sent it to me. I cannot understand what is the matter with him."

The inability to sell her property at a price she found acceptable prevented May from returning to Los Angeles in time to greet friends visiting from the East Coast, prompting her to send several long letters to Frederick Jr. and Rhoda filled with specific instructions on how she expected her guests to be treated. She directed them to take her guests on a ride along their private railway on the flatbed railcar, which Frederick Jr. and Rhoda had nicknamed the "go-devil," for the length of the ranch. "Take a nice lunch and take the maid along to make the coffee—take a table cloth and eat out of doors as we always do—have some asparagus made hot and some rolls to make hot and the other things you know about and some candy—they are both fond of it," she dashed off. "Now Rhoda and Frederick do not fail me do just as I have told you won't you—if you do not I will be heartbroken." The next day, she wrote Rhoda again, warning her, "Be careful of snakes on the Laudamus hill and on Pt Dume and everywhere on the ranch as March is the first month they are out." In case her point was not clear, May added, "I worried for fear you would not do as I liked in some way misunderstanding so I sent you a telegram this morning."

Weeks passed without any progress on the sale. For a diversion, one evening she and Samuel went to the Boston Grand Opera, where they sat amid a packed house for a performance of *Thaïs* directed by Oscar Hammerstein, whose grandson of the same name would later become one part of the most famous duo in Broadway history. "I loved it, but Mary Garden's voice was screechy on the very high notes," May would later confide to Rhoda. Even those nights spent with Samuel were not enough to quell her desire to leave the town, where the sight of Frederick's numerous gifts to Cambridge made her acutely aware of her loss. "Well, my dear I am just tired of being in Boston and I want to be at home, but I feel like a dog who is chasing a cat up a tree and my cat is only half up so I must wait until the game is finished," she wrote to Rhoda.

Finally, as the calendar turned to April, she had enough. "I raised ruckus last Saturday and said [they] would either have to buy me out by Monday or I would put the mills in the hands of a new commission house and go home. So Mr. Kelley called today after having a talk with the firm and had a note from Mr. Bremer saying Mr. Street the New York partner would be here in the morning—now we will see if there is enough business in him to put the deal through," May wrote. "I never saw such a lack of business in men who are supposed to do business in my life. Now will see what will be done tomorrow. . . . It does seem a thousand years since I was home and I feel so helpless to push things but I have them going now and <u>maybe</u> something will be accomplished in the morning."

May must have seemed an altogether different creature from any the men negotiating across from her had ever encountered. Assertive and unwavering at a time when few women could be found in boardrooms, May demonstrated the same force of will that had propelled Madam Preston to command a sect of followers. She could not count on the connections Frederick had always seemed to hold in his pockets like cards; nor did she generate the same feelings of goodwill he'd inevitably inspired. Yet she knew what she considered a fair price, and she would not back down until she got it. Fetching a high enough sum would also provide another prize: enough cash to retire the Rindge Company's debts, making her all the more independent. "They told Mr. Kelley and Mr. Clark Saturday that they wanted to buy me out and would get right down to business seeing they had to. Well I may get home some day at this rate—but think how nice it will be if I can bring home enough money to pay that terrible debt that has worried me so long. The big one to the Pacific Mutual." A few days later, she sent a telegram to Rhoda: "Sale closed this afternoon will start home Saturday."

Her adolescent children offered few protests as they saw their mother harden before their eyes, though they struggled to understand. Each had grown up in a world of privilege, accustomed to abundance in all its forms. They glided through social events while May often floundered, displaying a comfort in elite company that she would never acquire. The mind-set that life was an endless battle was as foreign to them as the daily presence of servants and cooks would have been to May when she was their age, toiling through days spent on the Michigan farm. As they edged closer to adulthood, the degree to which the Rindge children identified with the expectations set down by their gilded upbringing only grew, cleaving a rift between them and their mother that stretched a little wider by the day.

Chapter Fourteen

THE DEFINITION OF FREEDOM

WHILE MAY SUFFERED THE DAILY AGONY OF OPEN roads across Malibu, Los Angeles was just beginning to enjoy them. That they existed at all was something of a marvel. At the turn of the century, Americans were widely considered to drive, ride, and gallop along "the worst roads in the civilized world," in the blunt opinion of General Roy Stone, a Civil War veteran whom Congress appointed to investigate the condition of the nation's thoroughfares. In cities especially, horses, wagons, trolley cars, and coughing automobiles shared the same cacophonous space, all of it, more than likely, coated in the most foul-smelling muck imaginable. By some estimates, horses left behind 2.5 million pounds of manure and sixty thousand gallons of urine each and every day in New York City, literally flooding the streets with a stench so awful that it prompted one magazine editor to say that keeping up the roads was "so disastrously expensive that only a very rich country, like the United States, could afford them." Stone advocated that states take out what he called "very long loans" to finance the construction of decent roadways modeled with automobiles in mind.

The proposal attracted little attention until a Vermont physician by the name of Horatio Nelson Jackson set off eastward from San Francisco to win a fifty-dollar bet that he could become the first person to cross the continent behind the wheel of a car, an accomplishment that seemed so far out of the realm of possibility as to be scarcely imaginable. Until then, a trip across the country had been dictated by the timetables of others, whether a railroad or an ocean liner or the leader of a wagon train. Now it was as if the wall penning in American wanderlust had fallen, leaving only an open field in its place. Suddenly roads couldn't be built fast enough, and the more of them the better. California, already a place where moving fast was seen as a sign of strong character, followed Stone's proposal nearly as written. The State Legislature passed a series of highway bond acts to provide funding for the construction of some three thousand miles of roads built strictly for automobile traffic, the first time in its history that cars had merited such special treatment.

Drivers behind the wheel of Packards, Model T's, and other early automobiles who could not wait for the coming highways looked elsewhere for adventure. They soon discovered that the trail along the California coast that Frederick had once built with wagons in mind was a perfect diversion for their belching horseless carriages. Not only that, but its hard-packed dirt surface was in far greater shape than any other comparable route out of Los Angeles, even if the steep drops along its cliffs gave some drivers pause. Jaunts along the bluffs hugging the Malibu shore became one of the favorite pastimes of anyone wealthy or daring enough to take a car for a spin. In 1910, the *Los Angeles Times* was so impressed with a young woman referred to only as Miss Morrow that it wrote up a profile of her under the headline "Fair Autoist Is Courageous." The main point she had in her favor was her ability to brave the steep Malibu roads in her forty-horsepower Inter-State roadster without a man by her side. "Many men who regard themselves as competent enough to tackle practically all the bad roads in the south have discreetly fought shy of the territory," noted the *Times*.

Driving to Malibu became a spectacle in itself, and all of Los Angeles wanted in. The Automobile Club of Southern California, one of the first organizations that lobbied for more and better roads across the nation, chose Malibu as the destination for a car pageant it hoped would entice more men to plunk down the money for an automobile of their own and swell its ranks of dues-paying members. One spring morning in 1910, some three hundred automobiles, along with their owners, overwhelmed the intersection in front of the club's office in Bunker Hill, not far from the Conservative Life Insurance Building. The cars, decorated with flowers, banners, and pennants, set off on a parade toward the Malibu coast.

An hour later, a line of black cars crawled along the water's edge, each one steered by a driver fighting an inner war between concentrating hard enough to keep the car on the road and the temptation to stop and stare at a scene whose beauty was overwhelming. After driving across the Malibu ranch, a crowd of more than a thousand gathered on a spot on the coast and feasted on seven young steers, a meal that afforded several visitors in town from the East Coast their first taste of barbecued meat. The festivities culminated with a series of foot races, peaking with what everyone called without shame the "fastest fat man race." A 250-pound competitor named Tom Carrigan prevailed in the final heat, and afterward he told anyone who would listen that he was running for the honor of the Royal Tourist, the leading model of the Cleveland-based Royal Motor Car Company and the very vehicle he drove himself, and thus had known he could not lose.

The passions cars inspired among Angelenos were not alien to the Rindge family. At just sixteen years old and exhibiting the same iron will as her mother, Rhoda was behind the wheel in some of the first car races held in Los Angeles, piloting a British Sunbeam racer around tight curves at the then death-defying speed of forty miles per hour. When she wasn't driving in races, she was watching them. The Rindge home on Ocean Avenue in Santa Monica stood at the corner of some of the first road races through the city, at a point that drivers called "deadman's curve." One afternoon, Rhoda and her friend Jessie were along the wall when a driver lost control and skidded into a line of haystacks lining the course, barely avoiding the Rindge home itself.

May, too, yearned for the freedom of the automobile. She purchased two of the first six Pierce-Arrows ever shipped to Los Angeles, becoming the first local owner of a model so luxurious that President William Howard Taft would choose a pair to serve as the first official cars of the White House. She added a garage to the side of the Rindge home at Harvard Boulevard, and parked the two glimmering chassis within easy reach.

The rally in Malibu would prove to be more consequential than its jovial atmosphere suggested. Rumbling along the coast in your own car, at your own pace, with a great blue ocean licking the rocks at your side and sunshine warming your skin, was an experience so novel it can hardly be contemplated now. Those few who had done it rarely grew tired of relaying it in exacting detail to friends and relatives unable to make a trip themselves, building a swell of interest that seemed at times ready to boil over. The idea of combining cars and the coast seems intuitive today, but in the first years of the twentieth century it was positively intoxicating. The Auto Club put out a special edition of its magazine, *Touring Topics,* devoted solely to the drive across Malibu. Three years before, car travel had been such a novelty that the organization had taken it upon itself to post directional signs on California's highways. The turnout at the Malibu rally proved that those days were past. "There were fully 1,090 auto enthusiasts at the barbecue, and the way they boosted for the interest of the general public, whether autoist or not, in behalf of good roads, would cause any politician to sit up and take notice of the crystallization of the demand, for proper highways," noted the *Los Angeles Herald.*

Later that same year, a state engineer by the name of Nat Ellery ran for the Republican nomination for governor largely on what was called the "good roads" platform, a turn-of-the-century offshoot of the Progressive movement that considered building more highways and thoroughfares strictly for automobiles as the solution for all sorts of economic and social ills. A man driving in his own car at a speed of his choosing was the very definition of freedom, Ellery argued. The railroads, meanwhile, had controlled their monopoly on travel for so long that they had bred a culture of corruption in the state, which only the automobile could stamp out. "If you were to dump the Southern Pacific into the sea tomorrow the next day you would have a political boss. That is because of the vicious system that has grown up in this country. And we must eliminate that system," Ellery told a crowd of cheering men in Pasadena, who would soon be voting in the last gubernatorial election in California that barred women from participating.

Ellery would go on to lose the race to a man whose fight against the Southern Pacific was more personal. At the time, Hiram Johnson was a district attorney in San Francisco whose father, Grove L. Johnson, was one of the railroad's most important allies during his terms in office in both the State Legislature and as a member of the U.S. House of Representatives. Grove Johnson was an ornery, blunt man who often went directly for the jugular, no matter how small the matter. As a result, his sons hated him. Hiram went into law, searching for genteel ways to humiliate his father, while his brother, Albert, fell deep into the bottle. Grove would often remark that he "had two sons; one, Hiram, full of egotism, and the other, Albert, full of booze." After Albert died of liver failure, in 1907, Hiram set his eye on the governor's mansion, the ultimate comeuppance to his father, whose rise to power had stopped at the legislature. He toured the state in a sputtering open-topped crimson Locomobile, promising at each stop that he would "kick the Southern Pacific out of politics in California." The message worked, and he was soon voted into the governor's mansion in Sacramento. Upon learning that his son had won the election, the first thing Grove did was resign his seat in the legislature, preventing his son from ever directly outranking him. Hiram, for his part, would in one of his first official acts as governor pardon Chris Evans, a man who was routinely described in the press as a "bandit, train robber, and desperado of the most daring type." Evans had spent the last seventeen years in state prison as a consequence of waging a one-man war against the Southern Pacific, routinely holding up trains throughout the Central Valley in retaliation for how the railroad had treated farmers in the area. Johnson now told Evans that he was a free man, just as long as he left California.

Anger at the long-unchallenged reach of the power brokers in the state filtered down through every level of Johnson's administration, fueling what would become known as the golden era of the Progressive movement in California. At the first meeting of the new legislature, the chaplain opened the session by imploring the assorted representatives to "give us a square deal, for Christ's sake." Johnson pushed through such reforms as the introduction of the secret ballot, direct election of U.S. senators, and nonpartisan elections of judges, all in the service of breaking the monopolies that, Progressives argued, robbed the state of its potential and men of their freedom.

In 1911, Johnson directed Ellery, still in the employ of the state, to drive through the Malibu gates to conduct a survey for what legislators in Sacramento had begun calling the Coastline State Highway, an $18 million project that would build a ribbon of concrete along the shoreline from Oregon to San Diego, with outlets to each of the county seats along the way. Ellery motored along twelve miles of the ranch road but pronounced the route unsatisfactory. He returned the next day and began mapping out a plan to blast away rocks along the shoreline to carve a modern two-lane highway. "The road will be finished with a surface as smooth as our best county highways," he told the *Times*, with a note of triumph in his voice.

May, of course, would have none of it. As soon as she heard of Ellery's plans, she began preparing to sue the state should it try to make good on its engineer's boasts. Twenty years before, the mountains had widely been considered a no-man's-land, filled only with the sort of people for whom the prospect of not seeing another person for weeks at a time was a selling point, rather than a concern. Now, thanks to the automobile, the distance between Malibu and Los Angeles had shrunk to the size of a gas pedal. A journey that would have taken a day could now be completed in less than two hours, leaving those who made the drive to Malibu tempted to find a way to settle there. It wasn't only joyriders or homesteaders; even other cities bandied about ideas on how to secure a spot overlooking the sea. One group from Santa Monica, consisting of the mayor, the police chief, the head of the fire department, and the owner of that town's largest newspaper, circulated plans for the city to purchase a 160-acre former homestead high in Las Flores Canyon as a resort where influential men could discuss the affairs of the city in private. As soon as word got out of what they called "the Officials' City," the idea failed before coming to a vote.

More successful were the owners and members of the Crags County Club, a thirteen-hundred-acre mountaintop resort built in 1911 whose centerpiece was a two-story Swiss chalet–style clubhouse. The club limited itself to sixty members, each of whom was required to own an automobile as a prerequisite for admission. "You may tell it from me, there is not a more beautiful site in California for a club, nor in any other state that I've seen," said William M. Garland, the club's president, upon its opening.

No one at the club knew what to make of their closest neighbor, a scraggly-faced hermit by the name of Warren Udell. Fifteen years earlier, Udell and his wife had left Vermont and headed for California, eventually landing on 160 acres of land in the Santa Monica Mountains so remote that no one had ever claimed to be its owner. There, he built a two-room house, constructed a chicken coop, and dug a well, providing a close enough approximation to domestic life that he and his wife soon welcomed a daughter to the mix. Once the girl reached school age, however, Mrs. Udell took her and left to start a new life in Los Angeles, which offered something more than snakes and toil. For company, Warren turned to bees, thousands of them, which kept him stocked with honey and allowed him to earn a little money selling jars of it to his neighbors.

Even in a place that attracted those on the edge of reason, Udell stood out, and he was sent, against his will, to a state mental hospital several times. He always returned to his ranch soon after receiving his discharge papers, where he was known to keep a frighteningly large arsenal of rifles and other firearms. As the Crags Country Club was rising next door, he posted a handwritten sign on the property line that read, "Mt. Moriah. Come no higher. You've no business here." Club members complained to the sheriff about the constant sound of gunfire emanating from Udell's ranch, but none ever dared to wander over and ask him to stop.

EVEN AS EVIDENCE mounted to the contrary, May remained steadfast in her belief that she could keep everything in her life exactly as it had been in the days before Frederick's death. Each sign that she could not stop the march of time hit her as if a betrayal. Though she was slow to recognize it, her sons were no longer boys, but fully grown adults with lives of their own. In 1911, she attended Samuel's wedding and, two months later, Frederick Jr.'s.

The two men seemed to illustrate the twin sides of their late father's personality. And like him, each seemed determined to sprint into the future. Samuel, showing the same business instincts as Frederick Hastings Rindge, soon moved into a home off Wilshire and joined Citizens Trust and Savings Bank as one of its directors. He, too, began forming small companies, hoping to build a fortune of his own. Frederick Jr., meanwhile, chose to go north to the Sacramento delta, where he was more comfortable amid the family's vast agricultural holdings than he was in the hurry of Los Angeles. He expanded his farm until it stretched over twenty-five thousand acres; there, he would soon pioneer new methods of irrigation and tilling that would make his land some of the most productive in the state. His willingness to hire Japanese and Chinese farmworkers would prove an advantage, even as it resulted in his being called before a congressional board during a time of rampant bigotry against Asian immigrants. "Personally, I am a great admirer of the race; they are a people, who I take it, bear the torch," Frederick Jr.

told the hearing. In time, his unconventional methods would help him smash records of productivity per acre, earning him the nickname "the Potato King of the World."

The Harvard Boulevard mansion, once filled with the squeals of her children, echoed only with May's footsteps as she passed quiet hours among its endless rooms. A letter from Rhoda, away at Wellesley, would periodically break the spell of loneliness, yet that, too, would prove to be short-lived. May grew inward, unwilling to maintain focus on anything but the past. "Your pictures are such a comfort to me. They are still eleven strong on top of the bookcase just as you left them," she wrote to Rhoda one rainy evening in January 1911. "When is your Easter vacation? The suit will be postponed through Feb in order to get a new trial, a lot of work must be done. But anyway I am coming to you then and we will have a nice vacation together at Atlantic City." A day without a letter from Rhoda would seem an eternity, a fact that May subtly noted as she ended her letter: "I have not heard from you for over 4 or 5 days, but think it must be due to the snow blockades in the mountains."

Her days bled into one another, with little to distinguish them save the Malibu case. Each morning, a driver chauffeured her to the Rindge Building downtown, where she sat behind a desk in a top-floor office and signed off on every check cut by one of the companies she now headed in Frederick's place. The driver returned every afternoon, ferrying her back to the tony West Adams neighborhood, where she would spend the evenings in solitude, nursing the rancor she felt toward the settlers who had caused her so much trouble. Four years of testimony, and countless dollars in legal fees to O'Melveny's firm, had produced hundreds of depositions which together totaled over three million words, leaving one lucky company with what was called the biggest stenography job in the history of the state.

Finally, in 1913, came a breakthrough. Robert S. Bean, a federal judge from Oregon who had traveled south to act as an impartial arbitrator in the case, announced that the route along the coast was a public highway. Yet because the government had failed to establish that the paths the homesteaders had constructed across the ranch itself had ever been abandoned by the Rindge estate, he ruled that May was free to close them at her whim. She immediately instructed her lawyers to appeal the decision keeping the coastal route open, but jumped at the chance to close the Malibu interior. Her rancor at the settlers for the fire that had destroyed the Rindge home in Malibu had never abated, and she reveled in the opportunity to reclaim her land. She instructed Darlington to gather up every available stick of dynamite and blast away at each of the roads built by homesteaders until they were unrecognizable. When new paths began appearing in their place, she mounted a horse and rode into the hills alongside Darlington. There, she took up a shovel and, next to a team of bodyguards, began filling them in herself.

Each sign that the settlers were unwilling to leave only prompted her to escalate her next response. After learning that homesteaders had begun using a spot in Lechuza Canyon to pass through the Malibu ranch, she ordered her men to build an eight-foot-tall embankment topped by barbed wire. As an added deterrent, she told Darlington to bring in herds of hogs and pen them along the floor of the canyon, effectively creating a noisy obstacle course for anyone who wanted to slip through unseen. Along the coast itself, she abandoned the wagon trail Frederick had once built, which had since become a favorite for Southern California's growing number of drivers. In its place, May ordered Darlington to construct a new private road higher up on the bluff, which she lined with barbed wire and padlocked gates.

Floods destroyed the route along the coast itself the following spring, wiping away the only remaining public route to Los Angeles. After years of open travel, Malibu was suddenly closed, leaving the settlers at the unforgiving mercy of the mountains. Those who'd claimed their land after the federal injunction had opened the coast and the paths across the Malibu ranch were the most vulnerable. Used to relying on the proximity of Santa Monica for supplies, they had never needed to travel through the steep canyons for necessities. As stories reached Los Angeles of settlers unable to put food on their tables, the Venice Chamber of Commerce passed a resolution calling May's actions "contrary to religion, humanity and a sound and just public policy."

Alone in her mansion with the entire city cursing her name, May refused to reopen Malibu to the families who had only caused her sorrow. She sent a statement to the press that read, in part, "except as a scenic trip for automobilists, who can find ample gratification in that line elsewhere, there is not now, and has never been, any public or other necessity for any such road" in Malibu. The partial court victory emboldened May, leading her to believe that with enough money and time, the legal system would right any wrong. She began directing O'Melveny's firm to sue any perceived enemy for any perceived slight. One lawsuit charged Crags Country Club with appropriating water that should have been hers; another threatened the *Los Angeles Examiner*— owned by William Randolph Hearst, who, like Frederick, had once been a member of the A.D. Club while at Harvard—with libel after it ran an article alleging that many homesteaders were on the brink of starvation. "It's no exaggeration that many are in actual want and all due to the fact that we cannot get our produce out to the market and get to our families things that they should have to eat," one homesteader told the paper. When these and other targets of her legal attacks countersued, O'Melveny did whatever he could to slow down the proceedings, in hopes of bleeding more time and money out of the opposition until they gave up in frustration. His firm challenged court filings on the smallest technical details, one time alleging that an entire case should be thrown out because of an inconsequential error on the part of the court's clerical staff.

The law also protected May from herself, no more so than in early 1915, when she charged that city officials had taken bribes in exchange for their votes to expand Broadway between Pico Boulevard and Tenth Street, a project that would encroach on her property in the area. Nine city councilmen, two members of the Board of Public Works, and two other city officials announced that they intended to bring a criminal libel suit against her, seeking more than $1 million in damages. The measure fizzled out a few days later, once a city attorney informed the councilmen that May's charges, while annoying, were not actionable.

Nevertheless, the damage to her reputation was complete. What few connections had remained to Frederick's world of money and power now lay severed, leaving her alone in a city she no longer recognized.

Chapter Fifteen

BETWEEN THE MOUNTAINS AND THE SEA

IN PUBLIC, THE RINDGE CHILDREN, NOW ADULTS with families of their own, were silent as they saw their mother become a pariah. In private, however, they fumed as her barrage of lawsuits eroded the great fortune their father had built. Constructing the railroad to nowhere had already consumed millions. Adding to their worries, the notion that Malibu was not as remote as it had once seemed had recently dawned on the county tax assessors, prompting them to dramatically increase their estimates of the value of the land. The Sixteenth Amendment, ratified in 1913, had introduced a federal personal income tax to the nation, siphoning the once-endless Rindge coffers even more.

The lawsuits threatened to never end. In the spring of 1916, the county board of supervisors decided that if it could not prove that there were already roads through the Malibu ranch, then it would create them by force. The board voted to begin condemnation proceedings, the largest in the county's history, which would allow it to take portions of the ranch through the power of eminent domain. Through her attorney, May remained defiant. "We will not submit to trespass by the county or any of its residents," he warned.

For Samuel, it was the breaking point. He had long stood by as his mother refused to acknowledge that she could not keep Malibu untouched forever. The threat of an eminent domain suit finally spurred him to act: if successful, it would force the Rindges to sell strips of land to the government at a price that it deemed fair, which, Samuel reasoned, would be far below what the family could get from a private bidder should they subdivide the entire ranch by choice. Eminent domain cases were famously easy for the government to win, especially when something with an obvious public benefit, such as a road, was at hand, making May's stand seem all the more foolhardy. With the First World War raging in Europe, the War Department, meanwhile, was searching Southern California for a large unblemished tract to be used as a training ground where the military could conduct large-scale war games, and Malibu was widely thought to be its favored location.

In August 1916, Samuel filed a lawsuit demanding that his father's remaining stocks and property be liquidated and the proceeds disbursed between him, his siblings, and his mother. With Frank P. Flint, the former senator and a pallbearer at his father's funeral, serving as his attorney, Samuel alleged that the years of litigation went against his father's wishes and that, should Frederick have survived, he would have sold or developed the ranch by now. He named his mother as the defendant.

May had grown accustomed to disappointment in the years since Frederick's death, but nothing compared with this. The calluses built up from defending herself against an uncaring world vanished, letting the pain soak the raw skin underneath. In the moment, it was impossible to pinpoint which was the greater betrayal: that her firstborn son had turned against her or that he was now demanding that Malibu be taken away as well. She had long lived as if time had stopped on the day before Frederick's death, but never before had she been forced to explicitly choose between giving up the clutch she held on the past or letting go to take part in her family's future. She knew that opening Malibu to development would mend her ties with not only Samuel but with

Frederick Jr. and Rhoda as well. Yet she could not bring herself to do it. She had devoted her life to proving to the world that she could not be trampled on, never expecting that she would have to fight against her eldest son. In the end, not even he could sway her.

In the following weeks, she offered Samuel sole ownership of several hundred acres the family owned along Wilshire Boulevard between Fairfax and Highland in exchange for dropping the lawsuit and rescinding any further claims he had on the Malibu ranch. The land she presented was then nothing more than dairy farms and open fields, but Samuel accepted all the same. Once the deal was finalized, May broke off all contact with him, refusing to either see him or voice his name.

Samuel would go on to sell most of the land he received to a real estate developer named A. W. Ross, who saw in its barren fields the potential for a car-centered shopping district that would rival the city's downtown. As a catalyst, Ross placed parking lots behind his buildings, upending the notion that foot traffic was the key to bringing shoppers in. All over the city, other concessions to cars were in the making and offered hints of what Los Angeles would soon become. In 1924, the city's first automated traffic lights went up on a stone pedestal less than two miles from the Rindge mansion. Nearly seventy thousand cars passed through the intersection of Adams and Figueroa each day, making it the busiest junction in the United States. Drivers took a while to get used to following the mechanical rhythm of signs, rather than the officers who stood on soapboxes in the middle of intersections, a whistle in their mouths and white gloves on their hands. Yet the car had already diminished the human scale of the city. Over the next few years, the city's best department stores, including Desmond's and the May Company, opened multilevel bazaars along the land Ross purchased from Samuel, effectively pulling affluent shoppers away from its tight-packed downtown and toward its sprawling suburbs. The transformation from farms into a glittering district of upscale shops, Art Deco towers, and museums would give the strip the nickname the Miracle Mile.

May already felt as if she had lost her eldest son; that same spring, she would feel as if she lost her only daughter as well. Rhoda announced her plans to marry Merritt Adamson, a Los Angeles native who'd worked as superintendent of the Malibu ranch after his graduation from the University of Southern California's law school. May refused to speak to either of them, grumbling that Adamson was beneath Rhoda's station in life and the grand plans May held for her. The pair wed quietly in a small ceremony at the chapel of the Mission Inn in Riverside, east of Los Angeles, accompanied by Rhoda's two brothers. Frederick Jr. gave the bride away in his late father's place. May did not attend, choosing instead to remain in her nearly empty home with only servants for company. Frederick's maxims and mottos sat painted on the walls, surrounding her with his presence as she felt ever more alone.

AT THE RINDGE MANSION, months bled into one another in a monotony of sunny days, with only an occasional raindrop to suggest a change in the seasons. Finally, on April 9, 1917, came the news May had been waiting for. In a tersely worded decision, the state supreme court declared that all roads in question in Malibu, both along the coast and through its interior, were the private property of the Rindge family, who were free to regulate traffic however they saw fit. The judges ruled that there was no evidence that the roads had been constructed with public funds or built along established thoroughfares; nor were there any compelling reasons to build anything resembling them in an area locked between the mountains and the sea. "It is evident that if a public highway exists at all, it exists by prescriptive use and not by official acceptance of an offer of dedication, or by any official recognition of the existence of a highway," the decision read. "Indeed, it is quite plain that any county would be extremely slow to take into its charge and burden itself with the care of such a strip of ocean beach which, from the very nature of the country, would have slight use and less value."

After so many years of losing, May greeted vindication with impatience. The great gamble of her life had finally paid off, and she raced to make up for passed time. She ordered her men to build fifty miles of fences around the ranch's borders, the closest she could come to her dream of permanently cleaving it away from Los Angeles. In the kingdom itself, she made plans to rebuild, and in some cases enlarge, her memories. At the same spot where the 1903 fire had destroyed the family mansion, she told her architect to draw up plans for a home on the crest of Laudamus Hill, nearly double the size of its predecessor.

First, though, came the matter of gloating. All the years of silence had fostered a deep well of anger, which she gleefully spilled in public forums. "Your article in this morning's *Times* is a rank injustice to me, and for ten long years I have submitted to such tales as this being printed in your paper, for such has been the advice of my attorneys," May wrote in a long letter to the *Los Angeles Times* published two weeks after the court ruling. "Now, since Judge Bean and Judge Henshaw have decided that there is no road on the Malibu Rancho, and their integrity and ability cannot be questioned by any man, why should I be longer persecuted by the petty politicians of Los Angeles County?"

She then proceeded to unburden herself of the rage that had fermented for years. For the settlers who claimed to be on the edge of starvation, "They can get their supplies the way they came in," she offered, her tone dripping with sarcasm. "They gather our corn, dig our potatoes, steal our sheep and cattle, carry off our hay and grain by the wagons-full. Is it any wonder we object to these people going through our rancho? Would you stand for that, in order that a few politicians could be benefitted from a rise in the price of their lands? A two-week-old calf was found with its tail cut off close to its body, its ears cut off close to its head, and its eyes gouged out so it could not see. Of course, the Rindges love to have such people as these prowling over their rancho. Of course, the settlers can easily enough find where the does fall. I have been told that the only way to keep does from being shot is to keep a game warden in some of the settlers' back yards.

"My life has been threatened so often by them—one man going so far as to say he would beat me to death if he ever caught me alone; but I think the time has come to let the public know the kind of people they are sympathizing with," she continued. "Why are the papers so willing to continue to print articles reflecting on the owners of the Malibu Rancho and referring to the much-abused and so-called starving settlers, when in reality there are no such people in the mountains? It is a well known fact that several of the supposed settlers operate resorts in the mountains. Many of the employees of the Malibu Rancho have been dismissed when it has been learned that they have been frequenting these places." She ended with a flourish, signing "Very truly yours, May K. Rindge."

A few weeks later, a reporter from the *Times* paced up the imposing steps of the Rindge mansion in West Adams. He was there to interview the woman all of Southern California had grown to hate, and he wasn't sure what to expect. A door swung open, revealing May Rindge standing in a puddle of sunlight. She welcomed him into the home without hesitation, as if the last decade she had spent broiling over the newspaper's coverage was as temporary as a cloud in the Los Angeles sky. For a woman who had lost the favor of nearly everyone she had once called a friend and whose firstborn son would no longer speak with her, she seemed oddly buoyant. Her eyes twinkled at every joke, and she was quick to interject to keep the conversation flowing, skills that went beyond her nature but had been honed by the countless parties she had attended with Frederick.

Yet there was no mistaking that this was the same May Rindge who had endured twelve years of threats and abandonment and still refused to cave. Her eyes flashed when she spoke of the lawsuits or of Malibu, as if the single-minded devotion that burned within her was hot enough to sending embers flying. Now, with victory finally in her hand, she couldn't resist the temptation to savor it. "Most widows lose all their property before their children are old enough to know the value of what they have, and although litigation hovered around me like flies around a choice bit, I have endured and still retain our property, but am minus the cost of the suits," she said. "I still have a water-steal suit and a land-steal suit and a money-steal suit on my hands, which I hope before another year passes over my head will end as happily as those of the Malibu."

IN THE MALIBU HILLS, the court decision narrowed the lives of settlers to the question of survival. For nearly ten years, the government injunction had allowed them to cross the Malibu ranch at will, fostering a dependence on the city with which families had grown comfortable. With that ripped away, desperation sank in, leaving men to act on their craziest ideas.

Nearly all of them involved killing May. Every man, woman, and child living in the mountains knew what she looked like and had committed her habits to memory in order to sneak across the ranch when she was unlikely to be there. As the sun fell each Sunday evening, she left Malibu to head back to the West Adams mansion, a schedule as reliable as the ocean tides. That knowledge would soon be put to more sinister means. One afternoon two weeks after the interview with May ran in the *Los Angeles Times*, a settler by the name of Jack Henry, alongside two other men, eased three cars into a line along the Malibu shore, blocking the hard-packed dirt road, which, until recently, they had been free to use at will. As the waves boomed onto the coastline, they quickly drew out chains and tied their bumpers together into a makeshift barricade. Each man kept his gun at bay and waited.

A pair of headlights soon came into view. As the car carrying May raced down the coast, the late-afternoon sun flickered off the chrome lining its hood. As Henry and the men with him moved into position, the car, still far out of range, slowed and then stopped. The black limousine stood motionless for a few seconds, dust and dirt pluming around it. With a sudden jerk, the car hurried through a three-point turn before speeding back along its tracks. Once among the safety of her ranch hands, May ordered the men to send for help in Santa Monica. The foreman mounted a horse and raced down the ranch, outflanking the barricade and reaching the city late in the evening. More than a dozen deputies from the sheriff's office and the Santa Monica police force assembled and took off north, where they arrested the three men, still at their posts, without a struggle. Policemen drove on to the ranch house, where they found May, not the least bit shaken by the ordeal. They escorted her past the Malibu gates and on to her home in West Adams under armed guard, and kept a cruiser out front for a few days for good measure, as if the visible presence of the police would dispel all hard feelings.

It did little good. All of Los Angeles wanted the roads reopened in Malibu, and its people proved willing to try every method that presented itself. More than a dozen petitions circulated through town calling for the state to force a road through the Malibu ranch, the most popular of which garnered more than six thousand signatures. The mayor of Santa Monica came out in its support, as well as Abbot Kinney himself, the tobacco baron who had founded the neighboring city of Venice as a sunny haven for art and culture.

Settlers, however, turned to more violent means. One Sunday morning in September, on the eve of the annual shearing, workers on the Malibu ranch woke to the sight of more than two hundred dead and dying sheep. Among the bloated bodies were nearly all of the ranch's ewes, each less than a month away from bearing lambs. "We believe this wholesale attempt at poison," the Malibu foreman told the press, "is another of the many depredations the owners of the Malibu ranch have had to bear from some of the people living back in the Santa Monica mountains, who have been clamoring to use the private property of Mrs. Rindge."

May responded with a fury that unnerved even those who thought they had seen the depths of her rage. The next morning, explosions rocketed through the canyons of Malibu. A settler by the name of Hippolito Blendo, riding on horseback, discovered a deep hole at Las

Flores Canyon where the path had once been. A wall of rubble prevented him from crossing any farther. A similar obstruction was found in Carbon Canyon, a route that had long been the favorite of settlers coming down from the mountains to the coast. May, in her determination to prevent the settlers from doing any more damage to her or her property, elected to finally destroy the mountain passes that allowed them access. Settlers blocked by the debris soon erected a sign at Carbon Canyon that read, "Remember the Lusitania!," invoking the World War I cry for retribution spurred by the death of the 128 Americans who went down on the Cunard liner when it was hit by German torpedoes.

The bloody feud that Lawler had once warned would be the consequence of keeping the roads closed was now at hand. In February 1918, a doctor from Santa Monica responded to what he was only told was an emergency at the Malibu ranch. Once there, he discovered two men— May's personal chauffeur and one of the ranch hands—bleeding from gunshot wounds. The men refused to elaborate on the details, though the doctor soon pieced together a rough sketch of what had happened. Armed settlers, he learned, had gathered near the rubble in Carbon Canyon and spent the afternoon drinking moonshine, nursing their wrath toward Rindge. Talk soon gave way to action, and a loose-knit gang stormed onto the ranch, seeking revenge. Rindge's men shouted at the settlers to turn back, but they paid the workers no heed. Shots rattled across the canyons, coming in such bursts that it seemed as if the men were sending a message in Morse code. Rindge's men successfully turned the settlers back, but not before the two men now lying bleeding were hit.

Their wounds would ultimately prove to be minor, though that was of little consequence. Ranch hands turned to frontier justice to settle the score. In the following months, William D. Newell, one of the earliest homesteaders in Malibu and one of the most vocal about using any means necessary to fix the Rindge problem, went missing. At the request of G. L. Junge, a Venice grocer who counted Newell as one of his best customers, sheriff's deputies rode on horseback through the mountains, making inquiries into Newell's whereabouts at each homestead. The lawmen returned empty-handed. Whatever happened to Newell was a mystery locked in the hills, and no one was talking.

Chapter Sixteen

THE
PUBLIC GOOD

TRY AS SHE MIGHT, MAY COULD NEVER FULLY SHAKE Malibu free of other men's intentions. In the spring of 1918, the county of Los Angeles announced that it sought to use the power of eminent domain to build three roads across the Malibu ranch. Once so secure in her triumph, May braced for another court fight.

From the start it was clear that this would not be a rehash of the plodding case that had taken years to work its way to the courtroom. A state judge took up the case immediately, and the trial began days later. The issue at hand was no longer whether the roads already crossing the Malibu were public; instead, the county sought the power to build its own. It was the only option the government had left to open the great rancho to the metropolis flourishing just across the bay. Should the court rule against it, the board of supervisors knew that it could do nothing but wait for May's death and hope that her heirs would be more amenable. Given the hot impatience of the settlers, that day often seemed close at hand.

The board didn't have to wait long. On January 11, 1919, a state judge ordered the county to pay the Rindge estate $41,000—a figure that would now be worth more than $1 million—for land on which it could build a highway. At the same time, the court refused to issue an injunction that would prevent any work on the road's construction while May's attorneys appealed the decision. Teams of engineers soon spread out across the Malibu coast, surveying a route that was widely expected to become the most beautiful stretch of road in the country. "The opening of this route is but another link in our highway system, but its location is through a country of romance the equal of which is only approached by Helen Hunt Jackson's famous novel *Ramona*," noted the *Times* as the road plans took shape.

Desperate and with her options dwindling, May turned to the public she had so long scorned. She took out a full-page advertisement in the *Los Angeles Times* that, in two-inch-high block letters, railed against "THE AMAZING INJUSTICE WHICH COUNTY SUPERVISORS NOW THREATEN AGAINST THE PEOPLE OF THE COUNTY AND AGAINST THE RINDGE COMPANY"; several long paragraphs outlining her cause followed. "Never was there an act more unjust, indifferent to local consequences or disregardful of business prudence, than the avowed intentions of the Los Angeles County Supervisors to build a certain highway into Malibu Ranch," she wrote. The county's proposed road would likely cost more than half a million dollars of the taxpayers' money, she noted, while ignoring the less expensive option of going north along the other side of the mountains. "Should not our public officials in these road matters not only seriously consider but actually build their roads with a view to the greatest good to the greatest number—the greatest benefit to the taxpayers of the county and of the state whose servants they are?" she asked.

The advertisement belied how far she had fallen behind the times. In one of the first paragraphs, she wrote, "The County Highway as surveyed and contemplated utterly disregards the owner's interests as regards ocean frontage, and also ruthlessly cuts through and destroys the value of much of the arable lands." No one who looked at Malibu considered its possibilites as a farm, as Frederick had when he'd purchased it, twenty-seven years earlier. The allure was the promise of driving along its coast and marinating on its beaches, and there was little May could to do to make these any less appealing.

The state supreme court denied her appeal a year later, smothering May's hopes that she could eradicate the government's men from her land before they made any permanent marks. Where there had been engineers, the county now sent in full construction crews. None were happier to take part than Charles Decker, one of Marion's nephews, who'd grown up in the family clan in the mountains and made it a point to raise hell wherever and whenever he could. He took great joy in planting sticks of dynamite in the boulders along the coast that had long been the bane of his family and stood with a smile stretched across his face as he blasted each one into a confetti of stone. He was not the only one whose personal history ran parallel to the road. In a cruel twist, N. D. Darlington, May's onetime railroad engineer, returned to the ranch, this time as the head of the California Highway Commission, and went to work removing the last remnants of the railways he had once designed.

The first few miles of the county road up the coast opened in 1922 and set off a mania for every inch of beachfront property along the five-mile stretch between Santa Monica and the border of the Malibu ranch. "If it weren't for the motor car and the paved highway, that colony would not be there," said one Mrs. R. H. McDermoth, the head of a real estate firm in Los Angeles who helped sell the lots. Families trucked in their own lumber and constructed shacks on the sand, figuring that having anything standing was enough to lay claim. One man, realizing a little late that he had staked a lot on the beach too close to the water, put his house up on stilts that he drove into the low-tide line.

The road to Malibu was soon seen as one of the best diversions in a city that was beginning to be known for them. "The real and only genuine, honest-to-God last stand of the West is just an easy Sunday automobile ride from Los Angeles," the *Times* crowed. Strict adherence to facts didn't seem to matter; Malibu was sold as everything from an ancient Indian burial ground to an untapped goldfield, and the public loved every minute of it. Families jumped into their cars, hungry to see for themselves the place that the papers called more wild than any Hollywood party.

May could do nothing but post guards along the road and hope that their shotguns would be enough to scare any sightseers from trespassing onto the ranch itself. Tourists proved but one of her problems. In October 1919, the Prohibition movement, which Frederick had once nursed in Los Angeles, succeeded on a grand level, and the country officially turned dry. Americans didn't suddenly give up their thirst, however. The hidden coves of Malibu, so close to Los Angeles and a half day's voyage from Mexico, were too convenient for rumrunners to pass by. Bright moonlit nights were punctuated by shoot-outs between smugglers and ranch hands on the beaches. Finally bootleggers with a head on their shoulders realized that a few bottles of whiskey could buy silence, and the landings continued in relative peace.

After nearly two decades, May's stand to keep Malibu apart from the rest of Southern California seemed over. Then, in late 1922, her fortunes changed yet again. The United States Supreme Court announced that it would take up her case, finally settling the issue of whether taking portions of the Malibu ranch for construction of a public highway was legal. The battle for paradise headed three thousand miles to the east, where nine justices would determine the fate of an untouched link to the past.

ARGUMENTS BEGAN in April 1923 under a half dome in the north wing of the Capitol Building, which had been the home of the Supreme Court since 1860. (The court would not get its own space until 1935, when its current building opened across the street.) Each lawyer's voice echoed in the two-story amphitheater, trimmed in crimson and gold. High above them the last portrait George Washington sat for during his lifetime hung along the eastern wall.

In their allotted time before the court, May's attorneys ignored the question that underpins nearly all eminent domain cases: whether the road would be a public good. Instead, they attacked the idea that it was needed. A Dutch philosopher named Hugo Grotius—whose stature among his peers was heightened by the fact that he both escaped from prison and survived a shipwreck in his lifetime—introduced the concept of eminent domain in 1625 by arguing that "extreme necessity" was the only condition in which the state can seize private property for public purpose. That idea readily transferred over to the fledging American colonies, where as early as 1700 a law in Pennsylvania required that "no such road shall be carried through any man's improved lands, but where there is a necessity for the same." The proposed highway in Malibu, which crossed a rural ranch surrounded by fewer than twenty homesteaders, could hardly be called essential for public travel, May's attorneys argued. Nor would it offer any advantage to the military, which could easily pass over the ranch's private roads in the event of an emergency. Of course, "genuine" highways were a public necessity, May's attorneys offered. But "these particular roads," which would cost millions of dollars and benefit only a handful of settlers, were merely "shams under the name of public improvements."

Paul Vallée then rose to speak. In time, Vallée would go on to become the president of the State Bar of California, a judge, and a trusted confidant of California governor Earl Warren's before Warren became one of the most influential chief justices ever to serve on the Supreme Court. At that moment, however, Vallée was a relatively young and inexperienced attorney, speaking before the Supreme Court for the first time in his life. If he was nervous, he didn't show it. He acknowledged that the path along the sparsely populated coast served little practical purpose. Instead, he asserted that its true benefit was securing the public's access to beauty.

It was an argument that had never before been attempted in front of the Supreme Court. Fifteen years after the introduction of the Model T had turned the nation on to the automobile, Vallée was now insisting that roads could not only supply drivers with a means to get where they needed to go but could provide an experience so important as to outweigh the objections of a private landowner. Roads weren't just necessary conduits through space, he argued; they were a path toward human improvement. The idea was rooted in the City Beautiful movement, a turn-of-the-century groundswell that held that exposure to grandeur, whether natural or man-made, couldn't help but inspire moral and civic virtue and cleanse the nation's growing cities of the stink of poverty and crime. Until then, reformers inspired by the notion had mostly followed the model set by the 1893 Chicago World's Fair, in which Daniel Burnham and Frederick Law Olmsted, the chief designer of Central Park, built a dream city of classical buildings, free of any evidence of social ills, that became known as the White City. The success of the fair, which attracted over 27 million visitors, led to beautification efforts from Philadelphia to San Francisco and culminated in what became known as the McMillian Plan, which, beginning in 1902, remade the National Mall as the core of a new monument district within the nation's capital and sparked the construction of the Lincoln Monument along a riverbank that the Army Corps of Engineers had recently filled in with dredged dirt to prevent flooding.

Vallée aimed to convince the court that the beautification movement should not be limited to the nation's cities, but should be acted upon wherever possible. Automobiles provided the perfect method for bringing natural wonder within the reach of those who most needed it. Stephen T. Mather, the first head of the National Parks Service, was one of the first to see the possibility of the automobile in extending the ideals of the City Beautiful movement to the countryside. Just as classical architecture could inspire in its viewers a desire to heed their better nature, he held, so could coming into contact with a sweeping vista or standing in the shadow of a great mountain. Responding to complaints about litter left by tourists driving into previously pristine natural parks, Mather summarized his philosophy neatly: "We can pick up the cans; it's a cheap way to make better citizens."

The court asked few questions of Vallée, and adjourned that after-noon. It announced its decision six weeks later. On June 11, 1923, Justice Edward Terry Sanford, a Harvard Law graduate who had been confirmed to serve on the court just four months earlier, delivered the opinion. "A taking of property for a highway is a taking for public use which has been universally recognized from time immemorial," he began. He described all the reasons why, even if the road across Malibu did not connect with any other roads at the present time, it could still be considered public, before reaching the crux of the ruling. "These roads, especially the main road, through its connection with the public road coming along the shore from Santa Monica, will afford a highway for persons desiring to travel along the shore to the county line, with a view of the ocean on the one side and of the mountain range on the other, constituting, as stated by the trial judge, a scenic highway of great beauty. Public uses are not limited, in the modern view, to matters of mere business necessity and ordinary convenience, but may extend to matters of public health, recreation, and enjoyment," he read.

As he continued, it seemed as if Vallée had written the decision himself. Citing the decision in *Shoemaker v. United States*, an 1893 case that held that the government had the right to seize land in order to build a public park, Sanford announced that forcing a road through Malibu was also permissible because it would add to collective enjoy-ment. "A road need not be for a purpose of business to create a pub-lic exigency; air, exercise, and recreation are important to the general health and welfare; pleasure travel may be accommodated as well as business travel, and highways may be condemned to places of pleasing natural scenery. . . . In these days of general public travel in motor cars for health and recreation, such a highway as this, extending for more than twenty miles along the shores of the Pacific at the base of a range of mountains, must be regarded as a public use," Sanford concluded.

It was the first time a modern highway laden with cars zooming along at fantastic speeds received the same treatment as an untouched forest or seashore. The ruling soon fueled what was up to then one of the largest road-building programs ever launched. Within five years, there were over a thousand miles of roads under construction through the National Park System, all in order to make room for cars in the nation's most beautiful places. When planning the network of roads through Montana's Glacier National Park, for instance, a supervisor by the name of S. F. Ralston argued, "The roads to be built in the national parks should differ from the ordinary road, in that their purpose is to better display the natural scenic beauty of our national playgrounds and thereby encourage our own people to visit these spots of scenic interest and save to our country the wealth now annually contributed to Europe through the medium of the American tourist." The head of Yellowstone's road system noted that long, weaving roads should be more highly praised, even if they gobbled up more previously unsullied land, writing, "Diversion from a straight path to points of interest, regardless of expense, is important and necessary when designing [a road's] layout." Thanks to the court's decision, building roads had become synonymous with building happiness.

MAY HAD NO OPTIONS LEFT. She had held off the modern world for nearly eighteen years and had pursued her case as far as it could go. In a dark irony, the beauty of Malibu that had so captivated Frederick and inspired May to do everything to preserve it became, in the end, the reason why it was taken from her grasp.

Her defeat seemed to mark a turning point in California. With the last of the untouched Spanish land grants now open to outside travel, Southern California severed one of the final links to its frontier past. A generation earlier, it had been a place so empty that a man could stand on a hill and own every bit of land stretching to the horizon; now the state—and, in particular, Los Angeles—was attracting more people each year than it knew what to do with. "Although Mrs. May Rindge was an obstacle in the path of a much needed public improvement, her determination, her courage, and her tenacity in holding out for the rights of her property cannot help but command the admiration of every red blooded Californian," noted the *Times*, in a tribute to its vanquished foe.

A new war between California's past and its future, this time over water, was brewing. Ten years earlier, chief engineer William Mulholland had presided over the opening of the Los Angeles Aqueduct, promising that the water flowing down from the remote Owens Valley would meet the city's needs for the next hundred years. More than forty thousand people gathered on a San Fernando Valley hillside to watch as he waved an American flag, the signal to unleash the first torrent of water. "There it is!" he shouted in his Irish brogue. "Take it!" In Owens Valley, however, the destruction was just beginning. Its main lake and more than fifty miles of river were dry by the time Rindge lost her case, confirming the fears of the local farmers, whose protests had long been ignored. The following year, a group of Owens Valley farmers dynamited a section of the aqueduct, slowing the flow of water out of the parched land. Mulholland refused to bend, only saying that he "half-regretted the demise of so many of the valley's orchard trees, because now there were no longer enough trees to hang all the troublemakers who live there."

In perhaps the cruelest turn, when May now gazed down at Los Angeles from her West Adams mansion, she could no longer see Frederick's fingerprints. The frontier city he'd so loved had become the metropolis he'd always envisioned, and it had left his memory behind. Two years earlier, President Warren G. Harding had signed the Federal Highway Act of 1921, the first time Congress had set aside money for a national system of roadways. "We live in a motor age," Harding proclaimed in a speech to the nation. "The motor car reflects our standard of living and gauges the speed of our present-day life." In Los Angeles, horses were already a sight rarely seen on roadways. The city's fire department had closed its last stable in July 1921, giving those that remained of its once 163-strong herd a retirement in Griffith Park.

Three decades after the railroads brought upper-class families from the East Coast to settle amid the sun-filled valleys, the automobile age crafted new millionaires out of men like Earle C. Anthony, a one-time mechanic who opened the city's first Packard dealership, its first full-service gas station, and mounted the country's first neon sign. He soon began beaming the city's first 50,000-watt station from an antenna on his roof. He mostly filled the time advertising his automobiles, all the while repeating his personal motto: "Don't waste time dreaming about it! If it's worth thinking about, do it! If not, forget it!"

All of Los Angeles seemed to be living by the same instinct. The city itself seemed to be blessed, bathed in sunlight and opportunity. With Europe in ruins after the war and New York preoccupied with the collapse of the German economy, Los Angeles set about building structures as grand as its ambitions. In 1923, a mammoth stadium known as the Coliseum opened in Exposition Park, built as a memorial to veterans of the Great War. President Harding's sudden death of an apparent heart attack while lying in a bed at San Francisco's Palace Hotel in August of the same year did little to slow the city's momentum. Its economy continued to expand, and the Coliseum soon staged its first football game, in which the University of Southern California Trojans defeated Pomona College by a score of 23 to 7. In the Hollywood hills, architects crafted plans to build a shell over a modest wooden stage and amphitheater, the early beginnings of the Hollywood Bowl. A few miles away, workers painted forty-five-foot-high block letters a blinding white and anchored them to telephone poles set high above a new real estate development called Hollywoodland. At night, four thousand light bulbs flashed the name from the mountainside and across the wide city below, providing a beacon for dreamers.

Among them was a twenty-one-year-old animator from Missouri who had recently arrived in the city with just forty dollars in his pocket, all he could salvage after his first company, Laugh-O-Gram films, had gone bankrupt. Four months after the Supreme Court opened up Malibu for good, Walt Disney signed a contract with Margaret J. Winkler, a former secretary to one of the Warner brothers who had risen to the top of the nascent cartoon industry. She hired the young man to produce a series of comedies featuring a girl named Alice and an animated cat named Julius, and with it, the Disney Brothers Company was born.

As the city rushed to the future, the battle over Malibu quickly faded from memory. Two years after the Supreme Court decision, the county of Los Angeles issued May a check for $98,623—slightly more than $1.3 million today—for the land it had claimed through eminent domain. She refused to cash it, unwilling to acknowledge the validity of the state's claims to the end. Unknown to anyone outside the family, she desperately needed the money. The years of court costs had finally caught up to her, straining what was left of the fortune Frederick had built. Instead, she sought out a way to survive on her own terms. She soon came upon a plan that would transform Malibu into a modern paradise.

Chapter Seventeen

THE MANSION ON THE HILL

AFTER NEARLY TEN YEARS OF CONSTRUCTION CREWS blasting, scraping, and grinding away at rocks whose obstinacy at times seemed willful, the road along the Malibu coast finally opened on June 29, 1929. A caravan of fifteen hundred cars paraded in, packed together like a line of ants, along the bend of the ocean. In Sycamore Canyon, Governor C. C. Young, a Berkeley lawyer who would go on to become best known for his role in forging the Bay Bridge linking Oakland with San Francisco, spoke before a crowd gathered in front of a wooden stage draped with a giant American flag. After winding up a short speech praising the workers whose muscle had finally tamed the coastline, he gave a signal to two young women standing at opposite sides of the road; one wore a sash that read "Miss Mexico," the other "Miss Canada." As a brass band played, each lit one end of the banner stretched across the highway, and when it fell, Young declared the coastal route between America's northern and southern neighbors officially opened. Drivers attacked the road with something close to mania. By noon, dozens of black automobiles, their engines exhausted from running circuits up and down the coast, overflowed onto the rocks lining the highway's path.

As the public savored its freedom to move along the Malibu coast, May Rindge was nowhere to be seen. If she had received an invitation to the celebration of her defeat, she'd ignored it. Since the Supreme Court decision, which took away her hopes of keeping Malibu as she remembered it, she had refocused her life on repaying the costs of her long and unsuccessful legal fight. The process of ushering the Malibu ranch out of its long stillness had begun three years earlier, with the construction of a one-hundred-foot-tall dam in Malibu Creek that tamed its seasonal floods and created a nearly six-hundred-acre reservoir. Months later, she invited some of the finest architects and builders in Los Angeles to a long, slender factory that she built just yards from the waves. On display were tiles, hundreds of them, shimmering in the most brilliant assortment of reds, blues, and yellows found outside of the Middle East. The lot had been forged in one of the building's three kilns out of the clay found underfoot on the Malibu ranch. "It has always been my desire to utilize the natural nonmetallic minerals that occur in such large deposits on the property, before it would be opened for subdivision," May told the assorted crowd in a brief statement before slipping away from public view once more.

To head up the Malibu Potteries, as the tile factory would come to be known, May hired Rufus B. Keeler, a man widely considered a genius of no equal when it came to ceramics. He developed secret formulas that left each hand-painted tile glimmering with a shine that competitors would never manage to replicate. Keeler guarded his work with an all-consuming passion, vowing not only to fire any of his hundred-plus employees should they wander into the glaze room, even by mistake, but to blacklist them from ever getting a job in any other profession for the rest of their lives. As a final precaution, he slept each night in an army tent on the beach beside the factory, his mind fixed on preventing anyone from disturbing his work in progress.

For his staff, Keeler scoured California for the finest Italian artisans he could find. He allowed one break, at noon, which his employees often spent swimming in the ocean. Among them was a young immigrant from southern Italy by the name of Simon Rodia, who could often be seen leaving each evening with fragments of broken tile jutting out of his pockets. Rodia spent the rest of his lifetime transforming those shards into an otherworldly complex of sculptures on a small triangular plot of land in Watts. He called his project Nuestro Pueblo; today it is better known as the Watts Towers. Rodia died before his work was named a national historic landmark, and never realized the extent to which his artwork would be hailed as the mark of a genius. After his death, the Beatles included a photo of Rodia on the cover of *Sgt. Pepper's Lonely Hearts Club Band*, right next to Bob Dylan.

It wasn't long before Malibu tile became synonymous with luxury. The factory was soon churning out more than thirty thousand square feet of tile a month, shipping heavy crates to mansions springing up in Beverly Hills and beyond. William Wrigley, the Chicago chewing gum magnate, became so inspired by Keeler's work that he outfitted the grand casino he was then constructing on nearby Santa Catalina Island in the same style; the building, when completed, would include the first theater in the nation designed specifically for the novelty of movies with sound. In downtown Los Angeles, workers placed Malibu tile throughout the triumphant new city hall rising on Spring Street, a twenty-seven-story tower that sliced into the sky just three blocks from where Frederick Rindge had opened his first building forty years before.

MAY DIDN'T HAVE TO rely on tile alone to rebuild her wealth. She soon found herself immensely popular in a place perfectly unsuited for a woman who had little natural ability to charm: Hollywood. She had known the city when it was just orchards, and she'd thought more of it then. In 1887, the year May and Frederick first arrived in Los Angeles, a pair of midwesterners by the name of Harvey and Daeida Wilcox could often be found in a horse-drawn carriage, tracing the hills bounding the rural Cahuenga Valley. The couple had recently lost their nineteen-month-old son to illness, and the quiet hours spent watching the afternoon sun stretch across the sheep grazing in the open valley mended their pain.

While in an apricot orchard one day, they both felt a sensation that they were in a special place. Harvey, who already owned the land that eventually became the campus of the University of California, Los Angeles, soon bought the orchard and its surrounding 160 acres, and then started buying some more. A year later, Wilcox had crisscrossed his land with empty avenues, the beginning of what he envisioned as a model Christian community, with no saloons or liquor stores and free land available for any Protestant church within its limits. Harvey died before he could turn his idea of a Christian utopia into reality, and Hollywood—so named for the California holly bushes common to the area—became a farming town with a population of 106.

By the time D. W. Griffith, the son of a Confederate colonel, reached it in 1910, Hollywood still had a law on its books banning anyone from shepherding more than two thousand sheep along the street at any one time. At only the age of thirty-one, Griffith had already directed some 2,088 films, each one no longer than ten minutes, for the Biograph film studio in New York. He headed out to Los Angeles that winter with a small troupe of actors in order to take advantage of the warm weather. He installed them in a boardinghouse on Hollywood Boulevard, and within days he was filming *The Thread of Destiny*, a story set among the ranchos of Old California.

Lighting, camera work, actors: Griffith had to supply all the necessary elements of the production himself, as no one had ever filmed a movie in the town before. Until that time, nearly all film production took place in New York, not far from where Thomas Edison had invented the strip Kinetograph, one of the first cameras capable of taking pictures so fast they appeared to move, at his factory in northern New Jersey. Edison's Motion Picture Patents Company, commonly referred to as the

Trust, held the copyright to most film technology and often backed up its threats to shut a production down if a producer didn't meet its ever-increasing fees. Putting a continent's worth of distance between the making of a film and the Edison Trust was as much a part of the allure of Hollywood as the sunshine. Griffith would make twenty more films over the winter, nearly all of them starring a seventeen-year-old Canadian actress who called herself Mary Pickford.

A playwright by the name of Cecil Blount DeMille soon followed. He rented an L-shaped barn next to an orange grove at the corner of Selma and Vine, where he went to work filming *The Squaw Man*, which would clock in at a then absurdly long seventy-four minutes. Each day, DeMille, the scion of a family well known in the New York theater world, could be seen wearing a revolver on his hip as protection against both rattlesnakes and agents of the Trust, who once fired a rifle at him as he walked to his makeshift studio. Each night, DeMille would fall asleep to the howl of coyotes.

The finished product, a tale of an Englishman on the run from the law who escapes to live among Native American tribes in Wyoming, brought in fifteen times its budget of $16,000. After that, everyone wanted in. Within two years, scores of motion picture companies had set up offices in Hollywood, creating what would by the middle of the 1920s become America's fifth-largest industry, responsible for 90 percent of the world's films.

Hollywood would have stayed apart from Malibu if not for Harold G. Ferguson, a real estate developer who approached May in 1926 with the idea of turning a mile-long stretch of beachfront near the ranch's eastern edge into a beach colony. She initially blanched at the prospect of allowing anyone but a Rindge to live on the ranch itself, but relented after Ferguson agreed to her conditions: that each lease require any structure on the property to be torn down after ten years. May considered it insurance that she could shut down the colony, and erase all evidence of its existence, once her money situation improved. Despite the odd terms, Ferguson went to work, putting up billboards throughout the state depicting families playing on empty beaches. He let the artwork do most of the selling for him, including only a single word—"Privacy" on one billboard, "Tranquil" on the next—next to the address "Rancho Malibu Beaches."

He shouldn't have bothered. Anna Q. Nilsson, perhaps the most popular silent film actress at the time, rented the first lot that came available. Marie Prevost, whose large eyes and dark curls landed her roles as flappers in a string of popular comedies, came next, and then Raoul Walsh, a legendary one-eyed director who briefly made an eye patch a mark of sophistication, signed on, and before Ferguson knew it, he was fielding calls from seemingly every person in Hollywood for a spot in what was becoming the playground of the stars.

The Movie Colony, as it came to be known, was far from glamorous in itself. With the terms of the lease taking away any incentive to build something of substance, movie stars and directors who secured a piece of Malibu took to employing set designers and stagehands to build their beachfront cottages, with predictable results. The earliest homes baked in the daytime and froze at night, with each one barely held up by walls so thin that more than one drunken argument ended with a man punching his hand clear through to the cottage next door.

It was the company that mattered. For the first time, the idea that movie stars lived in their own charmed world was made literal. Stars posed in publicity photos, sunning themselves in their beachfront backyards, and gossiped about who would be able to make the transition from silent films to talkies. The public ate it up, if only because it confirmed their fantasies. The beaches of Malibu were described as a place where beautiful actresses "blend in with the seascape, being in much the same key; they too are dazzling, a little wearisome, and more than a little unreal; they too have that quality, that suggestion of having stepped out of somebody's fever dream, that goes with the Pacific Ocean and no other ocean," novelist James M. Cain wrote in a feature on life among the Hollywood elite. Early fan magazines like *Photoplay* and *Motion Picture Story* sent reporters up to Malibu, desperate for any news from the

Colony that would satisfy their readers' never-ending appetite. When Mary Pickford was seen volleying with Charlie Chaplin, shortly after the colony's first tennis court was completed, the photo was reprinted across the nation. The Colony soon had its own police force, courthouse, grocery, post office, and general store, giving the most famous one-mile stretch of beach in the country the outlines of a small town, albeit one whose gate was guarded at all times by armed patrolmen.

May put as much distance between herself and the stars as possible, never once venturing out to the Colony to mingle. She eventually granted one grudging interview to *Screen Book,* an early trade magazine. "I have been accused of many things, including a lack of public spirit," May told a reporter in an article carrying the headline "The Landlady of Malibu." "But it was sentiment which inspired me to forbid a road through the rancho. I knew that once we let down the bars, the ancient beauty of the place would be forever destroyed. I held out for years but finally lost in the courts." The influx of glamour along her coast seemed wasted on her. "Yes, I'm proud of my movie colony, I do not know a one of them personally and seldom go on the beach. They are excellent tenants and I never have any trouble with them. My favorite tenant? Oh, I have none, they are all fine," she said, before ending the interview with the admonishment "Give my movie people all the publicity you want, but leave me out of it."

The success of the Movie Colony, along with the tile factory farther up the beach, gave May her first new source of income in more than twenty years. She resolved to spend it in glorious fashion, constructing two proud monuments as proof that, although the Roosevelt Highway now cut through her ranch, she was not ruined. On a small promontory at the mouth of Malibu Lagoon once called Vaquero Hill, she began work on a beach house as gift for Rhoda and her family. Stiles O. Clements, one of the most prominent architects in Los Angeles at the time, designed a two-story home with whitewashed walls, shaded courtyards, and a red tile roof, evoking the ranchos that had spread across Southern California just a generation before and of which Malibu was the last.

Malibu tile covered nearly every surface of the seven-bedroom mansion, from the top of the oak table in the dining room to the white-and-blue trim of the dog bath in the rear courtyard.

Whatever restraint May showed in the construction of Rhoda's beachside mansion vanished when it came to designing her own. On the hill overlooking where the mansion lost in the fire of 1903 once stood, May began work on a fifty-four-room palace with wings for Frederick Jr.'s and Rhoda's families, all meant to serve as a symbol that the Rindge family would forever rule the kingdom of Malibu. She planned to pay whatever was necessary, not flinching when told that her plans could cost her upwards of $500,000—nearly $7 million in contemporary dollars. In Frederick Jr.'s bathroom alone, she told workers to build a thirteen-by-seventeen-foot swimming pool, which would prove to be neither the first nor the last pool to appear on the property. Tile lined every part of the home, often from the ceilings to the floors and even the doors themselves. Sewing rooms, butler's pantries, a music hall that was said to be large enough to fit in the Los Angeles Philharmonic—each room, no matter its importance, was set out with its own pattern of brilliant tile.

She paid for it all with gold bonds issued by the Marblehead Land Company, the corporation she had formed to manage what was left of Frederick's empire. As security, she pledged 7,965 acres of the Malibu ranch, along with 600 acres of what would become part of the exclusive Cheviot Hills neighborhood south of Pico Boulevard, and seventy-five lots on Crenshaw Boulevard between West Adams and Exposition Boulevard. Dividends from her stocks alone—a collection that included Union Oil of California, Union Oil Associates, Pacific Mutual Life Insurance, and the Artesian Water Company and together represented a market value of more than $1.4 million—paid more than $235,000 a year, she noted in a letter to potential bondholders. The leases at the Malibu Movie Colony brought in another $660,000, a sum more than enough to cover the annual interest charges of $360,000 without having to sell any part of the ranch. "We have never sold any portion of our

Malibu holdings, preferring to add to them rather to sell any part of the estate," May wrote.

In the spring of 1929, as the home began to take shape, she turned down an unsolicited offer of $17 million—worth $237 million in today's money—to develop Malibu into a resort, complete with a marina and hotels. The success of the last four years, coming on the heels of her greatest setback, had convinced her that she could withstand whatever the world conspired to throw at her. As the tower of her home rose above the open expanse of the Pacific on one side and the untouched green foothills of the mountains on the other, she assured herself that she was finally free to enjoy her kingdom without worry that it would be taken from her. At the foot of the stairway, she added a final touch: the Rindge family coat of arms, crafted out of a perfect patchwork of pastel tiles.

AS THE SUN ROSE above lower Manhattan in late October 1929, men poured out of the subway tunnels. Wall Street, typically deserted on a Sunday, was filled with the sounds of bankers and brokers sorting through the aftermath of a week that had broken all records of trading. Black cars were lined two deep along the curbs of the financial district. Messenger boys raced along cobblestoned streets, darting between tourists who had no business getting in the way. After quadrupling over the previous five years, the Dow Jones Industrial Average had taken a frightening plunge over the last week. Its ferocity spooked investors who had become accustomed to double-digit gains, so much so that President Hoover felt it necessary to tell the nation, in a radio address that weekend, "The fundamental business of the country . . . is on a sound and prosperous basis." Banks called in staff members on their day off to work through the wreckage, hoping to find evidence that the worst of it was already over. "The market appears already to have stabilized itself quickly and to a remarkable degree," the *New York Times* suggested on the morning of October 28, 1929.

By ten o'clock, those words were hopelessly out of date. As soon as the opening bell rang, the shares of venerable companies like General Electric and U.S. Steel began to dive, and the losses started to feed on themselves. The Dow collapsed 12.8 percent on Monday. The next day, which became known as Black Tuesday, traders said that they never even heard the opening bell, the cries of "Sell! Sell!" were so loud. Orders came in so fast that people didn't even know how much a stock was worth; they just wanted it gone. By the end of the day, the market had shed another 11.7 percent, producing more than fifteen thousand miles of ticker-tape paper, which engulfed the floor of the stock exchange and created drifts so high that traders resorted to storing them in trash cans. By the time the market hit a bottom, in November, more than $25 billion—or $319 billion in contemporary dollars—had vanished, ushering in the Great Depression. Well-dressed men could be seen walking around New York in shock, clutching ticker tape in their hands.

As the losses accelerated, so did the despair. After the market fell again, G. E. Cutler, the sixty-five-year-old head of a once-prosperous produce firm in the city whose savings were wiped out, jumped from the seventh-floor ledge of his attorney's office, landing on a car below. Around the world, Americans confronted the indignities of their financial downfall. In Paris, suddenly impoverished tourists jammed the offices of booking agents seeking the first ticket on a steamship home, creating a panic in the city not seen since the breakout of the Great War, fifteen years before. Banks started to refuse checks, drafts, and any form of IOUs, leaving the formerly wealthy trying to sell clothing, jewels, and even lingerie to get their hands on cash. Servants, cooks, and maids lined up outside the American Consulate building demanding assistance, telling anyone who would listen that their former employers were unable to support them and could not afford a ticket home themselves.

Wall Street lost nearly 90 percent of its value between its 1929 peak and the bottom of 1932, marring hopes that the good times would ever come back. May felt the pain of the decline intimately. Nearly all that was left of her remaining fortune was tied up in the shares of companies

Frederick had once owned, sparing her precious little cash to weather the storm. Orders at the Malibu Potteries shuddered to a halt, while the income from the Malibu Movie Colony had already been spent on the construction of her new mansion rising on the hill. Frederick Jr., too, saw his prospects crumple along with the price of potatoes, hemp, and wheat, leaving him dependent on his stake in the Marblehead Land Company for income. A fortune that had long seemed limitless disappeared slowly and then all at once, erased by payments on the bonds May issued just a year earlier. New York had never felt so close to Los Angeles, so ready to stomp on a person's dreams. More than the financial panic, however, the upper crust of Los Angeles feared that a lower stock of people would migrate west from the dust bowl and spoil their paradise by the sea. The All-Weather Club, an organization of businessmen formed to promote year-round tourism in the city, began running national advertisements that warned, "Come to Southern California for a glorious vacation. Advise others not to come seeking employment lest they be disappointed."

Families shuffling along the lines for soup kitchens searched for someone or something to give them a glimmer of hope. All those untouched hills of Malibu, just on the other side of the fences, provided a target too tempting to resist. In June 1930, nine months after the crash, an army of more than one hundred squatters tore down the barbed wire lining the Roosevelt Highway and raced onto the Malibu ranch. Each of them carried a typewritten piece of paper stating that, as Malibu had once been a Spanish land grant, Rindge had illegally taken land that should have been set aside for homesteading and they were now here to reserve a plot.

May's foreman led armed guards on horseback to meet them in the ranch canyons and, hoping to avoid a shootout, placed a call to the sheriff's office. A truck carrying a team of policemen arrived shortly after three in the morning carrying tear gas and a sheaf of warrants. Twelve squatters were arrested, including four husband-and-wife pairs. It was soon revealed that all one hundred members of the invading army had each paid $2,500 to a lawyer who'd promised that he could successfully challenge May's title to the property, a position that the registrar of the General Land Office called foolhardy in the extreme.

Having repelled one last invasion to her land, May soldiered on for three more years before capitulating to the downturn enveloping the country. She wrote a letter to investors in the Marblehead Land Company in March 1933, informing them that the company would be defaulting on loans she had taken out just before the crash. Fifteen months later, an auction house in San Francisco was filled with the contents of more than a dozen rooms of furniture once found in Frederick Jr.'s home in San Francisco, a white mansion that stood at 1900 Pacific Avenue. Frederick, who'd lost the home and furniture in a divorce seven years earlier and was now nearing bankruptcy, could only watch as a pink marble fountain from Italy, white marble benches, and several French Sèvres vases he had owned that were better suited for museums than private homes were sold for well below estimates.

In October 1935, a fire whose cause was never identified destroyed the Malibu Potteries, taking with it one of May's last sources of income. She arranged meetings with developers in hopes of spurring interest in selling portions of the ranch, yet no one was in the mood to build an upscale resort during the middle of the Depression. Merritt Adamson, the man she had once considered unfit for her daughter's hand, eventually came to her aid. He was one of the few with businesses the Depression had spared; with Rhoda, he had founded a dairy called Adohr Farms—Rhoda's name spelled backward—in nearby Tarzana in 1916 that went on to become one of the largest milk providers in the state. Bottles bearing its logo of a smiling baby—in reality a drawing of his daughter, Rhoda-May—became a staple throughout Los Angeles and its suburbs, providing Adamson with a reliable supply of cash. Shirley Temple would pose for portraits with two of the dairy's calves during the publicity tour for *Heidi*, offering an early form of celebrity endorsement. Over the next two years, Adamson would purchase a hundred acres of the Malibu ranch at a time, helping to keep control of the property within the family.

He could not afford to buy the whole thing, however, and there was finally nothing that could save May. In June 1938, with more than $10 million in unpaid federal taxes due and millions more in private debt outstanding, she lost control of Malibu. A federal bankruptcy court placed it in the hands of a new corporation run by the bondholders of the Marblehead Land Company. The unfinished hilltop mansion was left abandoned. Guards were posted at the gates of the Malibu ranch and given the instruction to prevent any member of the Rindge family from venturing onto the land without a pass. May kept a permit the size of a business card with her at all times, unable to let go of the place for which she had sacrificed so much.

In the following years, May would go for weeks without leaving her home in West Adams, having no one to see or any funds to spend, all the while dodging warrants to appear before the court in ongoing bankruptcy proceedings. When she could, she cajoled Merritt Adamson into hiring a chauffeur to drive her across Malibu, often with one of her granddaughters in tow. She would keep her eyes fixed out the window, glancing down only to write what she saw on a yellow legal pad in her lap. Then she would ask the driver to make the journey again, this time telling Rhoda-May to "write everything you find unusual—how many boats in the harbor? Where are the cattle?"

She lived in those memories while she passed hours alone in the West Adams mansion. All around her was the evidence that she had outlived her time. The neighborhood, once the most elite in Los Angeles, had begun fading after Mary Pickford and her husband, fellow film star Douglas Fairbanks, moved into a twenty-five-room mansion in the former farmland of Beverly Hills that the press dubbed Pickfair. Other stars soon followed, pulled by the prospect of building modern homes to suit their tastes. The oil barons and railroad magnates went next, drawing the center of the city's power west toward such neighborhoods as Hancock Park and Bel-Air.

Banks soon stopped making loans to potential home owners looking to buy in the neighborhood, the result of legislation signed in 1933 by

President Franklin Roosevelt that created what became known as the Home Owners' Loan Corporation. To convince investors that an area was safe, the quasi-governmental corporation hired thousands of real estate agents to create so-called safety maps, which showed block by block which areas of a city were desirable and which should be avoided. A bank officer would check the map in a back room before deciding whether to make a loan. A red-shaded area meant that banks would refuse to do business there—the source of the term "redlining" today. West Adams, the neighborhood Frederick Rindge had once developed with the expectation that it would be the den of power in the city for generations, was labeled yellow, only one block away from a group of red lots. In a final indignity, the streets surrounding Rosedale Cemetery, where Frederick was buried thirty years earlier, were redlined.

Affluent black families started moving into West Adams, hastening the flight of white home owners toward the west side or the San Fernando Valley. The neighborhood soon became known by the moniker Sugar Hill, and it would develop into one of the most prosperous black communities in the country, without the support of white-owned banks. Hattie McDaniel, who would become the first African American to win an Oscar, for her role as Mammy in *Gone with the Wind,* soon moved into a nine-bedroom white mansion topped by a red tile roof that stood three doors down from the Rindge mansion on Harvard Boulevard.

In early 1939, May ventured downtown to meet with Frederick Jr., one of her rare outings from her crumbling mansion. A sheriff's deputy spotted her and placed her under arrest outside the Federal Building, just a few blocks from where the Rindge Building once stood. She was immediately brought before a judge on the charges of avoiding warrants, issued in both 1936 and 1937, as a result of failing to pay a judgment of nearly $5,000 awarded on behalf of the Los Angeles Ice & Cold Storage Co. "We don't want any more trouble with you," the judge admonished May from the bench. "You must come to court the next time you are summoned or we'll send you to the county jail." Her attorney assured him that May would be present at the next hearing, which was scheduled for the following week. May barely spoke during the proceedings, her face almost entirely hidden by the ends of a fur neckpiece.

It was the last time she would be seen in public. May refused to answer any other demands from the court, and she rarely left her West Adams home during the final two years of her life. She fell ill in early 1941 and spent her last days in Wilshire Hospital, a few blocks from the site of the long-since-demolished train station where she had first arrived in Los Angeles as a newlywed, over fifty years before. On February 9, 1941, she died at the age of seventy-seven.

Even at a time when the country was engulfed in the question of whether to enter the Second World War, the death of the woman dubbed the Queen of Malibu landed on the front page of all of Los Angeles' papers. Her funeral service was held at the West Adams mansion where she had spent her final days and where, a lifetime earlier, senators and business titans had once gathered to mourn her husband. Her three children, nine grandchildren, and two great-grandchildren were among the few that attended. She was buried next to Frederick, under a simple stone monument, on a clear February morning. Even in death, May remained defiant. Her handwritten will, discovered in the days after her passing, left her remaining property to her daughter, Rhoda, and her grandson Frederick Hastings Rindge III. Once one of the wealthiest women in the country, May died with just $750 in cash to her name. "And to all others who would lay claim on my property I give one dollar," she ordered.

THREE MONTHS LATER, a small caravan pulled up in front of the abandoned hilltop estate in Malibu, the ruins of what would have been May's dream home. Leading the charge was a real estate agent by the name of Louis T. Busch, who faced the question of how to sell a half-finished mansion. Busch was trailed by an assistant, a photographer, and a reporter from the *Los Angeles Times*—who Busch hoped would write an article, stirring up enough publicity that the home would fetch a buyer. Bringing up the rear of the party was a pale, over-weight man in an ill-fitting suit and a black fedora. Frederick Rindge Jr. was the only member of the family that had once owned all of Malibu to come along, and the last to see the inside of the house his mother had hoped would stand as her lasting triumph.

The group made its way in through the garage, where more than nine thousand crates, each one filled with thousands of unused tiles, sat head-high among a thicket of spider webs. Dust-covered vases were jumbled among them in no apparent order, adding to the feeling of confusion. Once inside the main house, the visitors immediately noticed the pungent smell of feces, both animal and human. Everywhere they turned were signs of ruin. In what was to be the library, hand-carved wainscoting sat gathering dust on the ground. Hundreds of solid oak panels littered the floor of the music room, along with countless racks of molding, all of it seemingly dumped and forgotten. High above them echoed the squeaks of bats living somewhere up among the rafters.

At the center of the house, at the foot of a once-grand staircase now covered in dung, a mural was just visible under layers of filth. One member of the party grabbed a rag and, with a few wipes, revealed the Rindge coat of arms, still resplendent in shimmering pastel tiles. It was, for a moment, as if May had finally triumphed, and all of the years of heart-ache had vanished and been replaced by the reality she'd so desperately attempted to will into being. As quickly as it came, the moment passed. All that was left was the rotting home, a monument to a ruined future.

TRACKS IN
THE SAND

M AY RINDGE OUTLIVED HER HUSBAND BY THIRTY-SIX years, a span that saw the development of the automobile, the rise of the airplane, and the birth of Hollywood. It is tempting to wonder what Malibu would look like if it had been he, not she, whose hand had steered the rancho over that time. After researching this story, I am fully convinced that it would be a lesser place without her.

May never wavered in her principles, and she refused to give in even when it led to her ruin. It wasn't pragmatic, and she paid dearly for it, but she ultimately preserved the natural beauty of one of the most stunning places in the world. That sort of devotion can often veer into madness, yet she remained sharp and attuned to the ramifications of her decisions until her final days. In the end, she was tantalizingly close to succeeding. Had it not been for her folly of issuing millions of dollars in bonds just before the onset of the Great Depression, she could very well have lived her entire life without selling a single acre of the ranch she first saw while in the back of a horse-drawn carriage, nestled next to her husband.

Though Frederick wrote *Happy Days in Southern California*, extolling the beauties of the place, it's unlikely that he would have had the resolve required to maintain Malibu as his undisturbed cathedral of the sun once the costs of keeping it mounted. He was too level-headed, too much of a businessman, even if a romantic one. Had he lived longer, Malibu would likely have become the American Riviera he'd said it had the potential to be, full of hotels and marinas, and ultimately just another upscale place along a coast full of them.

MALIBU REMAINED largely untouched in the years immediately following May Rindge's death. Her family sold acres on the borders of the former rancho to satisfy the final claims on her estate, leaving their holdings a fraction of what they once were. In 1942, the unfinished mansion on the hill, once meant to symbolize her power, was purchased by a sect of Franciscan friars who intended to use it as a spiritual retreat. What land remained in Malibu was divided among her descendants, with Rhoda Adamson and her husband holding on to the majority.

Rhoda continued to live with her husband in the beachside house built on Vaquero Hill. There, she only had to look outside her window to watch Malibu evolve. In 1956, Frederick Kohner, a screenwriter who had immigrated to Hollywood twenty years before to escape Hitler, became fascinated with the strange new hobby of his fifteen-year-old daughter, Kathy. Her tales of surfing at a spot that everyone knew as Surfrider Beach provided the basis for a novel about a short surfer girl he called Gidget. When published the next year, it became a nationwide hit, spawning three movies and a television series that introduced the sport of surfing to a nation filled with teenagers looking for a good time. Thanks to Kohner, Malibu became one of the most famous surfing spots in the world.

Few seemed to notice the red-roofed house on the promontory just above where the waves at Surfrider Beach broke, a gift from May to her only daughter. After Rhoda passed away, in 1962, the state of California threatened to tear down the home and build a parking lot in its place. Malibu residents, along with members of the Rindge and Adamson families, protested the move and eventually secured a spot for it on the U.S. National Register of Historic Places. The chancellor of nearby Pepperdine University—a liberal arts college built on 138 acres of land donated by May's descendants—leased the home for ten years as his official residence. Now a museum and cared for by the California State Park system, the home is best known for its exquisite collection of Malibu tile, earning it the nickname "the Taj Mahal of Tile." The craftsmanship on display prompted two local artisans to spend two years in the 1970s re-creating the glaze, culminating in a business commissioning high-end reproductions of Malibu tile for clients such as George Lucas and Jane Fonda.

Now a popular venue for weddings, the Adamson House holds its own archives of Malibu history. Before her death, Rhoda's friend Jessie donated a collection of snapshots taken with Rhoda and May Rindge in the days when Malibu was still private. Tucked alongside a photo in which she is wearing the gun and cartridge belt May Rindge once gave her, Jessie wrote, "I don't remember my parents ever expressing any worry about me being armed to the teeth."

Frederick Jr. died in 1952, having never fully recovered from his bankruptcy. Samuel Rindge, the eldest son, spent a long career as a banker in Los Angeles, living the very life of a "slave to desk and electric light darkness in a back room" that his father had run away from in Cambridge. In 1926, ten years after he sued his mother in order to secure his inheritance, Samuel moved into an eight-bedroom Mediterranean Revival mansion in Hancock Park, designed by the same architects who built the Beverly Hills City Hall. In a nod to his mother's taste for the best, he had a pipe organ built into the home's fifty-two-foot ballroom and a vast wine cellar in the basement—labeled on the blueprints as a safe, of course, since the house was constructed during Prohibition. The home was less than four miles from the West Adams mansion where he spent much of his childhood, yet only on rare occasions did he make the trek over to see May in the years before her death.

She reconciled with him only at the debutante ball that ushered her granddaughter Ramona Rindge into the Los Angeles high society to which May herself was no longer welcome. He died in 1968, after a long career at Citizens Trust and Savings. His home is still standing, and in July 2014 it was sold for $11 million. His son, whom he named Frederick Hastings Rindge, spent forty-five years as a researcher on the staff at the American Museum of Natural History in New York City, where he developed one of the world's finest collections of moths, all the while delighting in the wonders of the natural world like his namesake.

Frederick and May's West Adams mansion, too, remains. Palm trees planted in the front yard, little more than shrubs when the family moved in, now tower seventy feet overhead. Yet where Frederick could once listen to the clop of passing horse-drawn carriages, a visitor to the home now hears the roar of the Santa Monica Freeway, built just a block away in the 1960s. The construction of the freeway obliterated what by then had become one of the most prosperous black neighborhoods in America, cleaving it away from the city proper and into what became known as South Central. In the years immediately after May's death, West Adams looked to be growing into a center of African American business and culture that could stand as a West Coast rival to Harlem. In 1945, the Los Angeles Superior Court threw out a lawsuit filed by a group of white home owners in West Adams that sought to enforce housing covenants that prohibited the sale of any property in the area to anyone but members of the "pristine white race" until at least 2035. The day after the court decision was announced, the *Los Angeles Sentinel*, one of the most influential African American newspapers in the country, ran a picture of Hattie McDaniel's West Adams home on its front page under the headline "California Negroes Can Now Live Anywhere! Homes Like These No Longer Out of Bounds." The victory emboldened affluent African Americans to further concentrate in the neighborhood, with the founder of the city's largest black-owned life insurance company living in a home just a few minutes' drive from the recording studio Ray Charles built for himself on Washington Boulevard. Hattie McDaniel died in 1952 and was buried in Rosedale Cemetery, in a plot not far from Frederick and May Rindge's.

In 1954, residents of West Adams formed the Adams-Washington Freeway Committee in the hope of convincing the California Highway Commission to move the proposed path of the Santa Monica Freeway away from the center of what was then considered the most beautiful black-owned neighborhood in the country. The freeway, local politicians warned, "would constitute a wall diagonally across this area" and make racial and economic boundaries firm. Their protests did little to sway the commission, and beginning in 1958, home owners received orders to move. The first section of the freeway opened in 1961, after a dedication that featured Governor Pat Brown surrounded by beauty contestants in bathing suits. Within a few years, West Adams became notorious as a center of prostitution, which often brought white customers into what had by then become a rough neighborhood. The crack epidemic in the 1980s hastened its decline.

Yet by the early 1990s, a wave of middle-class families, drawn by the stately homes still standing just south of downtown, began revitalizing the neighborhood. Today the neighborhood is in flux, home to both graduates from the nearby University of Southern California who have been priced out of the west side and long-term residents who still worry that the police aren't doing enough to keep the area clear of the sex trade. Across the street from the former Rindge mansion sits the First African Methodist Episcopal Church, which, with more than nineteen thousand members, is one of the largest black churches in the city. Some homes dating to the neighborhood's founding, such as Hattie McDaniel's former mansion, remain occupied and largely in their original condition, while others have been deemed uninhabitable by the city and are now mostly used in film shoots, to depict anything from haunted mansions to stately residences in period dramas.

After May Rindge's death, her West Adams mansion became a home for unwed mothers, operated by the Catholic Archdiocese of Los

Angeles. It was purchased in 1983 by an attorney named Harold Green-berg, who has since restored it to its original glory. Frederick's boyhood home, meanwhile, is still standing in Cambridge. Now divided into apartments, the building was a halfway house for a local mental health organization until 2014, when it was sold to a real estate developer. The Rindge home on Ocean Avenue in Santa Monica was demolished in the 1960s. The lot it sat on was purchased by the bandleader Lawrence Welk, who developed a twenty-story white skyscraper in its place. The structure, standing atop the Pacific Palisades, is now considered one of Southern California's most desirable office buildings.

Other buildings that played a part in the Rindge's story have also been erased. The site of the Rindge Building in downtown Los Ange-les, which Frederick constructed in his first year in the city and helped cement the growth of the city's core, is now a Carl's Jr. hamburger stand. Across the street sits the Bradbury Building, built in 1893 by Los Ange-les gold-mining millionaire Lewis L. Bradbury and now designated a National Historic Landmark, yet perhaps more familiar as the scene for more than twenty films, ranging from *Blade Runner* to *The Artist* to *500 Days of Summer*. A few blocks away is the spot where the Los Angeles City Hall once stood, and where Frederick had his first court standoff against Marion Decker and the other homesteaders. Now it holds noth-ing but a parking lot.

The Preston commune outside of Cloverdale, meanwhile, went undisturbed for years after Madam Preston's death. The hundreds of acres of the former community were under the watch of a caretaker hired by the Rindge family until they were purchased in 1943 by a cou-ple who planned to open a summer camp. There, they found buildings that had been untouched since Preston's death thirty-four years before. "Madam Preston's own mansion looks just as it must have been when she was there herself in imported gowns and jewels," the *Cloverdale Rev-eille* wrote in the 1950s. "Old silver and china ornaments glint in the sunlight from the long windows, imported tiles around the fireplaces gleam, the Victorian furniture appears reassuringly usable and not just to be looked at, and the graceful plush draperies look as fresh and rich as they must have been a half century ago."

A local doctor purchased the camp in the late 1960s and eventually turned it over to a group of hippies and artists, many of whom performed as musicians and actors in some of the first Renaissance Faires in the country. One group would later describe living in a 1950s Metro step van, traveling from fair to fair, and eventually venturing to Cloverdale after getting doused with tear gas during the People's Park riots in Berkeley. There, they found the ruins of the commune, including Madam Preston's mansion, a horse barn, a caretaker's house, a greenhouse, a schoolhouse, and a lake house. They spent hours in the church Frederick had built, playing music and making love. At other times, they explored what else was left over from the days of the commune. A musician by the name of Mickie Zekley later found a jar containing one of Preston's homemade remedies. After one of his friends sampled the concoction and claimed it made him feel great, Zekley asked a local doctor to analyze its contents. The mystery of why Preston's patients felt so good after taking her remedies was soon clear: it consisted mostly of alcohol, alongside tinctures of opium and cannabis.

ROADS, THE DOWNFALL of May's empire, continued to vex the residents of Malibu after her death. In 1961, the State Division of Highways proposed building an eight-lane double-decker freeway along the coast. Two years later, officials in Sacramento announced plans to build a nuclear power plant in Corral Canyon. The stars living in the Malibu Movie Colony rose up in protest, the beginning of a freeway revolt that would last for the next ten years and spread throughout Southern California. Their success was far from assured. In 1967, for instance, the head of the county regional planning commission announced that, thanks to the three freeways scheduled for construction through it, Malibu was expected to grow from a population of 22,000 residents to 275,000 by 1987.

Yet celebrity proved to be able to accomplish what May's long court stand could not. In 1970, Governor Ronald Reagan announced that all plans to build a freeway through Malibu would be shelved. Rockslides, congestion, and accidents continue to mar what is now called the Pacific Coast Highway. Caltrans, the state agency responsible for highways, devotes millions of dollars each year to clearing the road from fallen rocks. "If there weren't a highway there, we probably wouldn't build one," the agency's director of planning admitted in the 1980s, summing up the difficulty of caring for a road along a coastline that refuses to be fully tamed.

In an echo of Frederick and May Rindge's fight to keep paradise to themselves, those who have more recently purchased homes in Malibu have gone to great lengths to close off access to its coastline. Under California law, the length of the beach up to the high-tide line is considered public property. The California Coastal Commission often requires home owners who are remodeling or asking for zoning changes to offer an additional ten feet of dry sand as a public easement. The result is that billionaires such as media mogul David Geffen, who founded DreamWorks and Geffen Records, and Larry Ellison, the former chief executive of Oracle, have a few yards of public beach wedged between their mansions and the ocean. It's not at all unusual for beachgoers to suddenly be surrounded by private security guards demanding that they leave the area at once, or for home owners to post official-looking, but ultimately unenforceable, No Parking signs. One app, called Our Malibu Beaches, gives users a to-the-foot map of the Malibu coast, and relies on their phone's global positioning system to tell them whether they have strayed onto private property.

Malibu still seems to draw those who, like Frederick Rindge in his lifetime, see in its coastline and mountains a natural remedy for what plagues their bodies. Yet, ironically, the promise of health now looks to be one of the town's chief problems. There are now more than thirty-five state-licensed drug and alcohol rehabilitation facilities in the town of less than 13,000 residents, not counting an untold number of unlicensed sober-living homes. The largest, Passages, consists of a ten-acre campus where guests including Mel Gibson and Marc Jacobs have paid more than $64,000 a month for treatment that includes hypnosis and sound therapy. "These mega-facilities are buying up three and four properties and creating compounds that are changing the nature of Malibu's neighborhoods," the city attorney told the *New York Times*. "They're becoming hospital zones."

THE MEN AND WOMEN who played a part in the rise and fall of the Rindge kingdom in Malibu scattered throughout Los Angeles, leaving marks large and small. Henry E. Huntington, the man who developed West Adams with Frederick and once tried to build his own railroad through Malibu, died in 1927. His former estate is now the home of the Huntington Library, which houses the only remaining copy of the thousands of pages of court testimony from May Rindge's fight against the state and the source of much of the material in this book. Arthur Letts, the department store magnate who served as one of the pallbearers at Frederick's funeral, built a Gothic-Tudor mansion for his son, Arthur Letts, Jr., near the end of the Roaring Twenties. The home, with its twenty-two rooms, is now better known as the Playboy Mansion. Frank P. Flint, another one of Frederick's pallbearers, served one term as a U.S. senator and then became a real estate developer. The city of La Cañada Flintridge is named in part after him. The Williams Andrew Clark Memorial Library, housed in the former mansion of the multimillionaire nephew of another of Frederick's pallbearers, sits a half mile away from the Rindge mansion in West Adams, where it safeguards one of the finest rare-book collections in the country.

Many of the homesteaders whose presence had prompted the state to build a highway through Malibu left in the years after it was opened to the wider world. Warren Udell, the settler whose large arsenal of weapons frightened guests of one of the first country clubs in Malibu, eventually died alone on his ranch. In time, it became known as Udell

Gorge, and it is now part of Malibu Creek State Park. Most Americans have seen it, at least on-screen: in 1946, Twentieth Century Fox Studios purchased two thousand acres of land, where it filmed productions ranging from Elvis Presley musicals to the original *Planet of the Apes* to much of the television show M*A*S*H. It became a state park in 1976. The Crags Country Club, which had bedeviled Udell, closed in 1936; its crumbling foundation still sits on the mountainside, spooking hikers.

Other early Malibu settlers sold their plots quietly, making millions from the likes of King Gillette, the inventor of the safety razor, and entertainers such as Bob Hope. The Deckers, however, stayed on until rising property taxes slowly pushed nearly all of them away. In 2014, all that remained of the family's older generations was ninety-three-year old Millie Decker, whose failing health did not permit her to speak with me. Her husband, Jimmy, had gone into the family business, becoming known as "Dynamite Decker" for the glee he experienced while blowing up rocks and boulders across Malibu. Before his death, he used those skills to clear lots for the homes of such celebrities as Cary Grant. Over the years, Millie, too, has become a sort of folk hero in Malibu, known for wearing a cowboy hat and bolo tie and serving as a link to the city's rough-and-tumble past. That nearly all of her friendships were with the celebrities who had filled the hills next to her seemed to have no effect on her outlook. She continues to prize horses and self-reliance above all, even going so far as to refuse to leave during the wildfires that periodically threaten to destroy her home. "I knew old May Rindge when I was a little girl," Millie told the local community newspaper in 2010. "She scared me. She walked around with a gun holster strapped to her hip."

THERE ARE NO MONUMENTS to Frederick or May Rindge in Greater Los Angeles, nothing that outwardly commemorates their role in preserving its natural beauty long after other areas of Southern California were given over to tract homes and strip malls. The closest thing to a tribute is a pair of streets: Rindge Avenue, tucked away in an upscale neighborhood in Playa del Rey, at the western edge of Los Angeles, where each house overlooks the ocean, and Rindge Lane, a quiet street in Redondo Beach filled with upscale homes topped by red tile roofs. In the mid-1960s, the unfinished Rindge mansion purchased by the Franciscan sect caught fire. It was rebuilt and renamed the Serra Retreat, and it now anchors a gated community that is one of the most exclusive in Malibu.

In 1983, some of the worst storms in memory hit the Malibu coast, destroying homes in the area that once housed the Malibu Movie Colony and filling swimming pools in the hills with thick mud. When it was finally okay to return to the beach, residents were stunned to discover railroad tracks running along the coast. They were all that remained of the line May Rindge had constructed nearly eighty years before, unearthed once more.

In 2011, I visited the home of Frederick and May's great-grandson Grant Adamson, less than half a mile from the spot where the Rindges had built their first house in Malibu. A kind man whose easygoing manner belied the fact that he still controlled hundreds of acres of prime property in the town, Grant took me on a tour of the Serra Retreat neighborhood, where he lived with his wife and daughters. We passed the home of Britney Spears and those of other celebrities before ending up in his backyard, which had an unsullied ocean view that ran to Point Dume, several miles down the coast. He pointed to two undeveloped lots behind his property and explained that he was saving them for his daughters, one then in college and the other in high school, so they could build their own homes one day.

Grant, sadly, would not live to see that. He died in August 2013, when a hot-air balloon carrying him, his wife, and their daughters crashed in Switzerland after hitting a power line. His last act was to use his body to cushion the fall, a decision that saved his family's lives.

Grant was an enthusiastic supporter of this book, going so far as to invite me into his home office while he rummaged through a box of old files, searching for anything that could possibly be of interest. He considered his grandfather Merritt Adamson to be an unsung hero for buying up so much of Malibu from May Rindge, preventing it from falling into a developer's hands. An empty Adohr Farms bottle sat on his bookshelf. Yet Grant was proud of May, too. Tucked in a corner of his desk was the card issued by the bondholders of the Malibu ranch that May had once been forced to carry with her in order to pass through the gates of her former property, where she had spent the best days of her life in the company of her husband and children. Grant kept it as a reminder of what his family had gone through to hold on to paradise.

ACKNOWLEDGMENTS

I am grateful to the many people who contributed to this project.

The Rindge and Adamson families generously opened up their personal archives, sharing letters, diaries, photographs, and other materials that had never been made public. I am especially indebted to Deborah Miller and Ronald Rindge for fielding several rounds of questions, as well as Anne Rindge, Liza Rindge-Peterson, and Debbie Rindge for taking the time to assist in fact-checking the final manuscript.

Charles Sullivan and Kathleen Rawlins at the Cambridge Historical Commission were kind enough to help me navigate the materials related to Frederick's gifts to the city. Melissa Nykanen steered me through Pepperdine University's collection of items related to Malibu's history, while Heidi Bernard made the first introductions to members of the Rindge and Adamson families. William Clark and Glenn Howell, both formerly of the Malibu Adamson House Museum, were vital sources of information, and were kind enough to spend hours on the phone and in person answering my every question. Holly Hoods at the Healdsburg Museum and Historical Society shared her research into the life of Emily Preston and her followers. Harold Greenberg, who now owns the former Rindge mansion in

West Adams, was kind enough to field questions about the house and the inscriptions penned by Frederick Rindge that are still painted on its walls.

Special thanks go to my editor at W. W. Norton, Jill Bialosky, who championed this project from the get-go. The book is immeasurably better because of her. I am also deeply appreciative of Bonnie Thompson, my eagle-eyed copyeditor, and David High, of High Design, for a beautiful cover. Bill Rusin, Angie Shih, and Maria Rogers at Norton were also incredibly helpful while shepherding this book from manuscript to finished product.

This book wouldn't have been possible without the time and effort of my agents Larry Weissman and Sascha Alper, two of the kindest and most generous people I know. Every author should be lucky enough to work with them.

Thanks also go to friends and family who offered support and advice as I worked on this book, including Alan Yang, Matthew Craft, Sam Mamudi, Bill and Sydney Mueller, Linda Stern, Lauren Young, Brooke Kroeger, Helen Coster, Tom Gregorio, Hank Gilman, John and Carol Ordover, Rob and Gina Scott, Tony and Maryanne Petrizio, Ryan Randall, and my parents, Ken and Diane Randall.

And finally, infinite love and thanks go to Megan Randall, who not only served as my companion on several research trips to Malibu (a hard assignment if there ever was one), but offered unwavering encouragement and support at times I needed them most.

SELECTED BIBLIOGRAPHY
AND SOURCES

This book wouldn't have been possible without the assistance of the Rindge and Adamson families, who generously shared material held in their private collection that had never before been made public. Moreover, family members opened up their archives to me while knowing that they would have no editorial input on this project. For years, they had turned down other journalists who had inquired about the story, adhering to the motto that the only reason to have your name in the paper is when you are born, when you marry, and when you die. To say that I am grateful that they decided to open up their materials to me is an understatement.

In addition to the private family collection, I have relied heavily on the twenty volumes of court testimony from the main California state court case that are now housed at the Huntington Library in San Marino, California. Other key sources of materials include the Healdsburg Museum and Historical Society, the Rindge and Adamson Family Papers collection at Pepperdine University, the Malibu Adamson House Foundation Archives, and the Frederick Hastings Rindge Collection held by the City of Cambridge.

I am also extremely fortunate that Frederick Hastings Rindge was an accomplished and compulsive writer, leaving a wealth of diaries and books that let me follow him on a journey from a sleepy beachside hamlet in northeast Florida across the country to his days exploring the empty Malibu hills. Thanks to these and other letters, diaries, transcripts, and various court filings, everything that is housed between quotation marks in this book is a direct quote. I have not put words in the mouths of any characters, and where I have written what any person was thinking at any moment, I did so only in cases where there was ample evidence about their state of mind.

The archives of the *Los Angeles Times* and other newspapers were extremely helpful in filling in the gaps in the story, as well as giving a larger context as to what was happening in California as it transitioned from the frontier to the most populous state in the nation. The California Digital Newspaper Collection, hosted by the University of California, Riverside (my alma mater), allowed me to track down everything from advertisements for Madam Preston's lectures in San Francisco to Samuel Knight Rindge's business deals. What follows is a select bibliography for each chapter.

Introduction: THE BEACH

"Mrs. Rindge Besieged on the Malibu Ranch." *Los Angeles Times*. July 30, 1917.

Chapter One: A GREAT BEAST AWAKENING

Samuel Rindge letter. Private Rindge and Adamson family collection. Unpublished.

Waters, H. F. *The New England Historical and Genealogical Register*. Vol. 45. 1891.

Wood, John W. "Frederick Hastings Rindge." *Cambridge Historical Society*. Vol. 34. 1954.

Parker, Francis Jewett. "Memoir of Samuel Baker Rindge." Boston: David Clapp & Sons, 1891.

Associated Press. "Standard Time Zones in U.S. Mark 100 Years." *New York Times,* November 20, 1983.

Conwell, Col. Russell H. *History of the Great Fire in Boston.* Boston: B. B. Russell, 1873.

Abeel, Daphne. "Vita: Frederick Hastings Rindge. Brief Life of a Model Citizen." *Harvard Magazine* 11 (1998).

Karabel, Jerome. *The Chosen: The Hidden History of Admission and Exclusion at Harvard, Yale, and Princeton.* New York: Houghton Mifflin, 2005.

James, Henry. *The Portable Henry James.* New York: Penguin, 2004.

Tomes, Robert. "The Americans on Their Travels." *Harper's New Monthly Magazine* 31 (1865).

Smith, Harold Frederick. *American Travellers Abroad: A Bibliography of Accounts Published Before 1900.* Lanham, MD: Scarecrow, 1999.

Kilbride, David. *Being American in Europe, 1750–1860.* Baltimore: John Hopkins University Press, 2013.

Rindge, Frederick Hastings. "1878–1879 Diaries." Frederick Hastings Rindge Collection, Cambridge, MA. Unpublished.

Silliman, Benjamin. *A Visit to Europe in 1851.* New York: George Putnam, 1858.

Abbott, John S. C. "Ocean Life." *Harper's New Monthly Magazine* 5 (June–November, 1852).

Fox, Stephen. *Transatlantic: Samuel Cunard, Isambard Brunel, and the Great Atlantic Steamships.* New York: HarperCollins, 2003.

Butler, David Allen. *The Age of Cunard.* Annapolis, MD: Lighthouse, 2003.

Stowe, William W. *Going Abroad, European Travel in Nineteenth-Century American Culture.* Princeton, NJ: Princeton University Press, 1994.

Chapter Two: OH, THE HAPPY VAQUERO!

Rindge, Frederick Hastings. "1878–1879 Diaries." Frederick Hastings Rindge Collection, Cambridge, MA. Unpublished.

Rindge, Frederick Hastings. *Happy Days in Southern California.* Self-published, 1898.

Campbell, Reau. *Winter Cities in Summer Lands: A Tour Through Florida and the Winter Resorts of the South.* Cincinnati: Cincinnati, New Orleans & Texas Pacific Railway, 1885.

Bloomfield's Illustrated Historical Guide: Embracing an Account of the Antiquities of St. Augustine. St. Augustine, FL: Max Bloomfield, 1883.

"Opera Collection Spotlight: Denver's Tabor Grand Opera House." Autry National Center of the American West. Accessed at: http://theautry.org/collections/opera-5.

Spence, Clark C. "A Celtic Nimrod in the Old West." *Montana: The Magazine of Western History* 9, no. 2 (Spring 1959).

Wommack, Linda. *From the Grave: A Roadside Guide to Colorado's Pioneer Cemeteries.* Caldwall, ID: Caxton Press, 1998.

Miller, Mark. *Hollow Victory: The White River Expedition of 1879 and the Battle of Milk Creek.* Boulder: University of Colorado Press, 1997.

Swansburg, John. "The Passion of Lew Wallace." *Slate.* March 26, 2013.

Cummings, Amos Jay, and Milanich, Jerald T. *A Remarkable Curiosity: Dispatches from a New York City Journalist's 1873 Railroad Trip Across the American West.* Edited and compiled by Jerald T. Milanich. Boulder: University of Colorado Press, 2008.

Chapter Three: THE PROPHET OF PRESTON

Hine, Robert V. *California's Utopian Colonies.* New Haven: Yale University Press, 1953.

Sefton, W. M. "Preston: Recollections of 19th- and 20th-Century Communal Life at Preston Ranch." Self-published. Accessed at: http://larkcamp.com/Preston/PrestonHistory.html

Hoods, Holly. "Preston: History of a Late-Nineteenth Century Religious Community in Sonoma County, California." M.A. thesis, Sonoma State University, 2000.

Hoods, Holly. "The Prophet of Preston: Emily Preston and the Life of the Preston Colony." *Journal of the Sonoma County Historical Society* (2000).

Cross, Whitney. "The Burned-Over District: The Social and Intellectual

History of Enthusiastic Religion in Western New York, 1800–1850." *Journal of Southern History* 17, no. 1 (February 1951).

"A Free Lecture." *Daily Alta California.* March 26, 1884.

Preston, Emily. *Creed of the Free Pilgrim's Covenant Church.* Undated pamphlet. Preston papers, Healdsburg Museum.

Howell, Glen. "May Knight Rindge." *Malibu Lagoon Museum Newsletter.* Winter 2005.

Chapter Four: THE BOOMIEST BOOM

Netz, Joesph. "The Great Los Angeles Real Estate Boom of 1887." *Annual Publication of the Historical Society of Southern California* 10, no. 1–2 (1915–16).

Guinn, J. M. "The Great Real Estate Boom of 1887." *Historical Society of Southern California, Los Angeles* 1, no. 5 (1890).

Guinn, J. M. *A History of California and an Extended History of Los Angeles and Its Environs.* Vol. 1. Los Angeles: Historic Record Company, 1915.

"The Southern Boom." *Los Angeles Herald.* June 15, 1887.

Thompson, Gregory Lee. *The Passenger Train in the Motor Age: California's Rail and Bus Industries, 1910–1941.* Columbus: Ohio State University Press, 1993.

Starr, Kevin. *Americans and the California Dream, 1850–1915.* Oxford University Press, 1986.

Van Dyke, T. S. *Millionaires of a Day: An Inside History of the Great Southern California "Boom."* New York: Fords, Howard & Hulbert, 1890.

Dana, Richard Henry, Jr. *Two Years Before the Mast.* New York: Houghton Mifflin Company, 1911.

Bell, Major Horace. *Reminiscences of a Ranger; or, Early Times in Southern California.* Los Angeles: Yarnell, Caystile & Matker. 1881.

Brewer, William H. *Up and Down California in 1860–1864: The Diary of William H. Brewer.* Berkeley: University of California Press, 2003.

Southern California: An Authentic Description of Its Natural Features,

Resources, and Prospects. Southern California Bureau of Information, 1892.

Nordhoff, Charles. *Nordhoff's West Coast: California, Oregon, and Hawaii.* New York: Routledge, 2011.

Chapter Five: WHAT SHALL WE DO WITH THE MILLIONAIRES?

Guinn, J. M. *A History of California and an Extended History of Los Angeles and Its Environs.* Vol. 2. Los Angeles: Historic Record Company, 1915.

The Poems and Written Addresses of Mary T. Lathrap. Woman's Christian Temperance Union of Michigan. 1895.

Letters from Frederick and May Rindge. Private Rindge and Adamson family collection. Unpublished.

"The Public Library." *Cambridge Chronicle* 44, no. 2263 (July 6, 1889).

"A Generous Offer: Mr. Rindge Proposes to Give a Site for a High School." *Boston Daily Advertiser.* October 29, 1887.

"The Gifts of Mr. Rindge to Cambridge." *Boston Evening Journal.* November 14, 1887.

"Mr. Rindge's Benefactions: He is Not Expanding California Money on Eastern Institutions." *San Francisco Bulletin.* November 16, 1887.

"Cambridge's Benefactor." *New York Times.* November 16, 1887.

"Saw the Photographs." *Boston Daily Globe.* July 15, 1891.

The Rindge Gifts to the City of Cambridge, Massachusetts. Cambridge, MA: City Council, 1891.

Dole, Charles F. "What Shall We Do with the Millionaires?" *New England Magazine* 3 (September 1890).

"Fairmont Miramar: Yesterday, Today and Tomorrow." *Santa Monica Mirror.* July 2, 2011.

Chapter Six: HAPPY DAYS IN SOUTHERN CALIFORNIA

Robinson, W. W., and Lawrence Clark Powell. *The Malibu.* Los Angeles: Ward Ritchie, 1958.

Rindge, Frederick Hastings. *Happy Days in Southern California.* Self-published, 1898.

Totten, Sanden. "Geologist's Dream Unearthed by the 405 Construction Project." KPCC, November 26, 2013.

Perez, Cris. *Grants of Land in California Made by Spanish or Mexican Authorities.* Boundary Determination Office, State Lands Commission, Boundary Investigation Unit, August 23, 1982.

Newmark, Harris. *Sixty Years in Southern California, 1853–1913.* New York: Knickerbocker, 1916.

Rindge, May K. Transcripts of the Rindge Case. Held at the Huntington Library, San Marino, California.

Chapter Seven: FILLING THE MOUNTAINS WITH MEN

Decker, Marion. Transcripts of the Rindge Case. Held at the Huntington Library, San Marino, California.

Keller, Henry. Transcripts of the Rindge Case. Held at the Huntington Library, San Marino, California.

Letters from Frederick and May Rindge. Private Rindge and Adamson family collection. Unpublished.

Letter from May Rindge to Madam Preston. Collection of Healdsburg Museum. Unpublished.

Kinney, Abbot. *Eucalyptus.* Los Angeles: R. R. Baumardt, 1895.

"It Gets There." *Los Angeles Herald.* May 29, 1892.

"Supervisor James Hay." Los Angeles County Board of Supervisors records. Accessed at: http://file.lacounty.gov/lac/jhay.pdf.

Chapter Eight: CALIFORNIA SHALL BE OURS AS LONG AS THE STARS REMAIN

Decker, Marion. Transcripts of the Rindge Case. Held at the Huntington Library, San Marino, California.

Rindge, May K. Transcripts of the Rindge Case. Held at the Huntington Library, San Marino, California.

Lummis, Chas., and Charles Moody, eds. *Out West: A Magazine of the Old Pacific and the New.* 30 (January–June 1909). Los Angeles: Out West Magazine Company, 1910.

Letter from Frederick Rindge to Board of Supervisors. Private Rindge and Adamson family collection. Unpublished.

Haas, Walter. Transcripts of the Rindge Case. Held at the Huntington Library, San Marino, California.

"Santa Monica: County Surveyor Wright at Work in the Malibu District." *Los Angeles Times.* August 27, 1897.

"Going After Wealth on Malibu Ranch." *Los Angeles Times.* June 20, 1902.

"Work of the Government Land Survey—Interesting Developments." *Los Angeles Times,* January 4, 1897.

Davis, Margaret Leslie. *Dark Side of Fortune: Triumph and Scandal in the Life of Oil Tycoon Edward L. Doheny.* Berkeley: University of California Press, 2001.

"Frontier Still Rules in Malibu." *Los Angeles Times.* January 31, 1898.

"Entertainment of the Encampment of Knights of Pythias." *Los Angeles Times.* July 19, 1897.

"Santa Monica." *Los Angeles Times.* January 1, 1897.

Wallach, Ruth, et al. *Historic Hotels of Los Angeles and Hollywood.* Charleston, SC: Arcadia, 2008.

Letter from May Rindge to Madam Preston. Collection of Healdsburg Museum. Unpublished.

"Cambridge Demonstration: F. H. Rindge Visits the Manual Training School He Founded." *Los Angeles Times.* June 7, 1898.

"A Wheelman's Dream Which May Materialize." *Los Angeles Herald.* November 20, 1896.

Friedricks, William B. *Henry E. Huntington and the Creation of Southern California.* Columbus: Ohio State University Press, 1992.

"Industrial Growth Has Hardly Begun: Frederick E. Rindge Casts a Rosy Horoscope." *Los Angeles Times.* September 30, 1902.

"Five Story Building: Eighty-Thousand-Dollar Block Goes Up on Hill Street." *Los Angeles Times.* February 6, 1901.

"Real Estate and Building." *Los Angeles Herald.* March 3, 1901.

Rindge, Frederick. "Learn to Laugh." Private Rindge and Adamson family collection. Unpublished.

Lockwood, Charles. "Seminarians Live Where Stars Slept: Mansion on Adams Once Was Home to Film Celebrities." *Los Angeles Times.* September 20, 1987.

"Rindge Will Build Baronial Residence: A Fifty-Thousand-Dollar Home." *Los Angeles Times.* May 20, 1902.

"New Money and Brains: Important Additions to Local Enterprise." *Los Angeles Times.* January 16, 1902.

"Anti-Saloon Business Men: Wallace, Rindge and Others Stir a Crowd." *Los Angeles Times.* May 5, 1901.

Chapter Nine: THE FIRE

Rindge, May K. Transcripts of the Rindge Case. Held at the Huntington Library, San Marino, California.

"Rindge's Estimate of New President." *Los Angeles Times.* September 25, 1902.

Lummis, Charles, ed. *Out West: A Magazine of the Old Pacific and the New.* Vol. 18. Los Angeles: Out West Company, 1903.

Lech, Steve, ed. "The Beginning of a Landmark." *Journal of the Riverside Historical Society* 12 (February 2008).

"Santa Monica: Frederick H. Rindge, the Capitalist, Has Been Ill for Several Days at His Home on Ocean Avenue." *Los Angeles Times.* May 14, 1903.

"Rindge's Fine Shirt on the Way to Jail." *Los Angeles Times*. August 23, 1903.

Letter from May Rindge to Madam Preston. Collection of Healdsburg Museum. Unpublished.

"Flight for Life from Brush Fires." *Los Angeles Times*. December 6, 1903.

Chapter Ten: ONE LAST ADVENTURE

Articles of Incorporation of the Hueneme, Malibu and Port Los Angeles Railway. September 24, 1903.

"Further Particulars of Mr. Rindge's Death." *Cambridge Chronicle*. September 9, 1905.

"Mr. Rindge's Work: Now Building a Wagon Road Between Santa Monica and Malibu, His Big Ranch." *Cambridge Chronicle*. March 18, 1905.

Rindge, Frederick Hastings. *Songs of California and Other Verses*. Malibu Lagoon Museum, 2001.

Abeloe, William N., ed. *Historic Spots in California*. Stanford, CA: Stanford University Press, 1932.

Miller, Joaquin. *Unwritten History: Life Amongst the Modocs*. Hartford, CT: American Publishing, 1874.

Twain, Mark. *The Autobiography of Mark Twain*. New York: Harper Perennial Classics, 2000.

"A Grand Man Gone." *Los Angeles Times*. August 30, 1905.

"Millionaire Philanthropist Dies Suddenly in North." *Los Angeles Herald*. August 30, 1905.

Chapter Eleven: ARCH ROCK

"Loved Dead Laid to Rest: Funeral Rites of the Late Frederick H. Rindge." *Los Angeles Times*. September 2, 1905.

"Funeral of Rindge." *Los Angeles Times*. September 1, 1905.

"Loss to World Is Great, Says Minister at the Funeral of Frederick H. Rindge." *Los Angeles Herald*. September 2, 1905.

Wolfe, Susan. "Who Killed Jane Stanford?" *Stanford Alumni Magazine.* September–October, 2003.

"Coast Trolley to the North: Mrs. Rindge Heads Company Now Building Line." *Los Angeles Times.* October 7, 1905.

"Arch Rock Is Gone." *Los Angeles Times.* March 25, 1906.

"Arch Rock Mystery." *Los Angeles Times.* March 26, 1906.

"Arch Rock to Be Only a Memory." *Los Angeles Times.* July 25, 1915.

" 'Bean' Road Scares Espee." *Los Angeles Times.* April 4, 1906.

Letter from May Rindge to Emily Preston. Collection of Healdsburg Museum. Unpublished.

Rindge, May. Transcripts of the Rindge Case. Held at the Huntington Library, San Marino, California.

Hordern, Nicholas. "The Iron Mistress of Malibu." *Los Angeles Magazine.* 1970.

Chapter Twelve: TO FORCE HER GATES OPEN

Hindman, Jo. "The Big Ranch Fight." *Journal of Ventura County History* 52, no. 2 (2011).

"Rape of Locks Causes Stir." *Los Angeles Times.* April 24, 1907.

"Means Fight over Gates." *Los Angeles Times.* April 26, 1907.

"Movement to Make Malibu a National Park." *Los Angeles Herald.* May 1, 1908.

"Much Depends on This Demurrer: It May Settle Controversy over Rindge Roads." *Los Angeles Times.* August 21, 1907.

Keller, Henry. Transcripts of the Rindge Case. Held at the Huntington Library, San Marino, California.

Limerick, Patricia Nelson. *The Legacy of Conquest: The Unbroken Past of the American West.* New York: Norton, 1987.

"Private Snap of Reserve?" *Los Angeles Times.* February 10, 1907.

Aubrey, L. E. "Letters to the Times: Against Malibu Reserve." *Los Angeles Times.* February 17, 1907.

"Forest Reserves: Santa Monica Scheme Shut Down." *Los Angeles Times.* March 8, 1907.

"Wilderness Invaded: Los Angeles Business Men Become Squatters." *Los Angeles Times*. May 29, 1907.

"Los Angeles Auto Show." *Los Angeles Times*. January 23, 1907.

Thomson, Clive. "When Pedestrians Ruled the Streets." *Smithsonian*. December 2014.

"Around the Hotels." *Los Angeles Herald*. July 31, 1901.

Chapter Thirteen: OPEN ROADS

Guinn, J. M. *A History of California: An Extended History of Its Southern Coast Counties*. Los Angeles: Historic Record Company, 1907.

Clary, William W. *History of the Law Firm of O'Melveny & Myers, 1885–1965*. Vol. 1. Los Angeles: privately printed, 1966.

"Woman at War with Uncle Sam." *Los Angeles Herald*. December 4, 1907.

"Pioneers Testify as to Malibu Road." *Los Angeles Herald*. October 7, 1908.

"To Force Her Gates Open." *Los Angeles Times*. December 4, 1907.

"Gun Pointed at His Head." *Los Angeles Times*. December 5, 1907.

"For Opening Malibu Road." *Los Angeles Times*. December 17, 1907.

"Mrs. Rindge Answers." *Los Angeles Times*. October 24, 1908.

Sefton, W. M. *Preston: Recollections of 19th- and 20th-Century Communal Life at Preston Ranch*. Self-published. Accessed at: http://larkcamp.com/Preston/PrestonHistory.html.

Matheson, Jessie. Oral history on file at Adamson House Archives, Malibu, California.

Rindge, May. Letters to Rhoda Rindge Adamson. Rindge and Adamson Family Private Collection. Unpublished.

"Malibu Ranch Road Opened." *Los Angeles Times*. March 6, 1909.

"Woman Keeps Tab on Suit." *Los Angeles Times*. October 6, 1910.

"To Preserve Principality." *Los Angeles Times*. November 3, 1910.

"Malibu Problem: Deputy from US District Attorneys' Office Gathers Evidence Regarding Roads." *Los Angeles Times*. March 29, 1910.

Chapter Fourteen: THE DEFINITION OF FREEDOM

Swift, Earl. *The Big Roads: The Untold Story of the Engineers, Visionaries, and Trailblazers Who Created the American Superhighways*. New York: Houghton Mifflin Harcourt, 2011.

Burns, Ken, and Dayton Duncan. *Horatio's Drive: America's First Road Trip*. New York: Knopf, 2003.

"Fair Autoist Is Courageous." *Los Angeles Times*. August 28, 1910.

"Autoists Enjoy Run to Malibu." *Los Angeles Herald*. April 24, 1910.

"Three Hundred Cars Stretch to Malibu." *Los Angeles Times*. April 24, 1910.

Automobile Club of Southern California. *Touring Topics*. May 1910.

Matheson, Jessie. Oral history on file at Adamson House Archives, Malibu, California.

Rindge, May. Letters to Rhoda Rindge Adamson. Rindge and Adamson Family Private Collection. Unpublished.

"High-Powered Cars Coming." *Los Angeles Times*. August 25, 1912.

"Pierce-Arrow." The Revs Center for Automotive Research. Accessed at: http://revsinstitute.org/the-collection/1915-pierce-arrow-48-b-3/.

Starr, Kevin. *Inventing the Dream: California Through the Progressive Era*. New York: Oxford University Press, 1985.

"Great! Auto Route Along the Coast." *Los Angeles Times*. April 13, 1911.

"Coast Route Along Beach." *Los Angeles Times*. April 16, 1911.

"They Eat Dinner in Shirt-Sleeves: Los Angeles High-Brows in Rustic Paradise." *Los Angeles Times*. June 18, 1911.

Kilday, Ruth Taylor. "Settling Malibu Canyon: Tracing Warren's Footprints." *Malibu Lagoon Museum Newsletter*. Winter 2006–07.

Rindge, Frederick Hastings Jr. Quoted in "Japanese Immigration Hearings

Before the Committee of Immigration and Naturalization." House of Representatives, 66th Congress. July 15–20, 1920.

"Biggest Pothook Job: Transcript of Testimony in Malibu Road Suit Contains More Than Three Million Words." *Los Angeles Times*. June 18, 1913.

"Rindges Win Ten-Year War." *Los Angeles Times*. October 28, 1913.

"Demands Opening of Malibu Road: Venice Chamber of Commerce Calls on Supervisors for Action." *Los Angeles Times*. July 21, 1915.

"Crisis of Road War." *Los Angeles Times*. December 8, 1915.

"She Admits Nothing." *Los Angeles Times*. April 4, 1915.

"Monster Libel Suits Impend." *Los Angeles Times*. April 3, 1915.

Chapter Fifteen: BETWEEN THE MOUNTAINS
AND THE SEA

"War Threatens in the Malibu." *Los Angeles Times*. March 1, 1916.

"Force Keeps Fences Down." *Los Angeles Times*. March 2, 1916.

"Would Halt Malibu Sale: Samuel K. Rindge Says He Was Not Informed of Plan of Railroad Transfer." *Los Angeles Times*. May 18, 1916.

"Los Angeles May Get Field Artillery Post." *Los Angeles Times*. December 4, 1916.

"Asks Division of Big Estate: Minority Rindge Heir Sues Rest of Family." *Los Angeles Times*. August 16, 1916.

Wallach, Ruth. *Miracle Mile in Los Angeles: History and Architecture*. Charleston: History Press, 2013.

Deverell, William. *Whitewashed Adobe: The Rise of Los Angeles and the Remaking of Its Mexican Past*. Berkeley: University of California Press, 2004.

Epting, Charles. *University Park, Los Angeles: A History*. Charleston: History Press, 2013.

Masters, Nathan. "Should I Stop or Should I Go? Early Traffic Signals in Los Angeles." *Los Angeles Magazine*. January 4, 2013.

Reports of Cases Determined in the Supreme Court of the State of California. Vol. 174. San Francisco: Bancroft-Whitney, 1918.

"Does Slain in Malibu Hills." *Los Angeles Times*. April 15, 1917.

Rindge, May Knight. "Letter to the Editor: Says There's Two Sides to Story; Mrs. May K. Rindge Tells of Deer-Slaying." *Los Angeles Times*. April 26, 1917.

"New Era Dawns in the Malibu: Long Vast Legal Battlefield." *Los Angeles Times*. July 8, 1917.

"Up to Supervisors: Malibu Ranchers Want Short Way Across Ranch, Now That Supreme Court and Legislature Have Decided Against Them." *Los Angeles Times*. July 10, 1917.

"Dismiss Action Against Rancher: Chained Autos Together to Prevent Theft, He Says." *Los Angeles Times*. August 8, 1917.

"Petition for Way Through Malibu: Ranchers Demand a Road to Beach Thoroughfare." *Los Angeles Times*. August 31, 1917.

"Sheep Die by Hundreds in Malibu: Feud Sequel?" *Los Angeles Times*. September 11, 1917.

"Entrance Blocked to Malibu Ranch: Two Excavations Said to Be Due to Dynamite." *Los Angeles Times*. September 12, 1917.

"Rindges Blow Up Own Roads: Mysterious Destruction of Malibu Highways Solved." *Los Angeles Times*. September 13, 1917.

"Malibu Settler Abandons Home: Says Dynamiting of Trail Forced Him to It." *Los Angeles Times*. October 15, 1917.

"Hearst Sued for Rindge Road Item." *Los Angeles Times*. October 18, 1917.

"Turns Bloody: Anonymous Messages Hint at Bloody Doings on Malibu." *Los Angeles Times*. February 26, 1918.

Chapter Sixteen: THE PUBLIC GOOD

"For Road over Rindge Ranch: Condemnation Suit Ordered by Supervisors." *Los Angeles Times*. March 28, 1918.

"For Roads Through Malibu Rancho: Three Suits Against Rindge Company Will Go to Trial Today." *Los Angeles Times*. September 30, 1918.

"Rindges Lose Malibu Appeal." *Los Angeles Times.* May 13, 1919.

"New Fight on Road over Rindge Lands." *Los Angeles Times.* August 9, 1919.

"Court Actions Opens Malibu Ranch Road." *Los Angeles Times.* January 1, 1920.

"Decker Ranch Highway: Plan to Open Up Wildest Scenic Mountain Area in Southern California." *Los Angeles Times.* October 31, 1920.

"Mrs. Rindge Is Loser in Libel Suit Judgment." *Los Angeles Times.* December 15, 1920.

"The Amazing Injustice Which County Supervisors Now Threaten." Advertisement that ran in the *Los Angeles Times* and *Los Angeles Examiner,* April 4, 1920.

"Decision Ends Highway Fight: Supreme Court Denies Last Pleas of Rindge Family." *Los Angeles Times.* August 14, 1921.

"Rindge Office Building Sold." *Los Angeles Times.* November 11, 1921.

"Progress Threatens to Crumble Ancient Ranch." *Los Angeles Times.* March 25, 1923.

O'Malley, Penelope Grenoble. *Malibu Diary: Notes from an Urban Refugee.* Reno: University of Nevada Press, 2004.

Bird, Robert. Interview by author on April 28, 2011.

Rindge Company et al. v. County of Los Angeles. No. 237. United States Supreme Court.

Bird, Robert C. "Reviving Necessity in Eminent Domain." *Harvard Journal of Law & Public Policy* 33, no. 1 (2010).

Foresta, Ronald A. *America's National Parks and Their Keepers.* New York: RFF Press, 1984.

Proceedings of the National Park Conference. U.S. Government Printing Office, 1915.

McCelland, Linda Flint. *Building the National Parks: Historic Landscape Design and Construction.* Baltimore: John Hopkins University Press, 1998.

"An Old California Fighter." *Los Angeles Times.* October 26, 1923.

Reisner, Marc. *Cadillac Desert: The American West and Its Disappearing Water.* New York: Penguin, 1986.

Address of the President of the United States to the Congress, December 8, 1922. Washington, DC: U.S. Government Printing Office, 1922.

"The Era of the Horses." Los Angeles Fire Department Historical Archive. Accessed at: http://www.lafire.com/stations/fire_stations.html.

"Youth's Electric Carriage Led to an Empire." *Los Angeles Times.* June 21, 1998.

"Mrs. Rindge Declines to Take Check." *Los Angeles Times.* December 30, 1925.

Chapter Seventeen: THE MANSION ON THE HILL

"Malibu Ranch Scenic Wonders Open at Last." *Los Angeles Times.* June 30, 1929.

"Potteries Are Inspected." *Los Angeles Times.* July 27, 1926.

Rindge, Ronald. *Ceramic Art of the Malibu Potteries 1926–1932.* Malibu: Malibu Lagoon Museum, 1988.

The Towers of Simon Rodia. National Park Service. National Register of Historic Places Registration Form.

Stern, Bill. *California Pottery: From Missions to Modernism.* San Francisco: Chronicle Books, 2001.

Starr, Kevin. *Material Dreams: Southern California Through the 1920s.* New York: Oxford University Press, 1990.

———. *Inventing the Dream: California Through the Progressive Era.* New York: Oxford University Press, 1985.

Cain, James M. "The Widow's Mite; or, Queen of the Rancho." *Vanity Fair,* August 1933.

"Privacy Rancho Malibu Beaches Harold G. Ferguson Corporation." Duke University Library, Outdoor Advertising Association of America (OAAA) Archives, 1885–1990s.

"Castle That Malibu Queen Will Keep." *Los Angeles Times.* June 30, 1938.

Marblehead Land Company First Mortgage 6 Percent Sinking Fund Gold Bonds. Issued March 1, 1928.

"Settlers Name Lawyers." *Los Angeles Times.* November 24, 1926.

"Members of Film Colony Buy in Tract." *Los Angeles Times*. June 26, 1927.

"Wall Street Hums on the Day of Rest to Catch Up on Work." *New York Times*. October 28, 1929.

Suddath, Claire. "The Crash of 1929." *Time*. October 29, 2008.

Lowenthal, Bennett. "The Jumpers of '29: When the Market Crashed, Who Headed for the Windows?" *Washington Post*. October 25, 1987.

"Crash Maroons Tourists." *Los Angeles Times*. October 30, 1929.

"Rindge Estate Invaded by Band of Squatters." *Los Angeles Times*. June 16, 1930.

Giczy, Hailey. "The Bum Blockade: Los Angeles and the Great Depression." *Voces Novae: Chapman University Historical Review* 1, no. 1 (2009).

"Armed Men Guard Ranch." *Los Angeles Times*. July 8, 1930.

"Land Unit Defaults on Bonds." *Los Angeles Times*. March 1, 1933.

"Court Names Receiver for Rindge Case." *Los Angeles Times*. May 14, 1934.

"Grandeur for Sale: Famous Rindge Furnishings to Be Auctioned in San Francisco." *Los Angeles Times*. May 26, 1935.

"Rindge Sued as Bankrupt." *Los Angeles Times*. November 10, 1935.

"Mrs. May Rindge Loses Control of Great Rancho." *Los Angeles Times*. June 30, 1938.

"Mrs. Rindge Under Arrest." *Los Angeles Times*. May 12, 1939.

"Court Stay Won by May Rindge." *Los Angeles Times*. May 17, 1939.

Marciano, R.D. Goldberg, and C. Hou. "Redlining Map of Los Angeles." Courtesy of Testbed for the Redlining Archives of California's Exclusionary Spaces. Accessed online at: http://salt.unc.edu/T-RACES/holc.html.

"Mrs. Rindge, of Malibu Ranch, Taken by Death." *Los Angeles Times*. February 9, 1941.

"Mrs. Rindge Leaves Estate of Only $750 in Currency." *Los Angeles Times*. March 12, 1941.

Epilogue: TRACKS IN THE SAND

"Friars Buy Huge Rindge Mansion." Los Angeles Times. April 15, 1942.

"In Malibu, Gidget's Up." Washington Post. September 18, 2005.

"Tile Home a Link to Malibu's Past." Los Angeles Times. January 8, 1984.

Ward Biederman, Patricia. "Malibu Tile Is Feat of Clay: Artist Helps Revive Hand-Glazed Ceramics." Los Angeles Times. March 30, 1989.

Potenza, Flavia. "Bob Harris' Malibu Ceramic Works." Topanga Messenger. December 12, 2013.

"New Look, New Life for Fading Mansion." Los Angeles Times. October 14, 1999.

Hunt, Darnell, and Ana-Christina Ramon, eds. Black Los Angeles: American Dreams and Racial Realities. New York: New York University Press, 2010.

Banks, Sandy. "West Adams Neighbors Fight for Their Streets." Los Angeles Times. July 26, 2011.

Greenberg, Harold. Interview by author. January 19, 2015.

Groves, Martha. "Scouting Malibu Beaches? There's an App for That." Los Angeles Times. May 27, 2013.

Haldeman, Peter. "An Intervention for Malibu." New York Times. September 13, 2013.

Wanamaker, Marc. Westwood. Charleston, SC: Arcadia, 2010.

Malibu Creek State Park: General Plan and Final Environmental Impact Report. Vol. 1. California Department of Parks and Recreation. March 2005. Accessed at http://www.parks.ca.gov/pages/22491/files/malibu_creek_state_park_dpr_general_plan_final_version_march_2005.pdf.

"Jimmy Decker, 72: Pioneer of Malibu Lived Rural Life." Los Angeles Times. April 17, 1991.

Halpern, Jake. "The Last of the Malibu Hillbillies." LA Weekly. July 10, 2003.

"Millie Decker Celebrates Turning 90." Malibu Times. May 19, 2010.